T0224311

.NET DevOps for Azure

A Developer's Guide to DevOps Architecture the Right Way

Jeffrey Palermo

Apress®

.NET DevOps for Azure: A Developer's Guide to DevOps Architecture the Right Way

Jeffrey Palermo
Austin, TX, USA

ISBN-13 (pbk): 978-1-4842-5342-7   ISBN-13 (electronic): 978-1-4842-5343-4
https://doi.org/10.1007/978-1-4842-5343-4

Managing Director, Apress Media LLC: Welmoed Spahr
Acquisitions Editor: Joan Murray
Development Editor: Laura Berendson
Coordinating Editor: Jill Balzano

Cover designed by eStudioCalamar

Cover image designed by Freepik (www.freepik.com)

Distributed to the book trade worldwide by Springer Science+Business Media New York, 233 Spring Street, 6th Floor, New York, NY 10013. Phone 1-800-SPRINGER, fax (201) 348-4505, e-mail orders-ny@springer-sbm.com, or visit www.springeronline.com. Apress Media, LLC is a California LLC and the sole member (owner) is Springer Science + Business Media Finance Inc (SSBM Finance Inc). SSBM Finance Inc is a **Delaware** corporation.

For information on translations, please e-mail rights@apress.com, or visit http://www.apress.com/rights-permissions.

Apress titles may be purchased in bulk for academic, corporate, or promotional use. eBook versions and licenses are also available for most titles. For more information, reference our Print and eBook Bulk Sales web page at http://www.apress.com/bulk-sales.

Any source code or other supplementary material referenced by the author in this book is available to readers on GitHub via the book's product page, located at www.apress.com/9781484253427. For more detailed information, please visit http://www.apress.com/source-code.

Printed on acid-free paper

To my wonderful wife Liana.

Thank you for your help, your smile, and for keeping the kids out of my office while I finished the last chapter.

Table of Contents

About the Author

Jeffrey Palermo is currently the Chief Architect and CEO of Clear Measure, Inc., a DevOps-centered software engineering company. He is also the founder of the Azure DevOps Podcast and the Azure DevOps User Group. Previously he was a founding board member of AgileAustin, the founder of AzureAustin, and a leader in the Austin .NET User Group.

Jeffrey is a well-known author and international public speaker. He has received 13 Most Valuable Professional awards from Microsoft and has spoken at industry conferences such as Microsoft TechEd, Microsoft Ignite, Microsoft Build, DevTeach, VSLive, and various other regional conferences. Jeffrey has other books in the *ASP.NET MVC in Action* series as well as two video books on ASP.NET MVC and nearly a dozen magazine articles on various .NET development topics.

Jeffrey resides just outside of Austin, TX, with his wife, three children, and various livestock.

Acknowledgments

First, I must thank God and his son, Jesus, for giving me the ability to think and write. Next, I'd like to thank my beautiful wife, Liana, for being awesome at her job and affording me the flexibility to go away and concentrate for long periods of time while writing this text. With three kids in the household, she is an expert mother and homemaker, and this book would not exist without her expert work. Thank you to my kids, Gwyneth Rose, Xander Jeffrey-Boris, and Annika Noel. Thanks also to my parents, Peter and Rosemary Palermo, for instilling in me a love of books and learning from an early age. I also need to recognize my college professor at Texas A&M, Mike Hnatt, who, through his programming courses, business coaching, and ongoing friendship, has continued to mentor me. Additionally, I'd like to acknowledge Jack Welch, of whose MBA program I am a graduate. From him, his books, and his curriculum, I learned to use fewer words when presenting ideas and information.

To Steve Hickman, thank you for being my first and longest-tenured software mentor. Steve was my first boss. He hired me for my first programming position 22 years ago. He now mentors the software engineers and architects at Clear Measure, Inc. He has been instrumental in forming the vision for how to simplify software engineering on the .NET platform.

To Megan Beutler, thank you for your ongoing encouragement. Megan has been a part of Clear Measure for over five years and has been a constant source of encouragement and positivity. She brightens the day of anyone in her path.

To the engineers and architects at Clear Measure, Inc., who are blazing the trail of better .NET software methods and the DevOps approach illustrated in this book. Without the learning from the many client projects, the guidance of this book would not exist. Thank you to Rayne Fulton, Tony Fauss, Nick Becker, Scott Wilson, Troy Vinson, Danny Vandergriff, Vlad Serafimov, Eric Fleming, Colin Pear, Corey Keller, Kyle Nunery, Eric Williams, Mike Alpert, Mike Sigsworth, Zeeshan Ansari, Joe Lockbaum, Valerie Gurka, Haley Akchurin, Trish Polay, Eric Farr, Richard Hartness, Monica Pritchard, Jim Wallace, Justin Basinger, and Chris Thomas.

To Scott Guthrie, whose leadership at Microsoft not only with .NET but also with the Azure platform has made it the leading computing platform on the planet.

ACKNOWLEDGMENTS

I've considered Scott a friend since 2006. In 2017, I met with Scott at his office for almost an hour talking about the problem that is addressed in this book. That most .NET developers have too many options, too many disconnected tools, and that the DevOps environment for .NET and Azure isn't defined in a cohesive, simple way. Scott encouraged me to build the model that would show developers how to bring everything together.

To Scott Hunter, who heads up the .NET platform at Microsoft. Scott and I discussed this book in mid-2018 over lunch, mulling over the complexity of choices developers need to make when choosing how to bring together the different elements of the Microsoft platform in order to create an environment that causes the "pit of success" – where things fall into place because everything is integrated properly. Thank you, Scott, for being the sponsor of this book.

Finally, I'd like to mention some influential people who have taught me, knowingly or not, some key skills and habits along my career. Each of these has had either a direct or indirect impact on the synthesis of ideas and patterns in this book. First, Robbie McDonald, who took a chance on a cold resume for an internship at Dell. Through the chance he took on me, I was exposed very early in my career to very complex, sophisticated, and high-scale computer systems. Next, Eric Brand was the first architect I worked under. At that time, I didn't understand the difference between a software developer and a software architect. Eric was patient, encouraging, and always had time for questions. Under his projects, I became deeply adept with the .NET runtime and SQL Server, much more than I had been in the past. When the Iraq war started in 2003, my Army Reserve unit was called up for back-to-back tours in Iraq for 15 months. I was paired with Brett Rogers as co-truck-commanders in our HET tank transport company. Brett was also a .NET developer. Thanks, Brett, for the welcome .NET pair programming out in the Iraq desert. Next, I'd like to acknowledge Steve Donie. Steve taught me continuous integration and the mechanisms of build scripts. The build script in this book is an adaptation of build scripts he authored many years ago in both Ant and NAnt. Additionally, Jeremy Miller taught me dependency management and test-driven development. As the author of StructureMap, Jeremy afforded me an opportunity to contribute to that open source project as well as the deep learning applying it on some complex software projects. Paul Leury also played a key role in some of the patterns in this book. Paul hired me into my first management position. The team I managed under Paul built a significant native Windows desktop application. During that project, my thoughts on hub and spoke architecture and application buses solidified. The learning on that project made its way into the application bus pattern in the MvcContrib open source library as well as some projects that contributed to Jimmy Bogard's Mediatr library. Code in this example application is adapted from both of those open source projects. I next must thank Eric Hexter and Stephen Balkum for hiring me as an independent consultant advising one of their team architects, Blake Caraway, who has remained a good friend. Through that work, the guidance on team workflow and process emerged. Additionally, Eric has been a thought leader on deployment automation and production operations. I learned a great deal in those areas from him. He was a terrific asset as a cofounder of the MvcContrib OSS project as well as a coauthor with me on previous books in the "ASP.NET MVC in Action" series. Some of his work is cited in this book. Additionally, I thank my previous coauthors of various books. In working with them I became better at authoring larger bodies of work. Thanks to Ben Scheirman, Jimmy Bogard, Jeremy Skinner, Matt Hinze, and Eric Hexter. Finally, thanks to all the great people in the Microsoft MVP program. I've learned something from each of you since my time in the program from 2006 until now. Specifically, thanks to Carl Franklin, for helping me start the Azure DevOps Podcast and for your friendship.

My final acknowledgment goes to Kevin Hurwitz. We made the transition from developer to architect at a similar time. Kevin was instrumental as a sounding board, challenger, and coprofessional with me as we developed some of the ideas in this book while working on mutual projects. Notably was when Kevin introduced me to the SQL schema migration pattern that has now become industry standard and implemented by multiple libraries and products. The pattern he taught me is now recognized across the DevOps community and is in this book. Kevin has also contributed to many of the other ideas that have made their way into this book. Thank you, Kevin, for your ideas, innovation, and your friendship over the years.

Introduction

This book has been a culmination of long-time vision, some key leadership, and a confluence of industry events. Almost 15 years ago, the author gained a passion for helping developers succeed, for making the complex simple, and for finding rules of thumb that would work for 80% of situations. With too many options in the software world and too many answers of "it depends," the industry has been starved for the ability to do something "by the book." This book seeks to provide that text where a .NET developer can say "I'm doing DevOps with .NET and Azure by the book." In this manner, one would know what models and patterns were in play and what to expect from said environment. This book is being released while .NET Core 3 is in preview status; therefore, the version of the book should be considered preview as well. The examples largely use Visual Studio 2019 preview edition. The code itself and the Azure DevOps Services pipeline function perfectly well with .NET Core 2.2, however, and can be used to implement applications immediately. It is the intent of the author to release a .NET Core 3 edition aligning with Microsoft's release schedule. The example configuration used throughout this book can be leveraged through a public project and source code repository online at `https://dev.azure.com/clearmeasurelabs/Onion-DevOps-Architecture`.

CHAPTER 1

Introduction

You, dear reader, are starting down the path of excellence. By picking up this book, you are showing your leadership and resolve to equip your development organization to be world class, competing with any other development group on the planet. You are taking initiative. You are a software leader. You are confronting the challenge head-on. This book is for you. This book is a synthesis of practices, tools, and processes that, together, can equip a software organization to move fast and deliver software of the highest quality. In this chapter, we cover the relevant common problem our industry faces, the solution to that problem, and how to implement it for your team. This text goes hand in hand with a fully implemented example publicly available at `https://dev.azure.com/clearmeasurelabs/Onion-DevOps-Architecture`.

The Problem

Every day, millions of developers use .NET to build and operate mission-critical software systems for organizations around the world. Visual Studio, .NET, and Windows Server, whether on-premise or in Azure, provide astounding capabilities that enable any kind of software. The marketplace has scores of books, online courses, and tutorials teaching every technology framework and language feature. Microsoft's own online documentation is broad and comprehensive. The Microsoft platform, along with the marketplaces, extensions, and packages, has a building block for everything you can imagine. BUT, it is completely up to you to put it all the blocks together in just the right way for YOUR environment. This book seeks to change that.

© Jeffrey Palermo 2019
J. Palermo, *.NET DevOps for Azure*, https://doi.org/10.1007/978-1-4842-5343-4_1

The Challenge of Explosive Growth

By any measure, the number of professional developers has exploded over the last decade, surpassing the growth rate of the previous decade. As found in Figure 1-1, from Stack Overflow's 2018 survey, we can see that over half of professional developers entered the industry in the last five years.

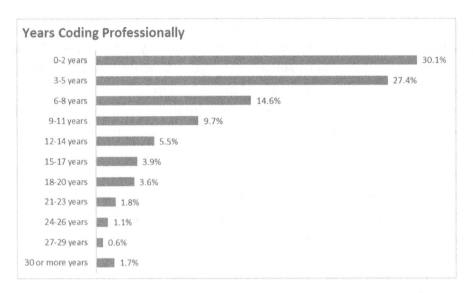

Figure 1-1. *Over half of developers have five years of professional coding experience or less – Stack Overflow*

If you have surpassed 20 years of development experience, you qualify at the top 5.2% of experience in the industry. We can see the inflection point between the 6-8 years and 3-5 years of experience. It's unclear how the growth will continue or if business demand will start to be saturated. Regardless of future growth, we have a challenge in our industry created by this explosive growth in the workforce. Consider this analogy. You are opening a new auto mechanic shop. Figure 1-2 is taken from Wikimedia Commons Site[I]

[I]Wikimedia Commons, 2010

Figure 1-2. *An auto mechanic shop must be set up in a way conducive to delivering quality and speed*

You purchase a fantastic location on a main road close to other centers of business. You spare no expense building the shop. You contact a local mechanic trade school and declare you wish to hire the top 7% of upcoming graduating class. You have budgeted for whatever pay it takes to hire the best and the brightest who have just been trained as new mechanics.

Along comes graduation day, and the next week, you are preparing to open for business. You gather in front of the shop next to pallets of just-delivery tools and shop equipment. You brief your new workforce expressing excitement saying, "Let's get the shop ready for opening. We start serving customers next week." Your staff's excitement turns to fear with wide eyes. Your grand opening is a disaster, and you wonder what you missed.

3

This manager hired staff who had been trained in how to fix and service automobiles. They were smart, skillful, and motivated. They were trained in an environment that was expertly configured. Alas, the curriculum did not include how to set up a new environment for themselves.

Unfortunately, more than a few team leaders and managers have experienced a similar situation. These teams have developers who know how to apply their training and practice. But in every trade that builds something, the jobsite, or environment, has a profound effect on the effectiveness of the team. The common curriculum has some gaps, and this is one of them. This book seeks to fill that gap in the curriculum. This book will equip you to build a highly effective DevOps environment for your team.

No End-to-end Reference Implementation

Along with documentation, open source projects, and samples, there does not exist any available end-to-end demonstration of a complete DevOps environment. Many have sought such a reference implementation. With a reference implementation, teams could emulate the patterns demonstrated and perform configuration rather than research and development in this area. And while tutorials and online videos exist, they demonstrate part of the solution and don't provide access to any functional implementation that can be evaluated and copied. This book changes that.

The Solution

This book provides the model for a world-class DevOps environment when working with Microsoft technologies. And while variances in tools, language, or requirements will change the needed implementation, the DevOps model shared in this text is the architecture for the working environment for your team. Modify parts of it as you see fit, but the architecture will enable all your teams and all your applications to accelerate in performance and push forward through the next decade.

Over the past 13 years of a 22+ year career in software engineering, this author has sought to synthesize research, patterns, methods, processes, and tools that would yield the best environment for development teams. Through early Agile transformations including Scrum, Extreme Programming, Kanban, Lean Software, and other methodologies, we can see that methodology alone with not guarantee software success. In addition, tools alone cannot remove all risk from a project. Only by combining the best elements of everything available can we create an environment where it is harder to fail than succeed. The DevOps environment described in this book seeks to pull good ideas from all available prior art, combining them in a unique way that any team can implement. It is this author's belief that any team can be WORLD CLASS when equipped with the right environment, tools, and process.

This book is written with a development leader in mind. Whether you are a software architect, lead engineer, manager, executive, or a passionate leader within a development team, this book is written so that you can take action to serve your team by equipping them for success. Our target reader is one who works to enable others to be productive in shipping great software that delights your customers. To start down this path, let's first cover the architecture of a DevOps environment.

DevOps Architecture

When designing software, or anything for that matter, one must draw what is to be built. In the software world, our best method for illustrating a software-related software architecture is Philippe Kruchten's 4+1 model. He writes about it in his IEEE paper, "Architectural Blueprints—The '4+1' View Model of Software Architecture."[II] In this model for emergent and iterative architecture, Mr. Kruchten defines four layers to illustrate the architecture and one list of scenarios, which are select use cases the architecture supports. The needed capabilities drive the architecture. Just like blueprints for a house will have layers such as floorplan, electrical, and plumbing, the four layers in this model for software architecture are

- Logical view

- Process view

- Physical view

- Development view

Logical View

Let's consider the very popular logo that has come to represent DevOps. Figure 1-3 is taken from the Wikimedia Commons site.[III]

[II]Kruchten
[III]Wikimedia Commons, 2016

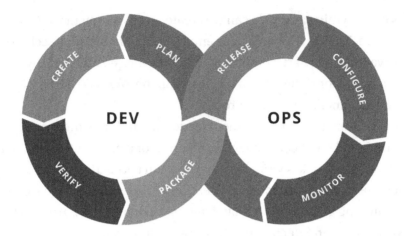

Figure 1-3. *The common logo for DevOps still does not combine Dev and Ops*

There are many versions of this same depiction of DevOps, but this author believes it is fundamentally wrong. It fails to unify development and operations. It still maintains that they are two. And if there are two that must work well together, then one would question: "where is product management" or "where is QA." And once these other groups are depicted, we have an organization that still hangs onto the silos. No, a much better logical view of DevOps is the following Figure 1-4.

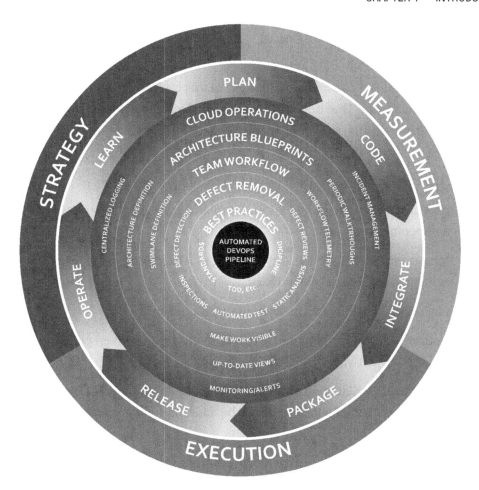

Figure 1-4. *Logically, DevOps seeks to drive a fast cycle time with a unified organization*

A more appropriate view of DevOps would untwist the sideways figure eight into a unified cycle. The goal of the unified team is to complete a cycle in as short a time as possible. The cycle includes

- Plan

- Code

- Integrate

- Package

- Release

- Operate

- Learn

In order to facilitate a constant acceleration of this cycle, we define a hub around which this cycle can spin. That hub is the automated DevOps pipeline. Built on top of that foundation, we also have several layers of capability to achieve in our team. Each layer needs

- Strategy: Decisions on what is to be done and how

- Execution: Competent and faithful implementation of the strategy on an ongoing basis

- Measurement: Inspecting and verifying that executing the strategy is achieving the desired objectives

The six layers of capability for the team in this model are

- Automated DevOps Pipeline: An automated way to convert code into production software

- Best Practices: Selection and appropriate implementation of the practices that are deemed to be the best for the software and the team's situation

- Defect Removal: Choice of defect prevention and defect removal techniques and the application thereof

- Team Workflow: Complete visibility into all the work the team is doing with the ability to see bottlenecks quickly

- Architectural Blueprints: The definition, maintenance, and inspection of clear blueprints for the software as is and as the software is to be in the next increment

- Cloud Operations: How the software is being operated, monitored, and customers supported in production

This is the logical model for a team's DevOps environment. As you evaluate these layers, you will not find a single cookie-cutter implementation that is right for every team, but each of these layers of capability must be addressed for every team. As you are analyzing this model for you team, don't hesitate to add an additional layer if your context deems that appropriate.

Remember that the most important element of this logical architecture is the cycle. Everything is subordinate to the ability to continually accelerate the team's ability to cycle of planning an idea to learning that the intended outcome had been accomplished. Only about 1/3 of ideas that are prioritized for a software system end up having the positive affect that is intended. Sam Guckenheimer, product owner for the Azure DevOps product line at Microsoft, has shared his analysis of relevant industry research in a 2018 podcast interview.[IV] At 15:43 of the interview, Mr. Guckenheimer relates the "rule of thirds" whereby

- One-third of prioritized features have the positive, intended effect.

- One-third of prioritized features have a neutral effect.

- One-third of prioritized features have a negative effect and should be reverted immediately.

If even the best, most sophisticated companies are still subject to this general rule, it is imperative that a software organization be able to execute a software cycle very quickly. Companies that can drive cycle time lower will have a sustained competitive advantage in the marketplace.

Process view

In 4+1 architecture, the process view follows the order in which things are done. This view, and the structure thereof, will guide many other implementation decisions as tools are integrated and methods chosen. As shown in Figure 1-5, that is an end-to-end process view for the model of DevOps that will be illustrated throughout this book.

[IV]Guckenheimer, 2018

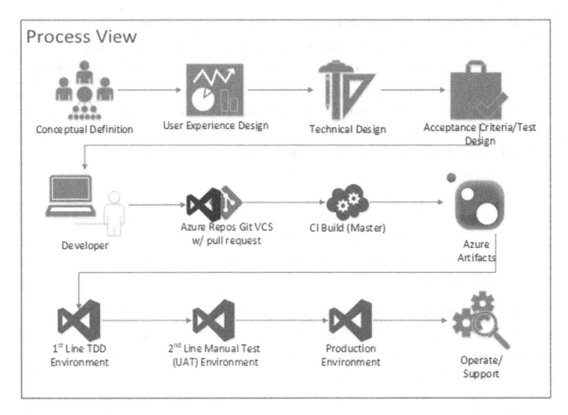

Figure 1-5. *The DevOps' architecture process view*

The process for a DevOps environment contains more than just automated builds and deployments. It starts by modeling the entire value chain from the time an idea is being discussed to when that idea has been put into the hands of customers as a new software capability. Before code is even touched, there are four distinct types of design that must be performed on a feature so that developers know how it should be implemented. Some small teams do not track their process to this level of granularity. Instead, they rely on conversations with a product owner, as in Scrum, to have questions answered. This can work fine at small scale, but a high-performing process enumerates every distinct type of work that must be performed and separates them in sequence. This allows for the measurement of work in process (WIP) and throughput of each workstation. The modern DevOps books that will be cited in this book all credit their thinking on the concept of flow to Eliyahu Goldratt, author of *The Goal: A Process of Ongoing Improvement*.[v] This is the same author of the popular book

---

[v]Goldratt, The Goal: A Process of Ongoing Improvement, 30th Anniversary Edition, 2014

Theory of Constraints.[VI] This concept of flow, as within a manufacturing plant, has us design the process so that we can visualize the amount of work at any given phase of work and make sure none of them become a bottleneck in the overall process. One step will mathematically always be the bottleneck, so our continual process improvements in search of an ever-quicker cycle time will be targeted at the phase of work that is the currently holding up further rates of throughput.

Physical View

The physical view of a software system is meant to represent the items that comprise it at runtime. With virtual being the new physical, and cloud being the new virtual, I'll simplify this view as the components that own their own memory space. If you are describing the physical view for an application in production, you might draw a single virtual machine, but that wouldn't be very descriptive for small applications. A better approach would be to draw the VM as a container and illustrate the different processes that might run on that VM and their dependency on one another. For the purposes of the DevOps environment that we are describing, please consider Figure 1-6.

[VI]Goldratt, Theory of Constraints, 1990

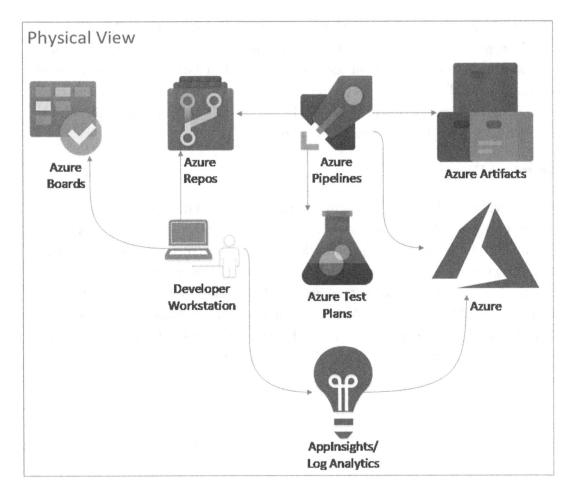

Figure 1-6. *The physical view of a .NET DevOps Environment*

The physical view of our DevOps architecture shows the products that must be online and connected with one another in order to enable our DevOps environment. As you add products and other tools, this view of the architecture will grow.

This is a high-level physical view, as the three environments that we see depicted in the local view are just represented by an Azure icon in this view. It would be appropriate to split that out if we wanted to specify different regions for our environments. At the highest level, this is our physical view.

Development View

The development view, within your 4+1 architecture, depicts the structure of a developer's workstation and surrounding resources in order to implement the system described by the architecture. This is shown in Figure 1-7.

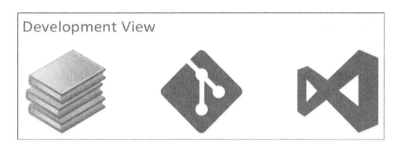

Figure 1-7. *The development view for the DevOps environment described in this book*

In order for you to develop your own world-class DevOps environment for your team, you will need the public Azure DevOps Services project provided with this book, the Git repository for the sample application, and this book along with access to the other books and text referenced in footnotes throughout this text. This book is not meant to stand alone. It is a guide through the complete .NET DevOps implementation provided with the book and delivered via Git and a public Azure DevOps Services project.

This book is not meant to stand alone. It is a guide through the complete .NET DevOps implementation provided with the book and delivered via Git and a public Azure DevOps Services project.

Now that we've reviewed the four views of the architecture for our DevOps environment, let's look at some scenarios that will be supported by this architecture.

Scenarios

The scenarios included with a 4+1 architecture are meant to illustrate the capabilities of the architecture. In the simplest form, scenarios can be use cases or even a list of capabilities the architecture provides. For complex scenarios, it can be useful to illustrate through drawing how data would flow through the system as someone used a capability of the system. For the purposes of our DevOps environment, being the system under design, a list of capabilities will suffice:

- A team member can see which features are in varying states of design by glancing at the project board.

- A developer can open a new feature branch from a feature work item that is in development.

- A developer can run a private build locally, without outside dependency, to validate readiness for a commit/push.

- A developer can execute unit tests and integration tests locally to validate changes before pushing code to the team's Git repository.

- A developer can see newly pushed code build in a continuous integration build and know that the new changes worked well with changes from other teammates.

- A developer receives notification of pass or fail of the full body of automated full-system tests that run in a fully deployed environment.

- Any team member can access versioned release candidate packages for any application components of any successful build.

- A developer can submit a pull request in order to have a teammate inspect the set of changes linked to the work item of the branch.

- A pull request inspector can see the successful CI build, deployment, and full-system test run along with static analysis results and test code coverage metrics while executing the pull request inspection checklist.

- A stakeholder can request on demand for a new build to be deployed automatically to an environment and see it deployed quickly, database and all.

- A team member can query the centralized logs from any environment in order to diagnose issues reported via configured alarms.

Every team's DevOps environment should include these base capabilities. Many teams will want even more capabilities. This book will enable you to design and implement a DevOps environment with the preceding capabilities. At this, the author hopes you are excited! If your team's working environment contained all these capabilities enumerated, would you produce faster or slower for your customers? Would you produce better quality or more bugs with the preceding capabilities? Certainly, any team would be better off with these capabilities.

DevOps Methodology

Before we begin discussing how to implement the architecture of a DevOps environment, let's review the state of the DevOps methodology in the industry. In his popular book, *The Phoenix Project: A Novel About IT, DevOps, and Helping ...,*[VII] Gene Kim enumerates three guiding principles of DevOps. He names them "The Three Ways." They are

1. The First Way: Systems thinking

2. The Second Way: Amplify feedback loops

3. The Third Way: Culture of continual experimentation and learning

These are quite abstract but look out for them as we implement our DevOps scenarios specified above. In our industry lies much confusion about DevOps. Having only been named as such in 2010, DevOps has been commercialized and marketed. You'll see job openings for "DevOps Engineer." This is akin to the "Senior Agile Engineer" job postings around the 2005 time frame. DevOps is a way of thinking. It is a mindset. There are practices that go very well with the DevOps way of thinking, just like test-driven development goes very well with the Agile way of thinking. Let's illustrate the Three Ways of DevOps briefly.

The First Way: Systems Thinking

The DevOps methodology is based on the principles known as The Three Ways. The first way is systems thinking, as shown in Figure 1-8.

Dev   Ops

Figure 1-8. *The first way is systems thinking*

[VII]Kim, Behr, & Spafford, 2013

There is a lot of thought packed into this first principle of DevOps. It encompasses the ability to create a smooth, predictable flow of working software from the imagination of the developers to the active use of the customer. In our world, regardless of job description or job title, if you are involved in building or changing the software, you are on the side of Dev. If you are someone who uses or consumes or depends on the software, then you are on the side of Ops. Other definitions of DevOps that don't include the user are at great risk.

The Second Way: Amplify Feedback Loops

In this principle, we create an environment where those using our software – those operating their business or departments with our software – provide continual feedback to those operating, developing, and changing the software, as shown in Figure 1-9.

Figure 1-9. *Those operating their departments using our software provide continual feedback to those changing the software*

We can put ourselves in the right DevOps mindset by translating the keywords as follows:

- Dev: Includes anyone who works to support, build, change, and improve the software or system

- Ops: Includes anyone who relies on the software to operate their business or department

If our company has a department known as IT Operations, or Support, or Data Center Operations, it's important not to confuse these groups as our customer. They don't use the software. They are merely part of our development capability – the capability to deliver valuable software to our customer so that our customer can operate the software in order to experience its value.

The Third Way: Culture of Continual Experimentation and Learning

If the first two ways were about completing a software release cycle in a streamlined and effective way. The third way is about making that cycle faster, as shown in Figure 1-10.

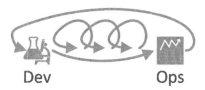

Figure 1-10. *The third way introduces smaller cycles within the cycle*

Companies such as Netflix showed us that software can be released not only daily but many times per day with no downtime and no defects (or close to that ideal). The third way causes us to think with that end in mind, solving any challenges that would prevent us from this ability. Even if the customer doesn't want software releases at that cadence, this way of thinking causes us to gain this capability so that we are ready on a moment's notice to release the software as it stands, always stable, always working, and always bug-free. This way of thinking also encourages us to stop thinking about software releases as a big ceremony. We will see in the coming chapters how to equip our teams with the ability to release changes big and small. We will see that the same process needed for small changes is effective for large changes when every small change has made a trip down the DevOps pipeline. Now that we have covered the architecture and the thinking of DevOps, let's see how to get started.

How to Get Started

The example application, along with the Azure DevOps Services configuration, is available online as a public project.

`https://dev.azure.com/clearmeasurelabs/Onion-DevOps-Architecture`

Keep the sample application and the Azure DevOps project handy as you move through this book. This working sample serves to demonstrate all the capabilities working together. No sample application will be sufficient to illustrate every scenario in the development world, but for the purposes of a DevOps environment, we have chosen the most common application type at the moment. Before we review the sample application, let's map common application components to their runtime components.

Application Runtime Architectures

You are building software with Visual Studio. Regardless of the libraries or frameworks you might choose, you have a finite set of runtime architectures to choose from. Popular today is a web architecture which consists of a ASP.NET web application and a SQL Server database. Or you might have a desktop WPF application communicating to ASP.NET Web API services that then use a SQL Server database. If you have an iPhone app, that might connect to your Web API services. Regardless of the combination of runtimes you take advantage of, the Microsoft platform has a finite set of choices, and the Azure cloud has a handful of ways to run each that must be deployed into the cloud.

Application architecture	Production Runtime
ASP.NET MVC	IIS/Azure App Service, etc.
ASP.NET Web Api	IIS/Azure App Service, etc.
SignalR	IIS/Azure App Service, etc.
Razor Pages	IIS/Azure App Service, etc.
SPA(Razor Components, Angular, React)	IIS/Azure App Service, etc.
Windows Service	VM, Webjob, Azure Function, etc.
Scheduled EXE	VM, Webjob, Azure Function, etc.
SQL Database	Azure SQL, Cosmos DB

Figure 1-11. *A small illustration of Azure runtimes covering the breadth of application architectures*

While this table is nowhere near being complete, we can see that through web applications, off-line jobs, and a relational database, we cover a high percentage of applications out in the wild. WPF, Winforms, and native iOS and Android applications are also supported by a small number of options. With each of these application types, we can choose a full range of runtime options from Infrastructure as a Service (IaaS) to Platform as a Service (PaaS).

The architectural point to consider when designing a DevOps capability is to realize that while implementing the first way, we need **not** support a unique configuration for every team or application. Once we understand how to deliver a web application of some form with a SQL database out to Azure, how many of our applications are now covered?

Most. I would venture to guess for each of you, dear readers, that a high number of your applications use those architectural components. We then add a capability for off-line jobs such as Windows services and scheduled tasks, and we cover a good part of the gap. Once we have these application types covered, you will see how much smaller of a leap it is to then cover your native mobile apps, and Windows desktop apps as well.

The Necessary Tools

In order to set up a professional DevOps environment targeting Azure, you'll need to have a few key tools to get started:

- An Azure subscription

- Visual Studio (2019 or VSCode)

- An Azure DevOps Services organization account

These tools are just the starting point, and throughout this book, we'll integrate more tools, libraries, frameworks from Microsoft, other vendors, as well as open source repositories. Remember, DevOps is about a way of thinking that leads to an outcome of shorter lead times, shorter cycle times, and fewer disruptions. Throughout this book, we'll put all these pieces together one by one.

If you are just getting started with Azure or Azure DevOps Services, don't skip Chapter 2. It will quickly introduce some basic capabilities in an interactive way without requiring you to write any scripting. But don't stop there. The steps shown in Chapter 2 are only to introduce first-time users of these tools. These techniques are not meant for long-term maintainability. For the professional way to set up your DevOps environment, move to Chapter 3 and beyond where we will go through each area in detail.

The Sample Application

While samples tend to be too simplistic or unnecessarily complex, the book uses an ASP.NET Core web application configured with a SQL Server database, using Entity Framework Core for an object-relational mapper (ORM). This application is properly factored into logical layers that control access to key dependencies. The application only does one thing, which is expose a Web API that retrieves expense report records. Our core object model has exactly one entity, ExpenseReport, and our SQL Server database schema has exactly one table, ExpenseReport. Rather than clutter this book with general coding practices, this sample provides some structural guidance with enough surface area to demonstrate all the necessary DevOps techniques. It does not see to illuminate coding patterns or frameworks.

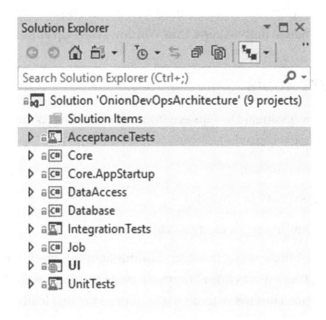

Figure 1-12. *Solution structure of the sample application*

The Visual Studio solution does conform to the Onion Architecture[VIII] dependency management model, by isolating key dependencies inside their own assembly and concentrating application and business logic in a dependency-free assembly called "Core."

- AcceptanceTests: The full-system acceptance tests reside in this project. They run as NUnit tests configured with Selenium and drive the Chrome browser to execute tests against a fully deployed instance of the application.

- Core: This project has no NuGet package dependencies as well as no project dependencies. It is best implemented as a .NET Standard library, and it should contain plain C# objects. The value of this library is that any code it contains is verified to be portable to any application type given that the assembly produced will have no other dependencies that the base class library and C# language features.

[VIII]Palermo, n.d.

- Core.AppStartup: This project exists to bootstrap the application, initiate the Inversion of Control (IoC) container, and instantiate any global resources or cache's that may be needed by the application. Some developers put this logic in the UI project because it is the startup point for the application, but since IoC has nothing to do with serving web pages, we have factored it out to its own very small project.

- DataAccess: This project maintains the responsibility of configuring and using the Entity Framework Core dependency. It contains logic to map our class to the SQL Server schema. It also contains any logic that requires using the EFCore APIs. No code outside of this project knows that the EFCore package exists.

- Database: The database project contains our SQL Server schema migration tooling and migration scripts necessary for incremental, automated changes to the database schema and nonuser data.

- IntegrationTests: This project houses our L1 tests, or integration tests. This is described more in Chapter 7.

- Job: This project houses a normal back-end job that runs on a scheduled interval.

- UI: This project is an ASP.NET Core project and serves our ValuesController, returning all ExpenseReport(s). It makes use of the capabilities of the Core project.

- UnitTests: This project houses the L0 tests, or unit tests for our code.

This application is about as simple as it gets. The Visual Studio solution, however, is factored in a manner that would be suitable for a larger application or service. The hope is that this sample may be a starting point for your own applications, and it would be unrealistic to provide a sample that contained only a single project with no logical separation or dependency isolation.

About the Book

Using the model described earlier for a complete DevOps environment, each of the chapters in this book highlights in detail how to think about each area. The relevant principles will be covered first along with how to implement that part of the environment. While some specifics are highlighted in the chapter, this text makes heavy references to other books, articles, and Microsoft documentation. Rather than duplicate other works and documentation, which will be updated more rapidly than this book, footnotes are used to direct you to the right resource. In addition, use the sample application and public Azure DevOps Services (sometimes abbreviated hereafter as "AzDO") to follow along while digging in as deep as you like. The number of integrations and settings required in order to establish a complete DevOps environment can be daunting. That's why this book needs to be published. While there is no practical way to publish every setting and script file in the text, you may use the accompanying video-recorded walkthrough of the public AzDO project in order to gain a detailed understanding of all the settings that were changed from their defaults.

Until you have a complete DevOps environment, go "by the book." Once everything is online and functioning, feel free to customize, change, and improve.

Now that you understand the challenge our industry is facing and the model for DevOps that will be implemented in this book, let's review what will be covered as you read through the chapters.

Chapter 2 is for those new to Azure DevOps and to Azure in general. It will cover how to set up the basics so that you can follow along with the rest of the book. If you are already a user of AzDO and Azure, feel free to quickly skim the chapter and move on.

Chapter 3 moves beyond the quick starts and online tutorials and describes the professional-grade development environment and the tools you should be using.

Chapter 4 dives into the first phases of work in our DevOps process, which is tracking work. You learn how to customize your own project board so that all work is visible.

Chapter 5 teaches how to track code using Azure Repos. More importantly, it teaches the natural rules for segmenting applications into Git repositories in a fashion suitable for the beginning of an automated DevOps pipeline.

Chapter 6 builds the code. The chapter covers the different types of builds and when to use each. After covering the steps that each type of build should contain, the reader is taken through the configuration of the continuous integration build in Azure Pipelines.

Chapter 7 is the quality control chapter, illustrating how to think about code validation in your DevOps environment. This chapter relates relevant quality research along with rules of thumb for implementing the three required defect removal methods necessary in any DevOps environment.

Chapter 8 creates a versioned, deployable release candidate. This chapter shows how to decide the boundaries of application packaging, how many packages you should have, and how to create them in a deployable format and store them in Azure Artifacts.

Chapter 9 provisions, configures environments, and deploys our release candidates across the environments in Azure. This chapter covers the three distinct types of environments, the difference among them, and how to dynamically create each using PowerShell, Azure Resource Manager (ARM) templates, and Azure Pipelines. It also takes the reader through the deployment steps needed for the three environment types and the configuration settings in Azure Pipelines that allow for total control of when and how software is released.

Chapter 10 rounds out the book by covering how to monitor and support software that has been deployed to a production environment. This chapter shows how to implement and centralize logs and other diagnostics so that they are available for analysis both for proactive alarms using Azure Monitor as well as for on-demand investigation.

Wrap Up

This is the beginning of a new era for your software team. Use the methods and examples in this book to constantly accelerate your team's cycle time. Analyze any part of the process that causes delays or bottlenecks and squeeze those problems out. Now let's get on with the book!

Bibliography

Goldratt, E. M. (1990). *Theory of Constraints*. North River Press. Retrieved from www.amazon.com/Theory-Constraints-Eliyahu-M-Goldratt-ebook/dp/B00L7XYW2Q

Goldratt, E. M. (2014). *The Goal: A Process of Ongoing Improvement, 30th Anniversary Edition*. North River Press. Retrieved from www.amazon.com/Goal-Process-Ongoing-Improvement/dp/0884271951

Guckenheimer, S. (2018, 9 24). Sam Guckenheimer on Testing, Data Collection, and the State of DevOps Report – Episode 003. (J. Palermo, Interviewer) Retrieved from http://azuredevopspodcast.clear-measure.com/sam-guckenheimer-on-testing-data-collection-and-the-state-of-devops-report-episode-003

Kim, G., Behr, K., & Spafford, G. (2013). *The Phoenix Project: A Novel About IT, DevOps, and Helping Your Business Win*. Retrieved February 18, 2019, from https://amazon.com/phoenix-project-devops-helping-business/dp/0988262592

Kruchten, P. (n.d.). Retrieved from Architectural Blueprints—The "4+1" View Model of Software Architecture: www.cs.ubc.ca/~gregor/teaching/papers/4+1view-architecture.pdf

Palermo, J. (n.d.). *The Onion Architecture*. Retrieved March 21, 2019, from http://jeffreypalermo.com/blog/the-onion-architecture-part-1/

Wikimedia Commons (2010). ANT Berezhnyi [CC BY 3.0 https://creativecommons.org/licenses/by/3.0)].*File:*https://commons.wikimedia.org/wiki/File:Chery_A1_-_service_shop_in_Ukraine_(7).jpg Retrieved from https://commons.wikimedia.org/wiki/File:Chery_A1_-_service_shop_in_Ukraine_(7).jpg

Wikimedia Commons (2016). Inedo (Karl Harnagy) *File:Devops-toolchain.svg*. Retrieved from https://commons.wikimedia.org/wiki/File:Devops-toolchain.svg

CHAPTER 2

Zero to Azure in 60 Minutes

—Contributed by Cam Soper and Scott Addie, © Microsoft

"I am very grateful for this chapter's contribution to the book. If you, dear reader, are new to the Microsoft platform, to Azure, or to Visual Studio, this chapter will help you understand the building blocks we will be working with in this book. If you have never used Azure DevOps Services in any way, this chapter will introduce you to that product family. I thank Cam Soper and Scott Addie, members of the Microsoft documentation team, for the contribution of this chapter to the book"—Jeffrey Palermo

To give you a hint of the capabilities available to ASP.NET Core developers on Azure, let's take a quick tour through Azure App Service and Azure DevOps.

Deploy an App to App Service

Azure App Service is Azure's web hosting platform. Deploying a web app to Azure App Service can be done manually or by an automated process. This section of the guide discusses deployment methods that can be triggered manually, by script using the command line, or triggered manually using Visual Studio.

In this section, you'll accomplish the following tasks:

- Download and build the sample app.
- Create an Azure App Service web app using the Azure Cloud Shell.
- Deploy the sample app to Azure using Git.
- Deploy a change to the app using Visual Studio.
- Add a staging slot to the web app.
- Deploy an update to the staging slot.
- Swap the staging and production slots.

© Jeffrey Palermo 2019
J. Palermo, *.NET DevOps for Azure*, https://doi.org/10.1007/978-1-4842-5343-4_2

Download and Test the App

The app used in this guide is a pre-built ASP.NET Core app, Simple Feed Reader. It's a Razor Pages app that uses the Microsoft.SyndicationFeed.ReaderWriter API to retrieve an RSS/Atom feed and display the news items in a list.

Feel free to review the code, but it's important to understand that there's nothing special about this app. It's just a simple ASP.NET Core app for illustrative purposes.

From a command shell, download the code, build the project, and run it, as shown in Figure 2-1.

Note   Linux/macOS users should make appropriate changes for paths, for example, using forward slash (**/**) rather than back slash (****).

---

1. Clone the code to a folder on your local machine.

   git clone https://github.com/Azure-Samples/simple-feed-reader/

2. Change your working folder to the simple-feed-reader folder that was created.

   cd .\simple-feed-reader\SimpleFeedReader

3. Restore the packages and build the solution.

   dotnet build

4. Run the app.

   dotnet run

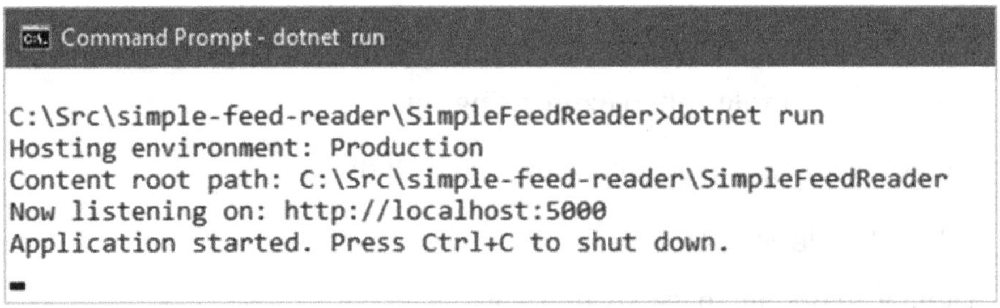

```
Command Prompt - dotnet run

C:\Src\simple-feed-reader\SimpleFeedReader>dotnet run
Hosting environment: Production
Content root path: C:\Src\simple-feed-reader\SimpleFeedReader
Now listening on: http://localhost:5000
Application started. Press Ctrl+C to shut down.
```

Figure 2-1. *Command Prompt- dotnet run*

5. The dotnet run command is successful.

6. Open a browser and navigate to **http://localhost:5000**. The app allows you to type or paste a syndication feed URL and view a list of news items. Refer to Figure 2-2.

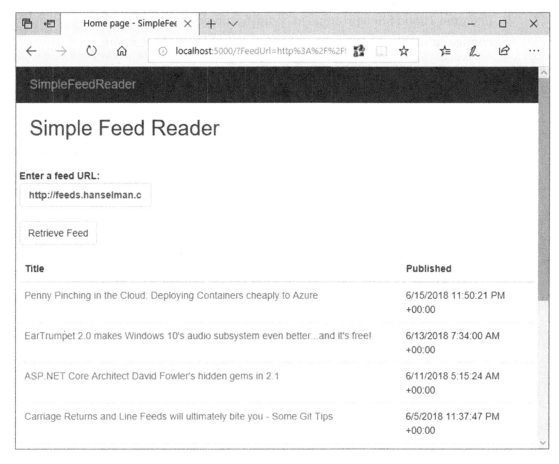

Figure 2-2. *Simple Feed Reader*

7. The app displaying the contents of an RSS feed.

8. Once you're satisfied the app is working correctly, shut it down by pressing Ctrl+C in the command shell.

Create the Azure App Service Web App

To deploy the app, you'll need to create an App Service web app. After creation of the web app, you'll deploy to it from your local machine using Git.

1. Sign in to the Azure Cloud Shell. Note: When you sign in for the first time, Cloud Shell prompts to create a storage account for configuration files. Accept the defaults or provide a unique name.

2. Use the Cloud Shell for the following steps:

   - Declare a variable to store your web app's name. The name must be unique to be used in the default URL. Using the $RANDOM Bash function to construct the name guarantees uniqueness and results in the format webappname99999.

     `webappname=mywebapp$RANDOM`

   - Create a resource group. Resource groups provide a means to aggregate Azure resources to be managed as a group.

     `az group create --location centralus --name AzureTutorial`

   The **az** command invokes the Azure CLI. The CLI can be run locally but using it in the Cloud Shell saves time and configuration.

   - Create an App Service plan in the S1 tier. An App Service plan is a grouping of web apps that share the same pricing tier. The S1 tier isn't free, but it's required for the staging slots feature.

     `az appservice plan create --name $webappname --resource-group AzureTutorial --sku S1`

   - Create the web app resource using the App Service plan in the same resource group.

     `az webapp create --name $webappname --resource-group AzureTutorial --plan $webappname`

- Set the deployment credentials. These deployment credentials apply to all the web apps in your subscription. Don't use special characters in the user name.

```
az webapp deployment user set --user-name REPLACE_WITH_USER_
NAME --password REPLACE_WITH_PASSWORD
```

- Configure the web app to accept deployments from local Git and display the Git deployment URL. Note this URL for reference later.

```
echo Git deployment URL: $(az webapp deployment source
config-local-git --name $webappname --resource-group
AzureTutorial --query url --output tsv)
```

- Display the web app URL. Browse to this URL to see the blank web app. Note this URL for reference later.

```
echo Web app URL: http://$webappname.azurewebsites.net
```

3. Using a command shell on your local machine, navigate to the web app's project folder (e.g., **.\simple-feed-reader\ SimpleFeedReader**). Execute the following commands to set up Git to push to the deployment URL:

- Add the remote URL to the local repository.

```
git remote add azure-prod GIT_DEPLOYMENT_URL
```

- Push the local master branch to the azure-prod remote's master branch.

```
git push azure-prod master
```

You'll be prompted for the deployment credentials you created earlier. Observe the output in the command shell. Azure builds the ASP.NET Core app remotely.

4. In a browser, navigate to the *web app URL,* and note the app has been built and deployed. Additional changes can be committed to the local Git repository with **git commit**. These changes are pushed to Azure with the preceding **git push** command.

Deployment with Visual Studio

Note   This section applies to Windows only. Linux and macOS users should make the change described in step 2 below. Save the file and commit the change to the local repository with **git commit**. Finally, push the change with **git push**, as in the first section.

The app has already been deployed from the command shell. Let's use Visual Studio's integrated tools to deploy an update to the app. Behind the scenes, Visual Studio accomplishes the same thing as the command-line tooling, but within Visual Studio's familiar UI.

1. Open *SimpleFeedReader.sln* in Visual Studio.

2. In Solution Explorer, open *Pages.cshtml*. Change **<h2>Simple Feed Reader</h2>** to **<h2>Simple Feed Reader - V2</h2>**.

3. Press **Ctrl+Shift+B** to build the app.

4. In Solution Explorer, right-click the project, and click **Publish**, as shown in Figure 2-3.

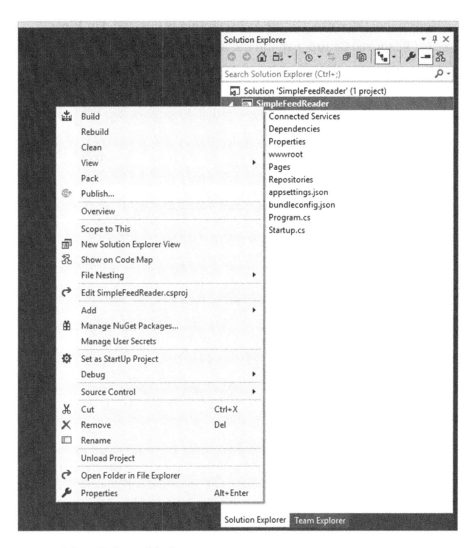

Figure 2-3. *Right-click, Publish*

5. Visual Studio can create a new App Service resource, but this
    update will be published over the existing deployment. In the **Pick
    a publish target** dialog, select **App Service** from the list on the
    left, and then select **Existing**. Click **Publish**.

6. In the **App Service** dialog, confirm that the Microsoft or
    organizational account used to create your Azure subscription is
    displayed in the upper right. If it's not, click the drop-down and
    add it.

7. Confirm that the correct Azure **Subscription** is selected. For **View**, select **Resource Group**. Expand the **AzureTutorial** resource group, and then select the existing web app. Click **OK**. Refer to Figure 2-4.

Figure 2-4. *Publish App Service dialog*

Visual Studio builds and deploys the app to Azure. Browse to the web app URL. Validate that the **‹h2›** element modification is live. Refer to Figure 2-5.

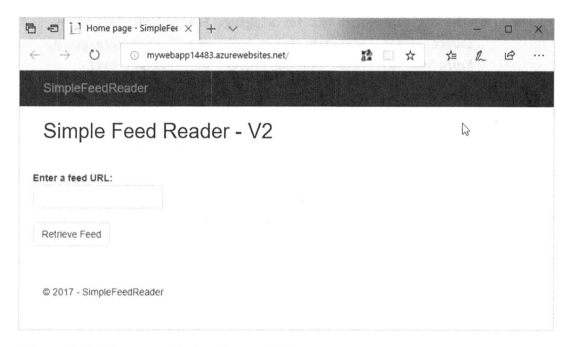

Figure 2-5. *The app with the changed title*

Deployment Slots

Deployment slots support the staging of changes without impacting the app running in production. Once the staged version of the app is validated by a quality assurance team, the production and staging slots can be swapped. The app in staging is promoted to production in this manner. The following steps create a staging slot, deploy some changes to it, and swap the staging slot with production after verification.

1. Sign in to the Azure Cloud Shell, if not already signed in.

2. Create the staging slot.

   - Create a deployment slot with the name *staging*.

     az webapp deployment slot create --name $webappname --resource-group AzureTutorial --slot staging

   - Configure the staging slot to use deployment from local Git and get the **staging** deployment URL. **Note this URL for reference later.**

```
echo Git deployment URL for staging: $(az webapp deployment
source config-local-git --name $webappname --resource-group
AzureTutorial --slot staging --query url --output tsv)
```

- Display the staging slot's URL. Browse to the URL to see the empty staging slot. **Note this URL for reference later**.

```
echo Staging web app URL: http://$webappname-staging.
azurewebsites.net
```

3. In a text editor or Visual Studio, modify *Pages/Index.cshtml* again so that the `<h2>` element reads `<h2>Simple Feed Reader - V3</h2>` and save the file.

4. Commit the file to the local Git repository, using either the **Changes** page in Visual Studio's *Team Explorer* tab or by entering the following using the local machine's command shell:

```
git commit -a -m "upgraded to V3"
```

5. Using the local machine's command shell, add the staging deployment URL as a Git remote, and push the committed changes:

   - Add the remote URL for staging to the local Git repository.

   ```
   git remote add azure-staging <Git_staging_deployment_URL>
   ```

   - Push the local *master* branch to the *azure-staging* remote's *master* branch.

   ```
   git push azure-staging master
   ```

   Wait while Azure builds and deploys the app.

6. To verify that V3 has been deployed to the staging slot, open two browser windows. In one window, navigate to the original web app URL. In the other window, navigate to the staging web app URL. The production URL serves V2 of the app. The staging URL serves V3 of the app. Refer to Figure 2-6.

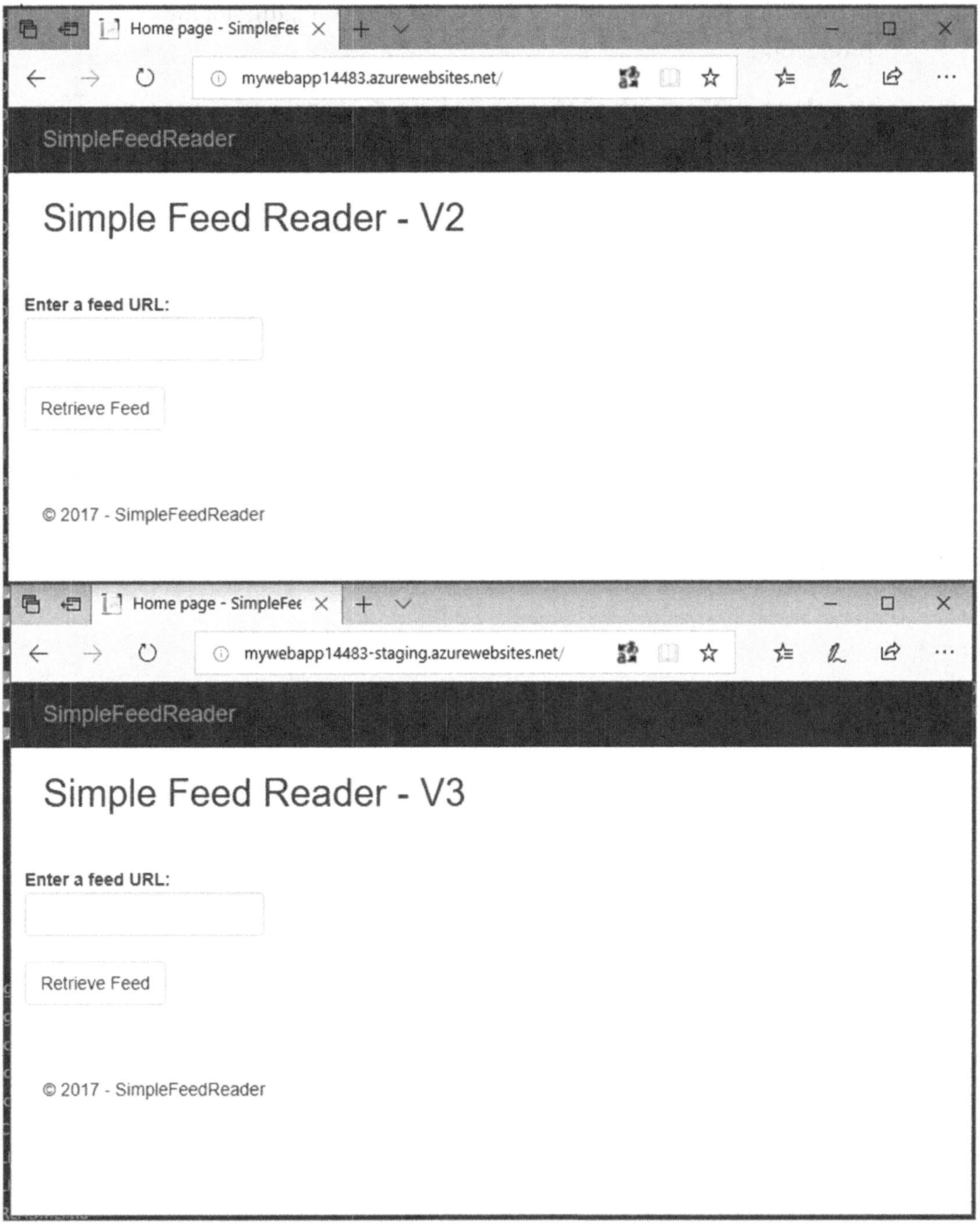

Figure 2-6. *Comparing the browser windows*

7. In the Cloud Shell, swap the verified/warmed-up staging slot into production.

    ```
    az webapp deployment slot swap --name $webappname --resource-group
    AzureTutorial --slot staging
    ```

8. Verify that the swap occurred by refreshing the two browser windows. Refer to Figure 2-7.

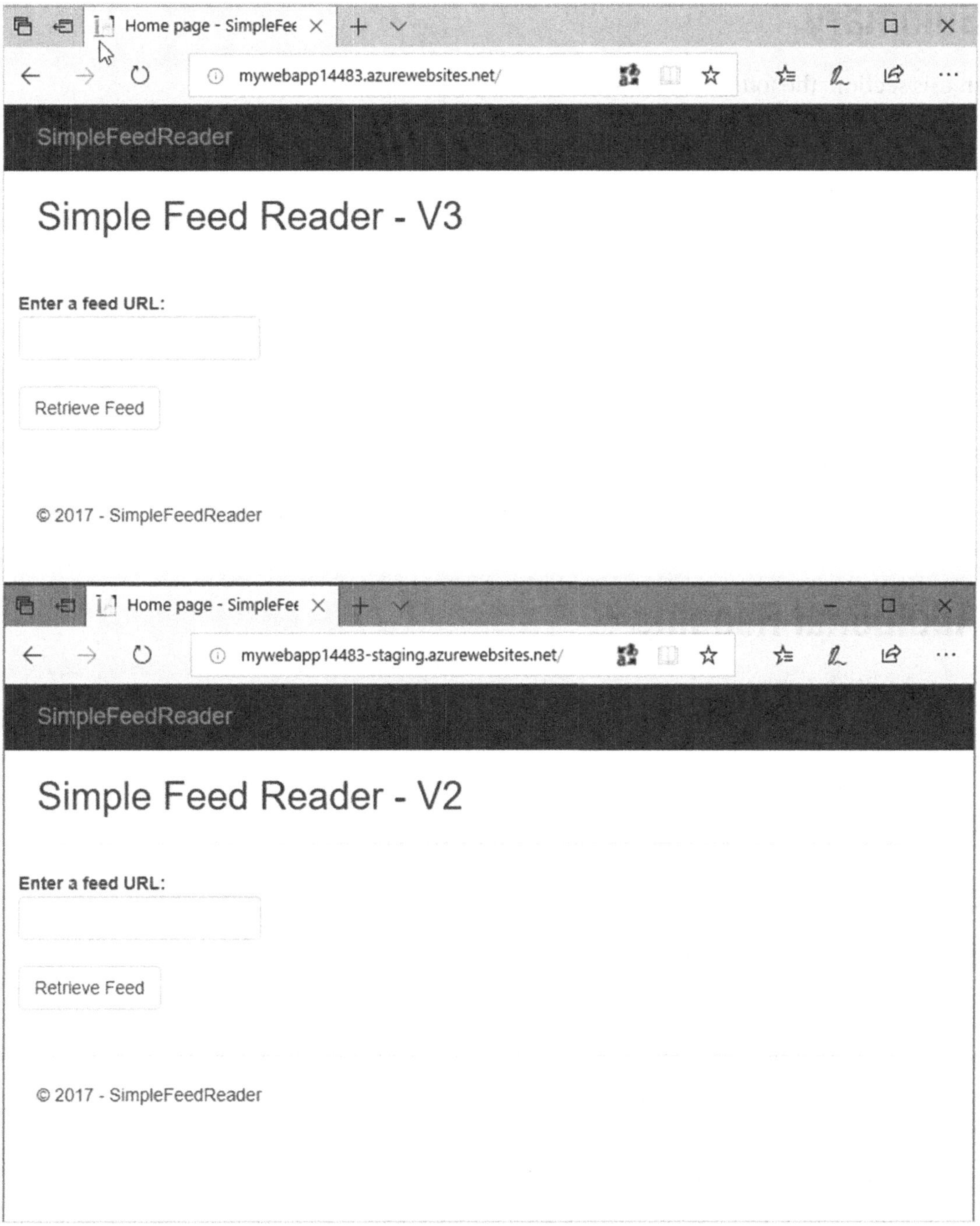

Figure 2-7. *Comparing the browser windows after the swap*

Summary

In this section, the following tasks were completed:

- Downloaded and built the sample app.

- Created an Azure App Service web app using the Azure Cloud Shell.

- Deployed the sample app to Azure using Git.

- Deployed a change to the app using Visual Studio.

- Added a staging slot to the web app.

- Deployed an update to the staging slot.

- Swapped the staging and production slots.

In the next section, you'll learn how to build a DevOps pipeline with Azure Pipelines.

Additional Reading

- Web Apps overview

- Build a .NET Core and SQL Database web app in Azure App Service

- Configure deployment credentials for Azure App Service

- Set up staging environments in Azure App Service

Continuous Integration and Deployment

In the previous chapter, you created a local Git repository for the Simple Feed Reader app. In this chapter, you'll publish that code to a GitHub repository and construct an Azure DevOps Services pipeline using Azure Pipelines. The pipeline enables continuous builds and deployments of the app. Any commit to the GitHub repository triggers a build and a deployment to the Azure Web App's staging slot.

In this section, you'll complete the following tasks:

- Publish the app's code to GitHub.

- Disconnect local Git deployment.

- Create an Azure DevOps organization.

- Create a team project in Azure DevOps Services.

- Create a build definition.

- Create a release pipeline.

- Commit changes to GitHub, and automatically deploy to Azure.

- Examine the Azure Pipelines pipeline.

Publish the App's Code to GitHub

1. Open a browser window and navigate to **https://github.com**.

2. Click the + drop-down in the header, and select **New repository** (refer to Figure 2-8):

Figure 2-8. *GitHub New Repository option*

3. Select your account in the **Owner** drop-down, and enter *simple-feed-reader* in the **Repository name** text box.

4. Click the **Create repository** button.

5. Open your local machine's command shell. Navigate to the directory in which the *simple-feed-reader* Git repository is stored.

6. Rename the existing *origin* remote to *upstream*. Execute the following command:

```
git remote rename origin upstream
```

7. Add a new *origin* remote pointing to your copy of the repository on GitHub. Execute the following command:

    git remote add origin https://github.com/<GitHub_username>/simple-feed-reader/

8. Publish your local Git repository to the newly created GitHub repository. Execute the following command:

    git push -u origin master

9. Open a browser window and navigate to **https://github.com/<GitHub_username>/simple-feed-reader/**. Validate that your code appears in the GitHub repository.

Disconnect Local Git Deployment

Remove the local Git deployment with the following steps. Azure Pipelines (an Azure DevOps Service) both replaces and augments that functionality.

1. Open the Azure portal, and navigate to the *staging (mywebapp<unique_number>/staging)* web app. The web app can be quickly located by entering *staging* in the portal's search box (refer to Figure 2-9):

Figure 2-9. *Staging web app search term*

2. Click **Deployment options**. A new panel appears. Click **Disconnect** to remove the local Git source control configuration that was added in the previous chapter. Confirm the removal operation by clicking the **Yes** button.

3. Navigate to the *mywebapp* App Service. As a reminder, the portal's search box can be used to quickly locate the App Service.

4. Click **Deployment options**. A new panel appears. Click **Disconnect** to remove the local Git source control configuration that was added in the previous chapter. Confirm the removal operation by clicking the **Yes** button.

Create an Azure DevOps Organization

1. Open a browser, and navigate to the Azure DevOps organization creation page.

2. Type a unique name into the **Pick a memorable name** text box to form the URL for accessing your Azure DevOps organization.

3. Select the **Git** radio button, since the code is hosted in a GitHub repository.

4. Click the **Continue** button. After a short wait, an account and a team project, named *MyFirstProject*, are created. Refer to Figure 2-10.

Figure 2-10. *Azure DevOps organization creation page*

5. Open the confirmation email indicating that the Azure DevOps organization and project are ready for use. Click the **Start your project** button (refer to Figure 2-11):

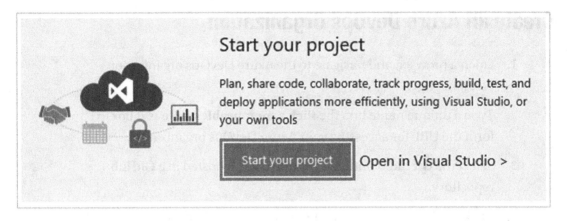

Figure 2-11. *Start your project button*

6. A browser opens to *<account_name>*.visualstudio.com. Click
    the *MyFirstProject* link to begin configuring the project's DevOps
    pipeline.

Configure the Azure Pipelines Pipeline

There are three distinct steps to complete. Completing the steps in the following three
sections results in an operational DevOps pipeline.

Grant Azure DevOps Access to the GitHub Repository

1. Expand the **or build code from an external repository**
    accordion. Click the **Setup Build** button (refer to Figure 2-12):

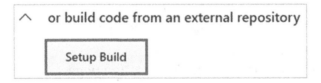

Figure 2-12. *Setup Build button*

2. Select the **GitHub** option from the **Select a source** section
    (refer to Figure 2-13):

Figure 2-13. *Select a source – GitHub*

3. Authorization is required before Azure DevOps can access your
    GitHub repository. Enter *GitHub connection* in the **Connection
    name** text box, as shown in Figure 2-14. For example:

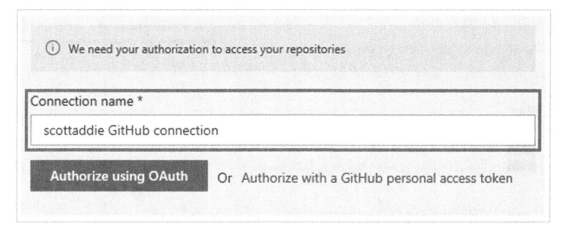

Figure 2-14. *GitHub connection name*

4. If two-factor authentication is enabled on your GitHub account, a
    personal access token is required. In that case, click the **Authorize
    with a GitHub personal access token** link. See the official GitHub
    personal access token creation instructions for help. Only the *repo*
    scope of permissions is needed. Otherwise, click the **Authorize
    using OAuth** button.

5. When prompted, sign in to your GitHub account. Then select
    Authorize to grant access to your Azure DevOps organization.
    If successful, a new service endpoint is created.

6. _ Click the ellipsis button next to the **Repository** button. Select the /
   simple-feed-reader repository from the list. Click the **Select** button.

7. Select the _master_ branch from the **Default branch for manual
   and scheduled builds** drop-down. Click the **Continue** button.
   The template selection page appears.

Create the Build Definition

1. From the template selection page, enter _ASP.NET Core_ in the
   search box, as shown in Figure 2-15:

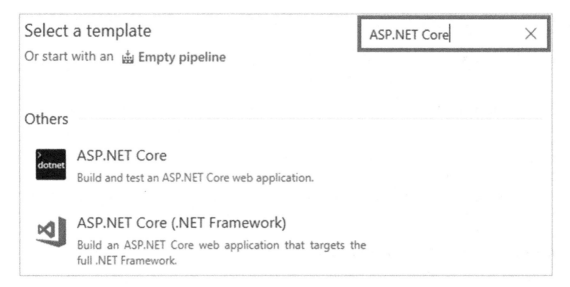

**Figure 2-15.** _ASP.NET Core search on template page_

2. The template search results appear. Hover over the **ASP.NET Core**
   template, and click the **Apply** button.

3. The **Tasks** tab of the build definition appears. Click the **Triggers**
   tab.

4. Check the **Enable continuous integration** box. Under the **Branch
   filters** section, confirm that the **Type** drop-down is set to _Include_.
   Set the **Branch specification** drop-down to _master_, as shown in
   Figure 2-16.

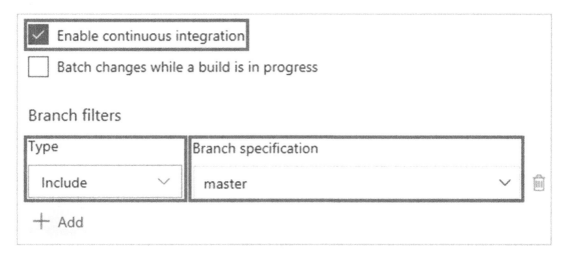

Figure 2-16. *Enable continuous integration settings*

These settings cause a build to trigger when any change is pushed to the *master* branch of the GitHub repository. Continuous integration is tested in the Commit changes to GitHub and automatically deploy to Azure section.

5. Click the **Save & queue** button, and select the **Save** option, as shown in Figure 2-17:

Figure 2-17. *Save button*

6. The following modal dialog appears, as shown in Figure 2-18:

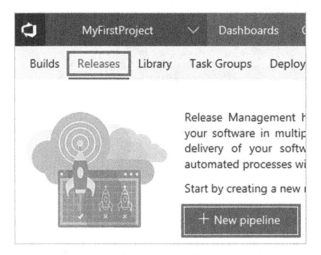

Figure 2-18. *Save build definition – modal dialog*

Use the default folder of \ and click the **Save** button.

Create the Release Pipeline

1. Click the **Releases** tab of your team project. Click the **New pipeline** button. Refer to Figure 2-19.

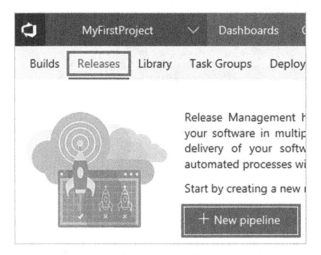

Figure 2-19. *Releases tab – new definition button*

The template selection pane appears.

2. From the template selection page, enter *App Service* in the
search box, as shown in Figure 2-20:

Figure 2-20. *Release pipeline template search box*

3. The template search results appear. Hover over the **Azure App
Service Deployment with Slot** template, and click the **Apply**
button. The **Pipeline** tab of the release pipeline appears, as shown
in Figure 2-21.

Figure 2-21. *Release pipeline tab*

4. Click the **Add** button in the **Artifacts** box. The **Add artifact** panel
appears, as shown in Figure 2-22:

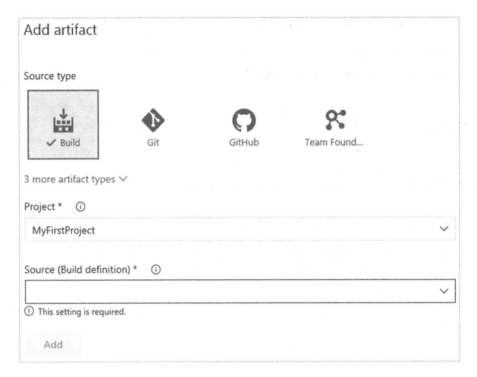

Figure 2-22. *Release pipeline –Add artifact panel*

5.   Select the **Build** tile from the **Source type** section. This type allows for the linking of the release pipeline to the build definition.

6.   Select *MyFirstProject* from the **Project** drop-down.

7.   Select the build definition name, *MyFirstProject-ASP.NET Core-CI*, from the **Source (Build definition)** drop-down.

8.   Select *Latest* from the **Default version** drop-down. This option builds the artifacts produced by the latest run of the build definition.

9.   Replace the text in the **Source alias** text box with *Drop*.

10.   Click the **Add** button. The **Artifacts** section updates to display the changes.

11.   Click the lightning bolt icon to enable continuous deployments, as shown in Figure 2-23:

Figure 2-23. *Release pipeline artifacts – lightning bolt icon*

With this option enabled, a deployment occurs each time a new build is available.

12. A **Continuous deployment trigger** panel appears to the right. Click the toggle button to enable the feature. It isn't necessary to enable the **Pull request trigger**.

13. Click the **Add** drop-down in the **Build branch filters** section. Choose the **Build Definition's default branch** option. This filter causes the release to trigger only for a build from the GitHub repository's *master* branch.

14. Click the **Save** button. Click the **OK** button in the resulting **Save** modal dialog.

15. Click the **Environment 1** box. An **Environment** panel appears to the right. Change the *Environment 1* text in the **Environment name** text box to *Production*, as shown in Figure 2-24.

Figure 2-24. *Release pipeline – Environment name text*

16. Click the **1 phase, 2 tasks** link in the **Production** box, as shown in Figure 2-25:

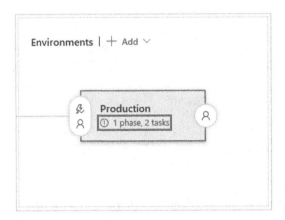

Figure 2-25. *Release pipeline – production environment link.png*

The **Tasks** tab of the environment appears.

17. Click the **Deploy Azure App Service to Slot** task. Its settings appear in a panel to the right.

18. Select the Azure subscription associated with the App Service from the **Azure subscription** drop-down. Once selected, click the **Authorize** button.

19. Select *web app* from the **App type** drop-down.

20. Select *mywebapp/* from the **App service name** drop-down.

21. Select *AzureTutorial* from the **Resource group** drop-down.

22. Select *staging* from the **Slot** drop-down.

23. Click the **Save** button.

24. Hover over the default release pipeline name. Click the pencil icon to edit it. Use *MyFirstProject-ASP.NET Core-CD* as the name, as shown in Figure 2-26.

Figure 2-26. *Release pipeline name*

25. Click the **Save** button.

Commit Changes to GitHub and Automatically Deploy to Azure

1. Open *SimpleFeedReader.sln* in Visual Studio.

2. In Solution Explorer, open *Pages.cshtml*. Change `<h2>Simple Feed Reader - V3</h2>` to `<h2>Simple Feed Reader - V4</h2>`.

3. Press **Ctrl**+**Shift**+**B** to build the app.

4. Commit the file to the GitHub repository. Use either the **Changes** page in Visual Studio's *Team Explorer* tab, or execute the following using the local machine's command shell:

   ```
   git commit -a -m "upgraded to V4"
   ```

5. Push the change in the *master* branch to the *origin* remote of your GitHub repository:

   ```
   git push origin master
   ```

   The commit appears in the GitHub repository's *master* branch, as shown in Figure 2-27:

Figure 2-27. *GitHub commit in master branch*

The build is triggered, since continuous integration is enabled in the build definition's **Triggers** tab, as shown in Figure 2-28:

Tasks
Variables
Triggers
Options
Retention
History
Save & queue
Continuous integration
scottaddie/simple-feed-reader
Enabled
scottaddie/simple-feed-reader
Enable continuous integration

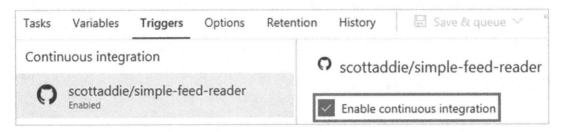

***Figure 2-28.** Enable continuous integration*

6. Navigate to the **Queued** tab of the **Azure Pipelines ➤ Builds** page in Azure DevOps Services. The queued build shows the branch and commit that triggered the build, as shown in Figure 2-29:

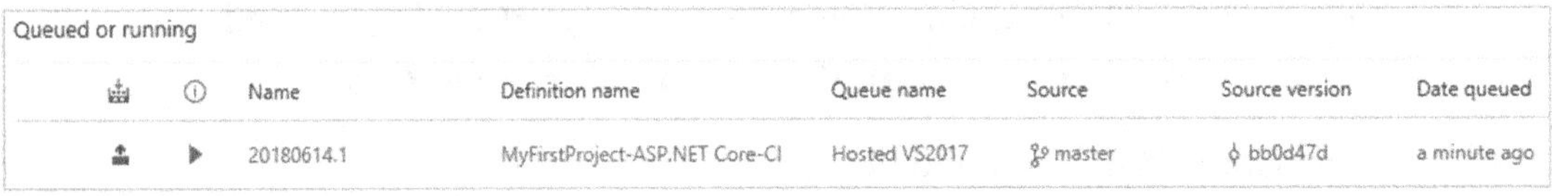

Queued or running
Name
Definition name
Queue name
Source
Source version
Date queued
20180614.1
MyFirstProject-ASP.NET Core-CI
Hosted VS2017
master
bb0d47d
a minute ago

***Figure 2-29.** Queued build*

7. Once the build succeeds, a deployment to Azure occurs. Navigate to the app in the browser. Notice that the "V4" text appears in the heading, as shown in Figure 2-30:

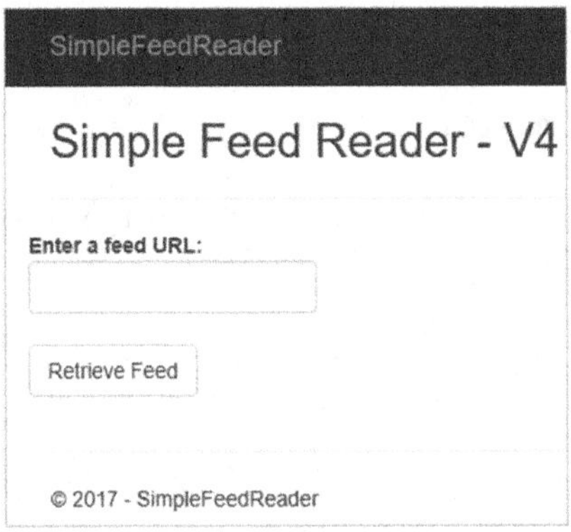

SimpleFeedReader
Simple Feed Reader - V4
Enter a feed URL:
Retrieve Feed
© 2017 - SimpleFeedReader

***Figure 2-30.** Updated app*

Examine the Azure Pipelines pipeline

Build definition

A build definition was created with the name *MyFirstProject-ASP.NET Core-CI*. Upon completion, the build produces a *.zip* file including the assets to be published. The release pipeline deploys those assets to Azure.

The build definition's **Tasks** tab lists the individual steps being used. There are five build tasks, as shown in Figure 2-31.

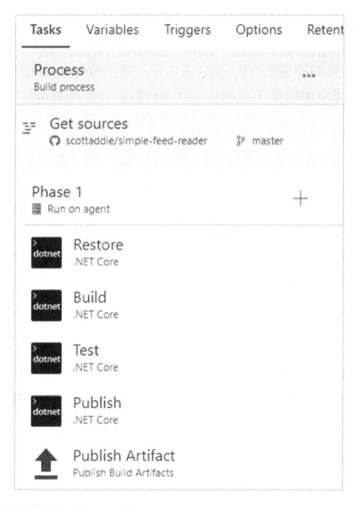

Figure 2-31. *Build definition tasks*

1. Restore: Executes the **dotnet restore** command to restore the app's NuGet packages. The default package feed used is nuget.org.

2. Build: Executes the **dotnet build --configuration release** command to compile the app's code. This **--configuration** option is used to produce an optimized version of the code, which is suitable for deployment to a production environment. Modify the *BuildConfiguration* variable on the build definition's **Variables** tab if, for example, a debug configuration is needed.

3. Test: Executes the **dotnet test --configuration release --logger trx --results-directory <local_path_on_build_ agent>** command to run the app's unit tests. Unit tests are executed within any C## project matching the ****/*Tests/*. csproj** glob pattern. Test results are saved in a *.trx* file at the location specified by the **--results-directory** option. If any tests fail, the build fails and isn't deployed.

Note   To verify the unit tests work, modify *SimpleFeedReader.Tests.cs* to purposefully break one of the tests. For example, change **Assert.True(result. Count > 0);** to **Assert.False(result.Count > 0);** in the **Returns_ News_Stories_Given_Valid_Uri** method. Commit and push the change to GitHub. The build is triggered and fails. The build pipeline status changes to **failed**. Revert the change, commit, and push again. The build succeeds.

---

4. Publish: Executes the **dotnet publish --configuration release --output <local_path_on_build_agent>** command to produce a *.zip* file with the artifacts to be deployed. The **--output** option specifies the publish location of the *.zip* file. That location is specified by passing a predefined variable named **$(build. artifactstagingdirectory)**. That variable expands to a local path, such as *c:_work, on the build agent.

5. Publish Artifact: Publishes the *.zip* file produced by the **Publish** task. The task accepts the *.zip* file location as a parameter, which is the predefined variable **$(build.artifactstagingdirectory)**. The *.zip* file is published as a folder named *drop*.

Click the build definition's **Summary** link to view a history of builds with the definition, as shown in Figure 2-32:

Figure 2-32. *Build definition history*

On the resulting page, click the link corresponding to the unique build number, as shown in Figure 2-33:

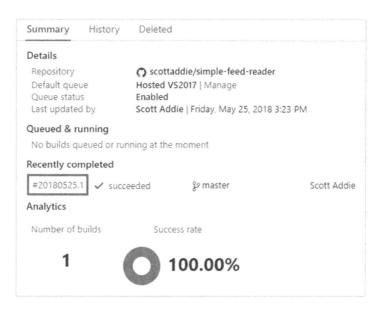

Figure 2-33. *Build definition summary page*

A summary of this specific build is displayed. Click the **Artifacts** tab, and notice the *drop* folder produced by the build is listed, as shown in Figure 2-34:

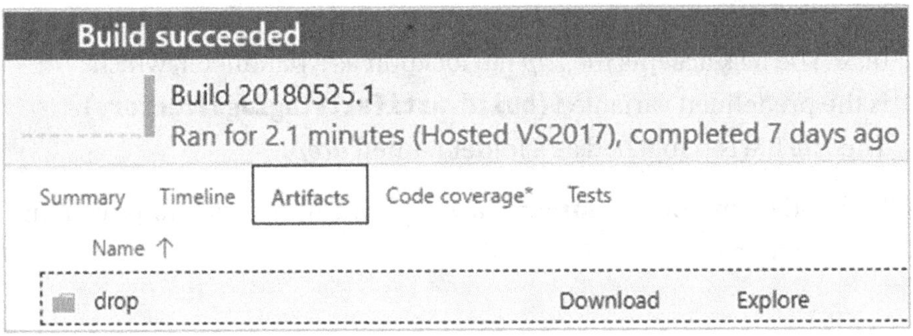

Build succeeded

Build 20180525.1
Ran for 2.1 minutes (Hosted VS2017), completed 7 days ago

Summary   Timeline   Artifacts   Code coverage*   Tests

Name ↑

drop   Download   Explore

Figure 2-34. *Build definition artifacts – drop folder*

Use the **Download** and **Explore** links to inspect the published artifacts.

Release Pipeline

A release pipeline was created with the name *MyFirstProject-ASP.NET Core-CD,*
as shown in Figure 2-35:

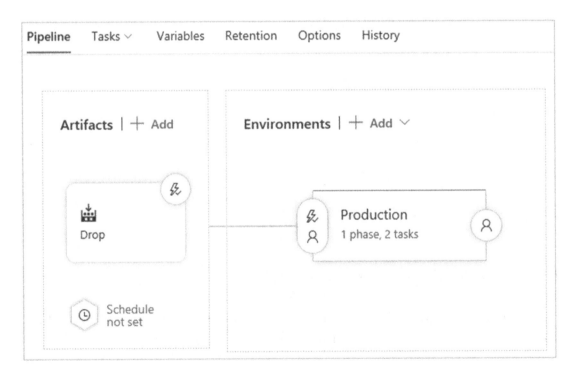

Figure 2-35. *Release pipeline overview*

The two major components of the release pipeline are the **Artifacts** and the **Environments**. Clicking the box in the **Artifacts** section reveals the following panel, as shown in Figure 2-36:

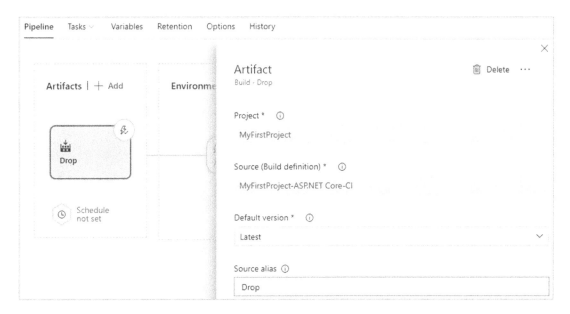

Figure 2-36. *Release pipeline artifacts*

The **Source (Build definition)** value represents the build definition to which this release pipeline is linked. The *.zip* file produced by a successful run of the build definition is provided to the *Production* environment for deployment to Azure. Click the *1 phase, 2 tasks* link in the *Production* environment box to view the release pipeline tasks, as shown in Figure 2-37:

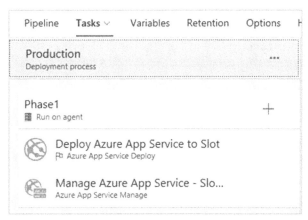

Figure 2-37. *Release pipeline tasks*

The release pipeline consists of two tasks: *Deploy Azure App Service to Slot* and *Manage Azure App Service – Slot Swap*. Clicking the first task reveals the following task configuration, as shown in Figure 2-38:

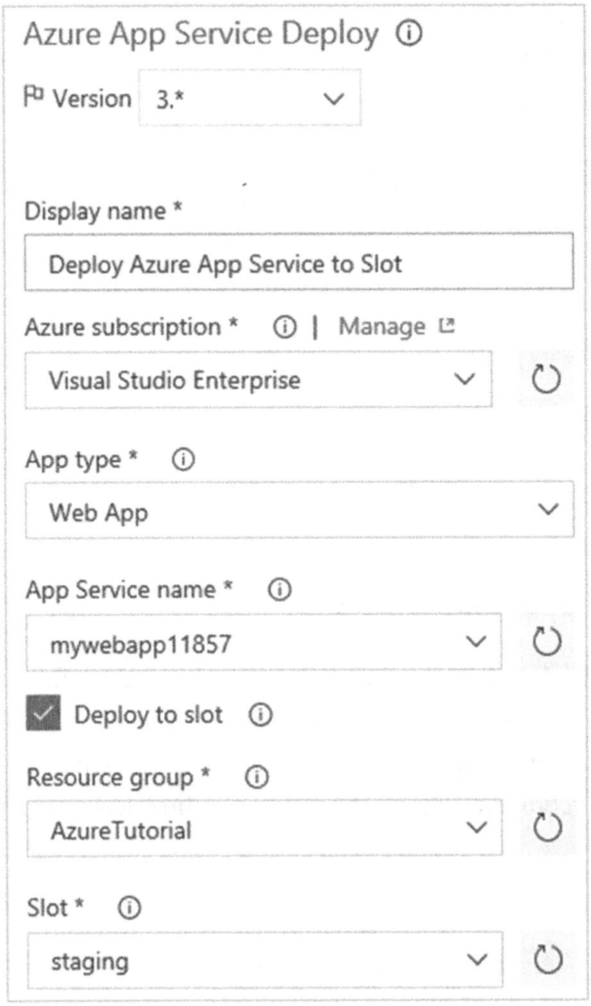

Figure 2-38. *Release pipeline deploy task*

The Azure subscription, service type, web app name, resource group, and deployment slot are defined in the deployment task. The **Package or folder** text box holds the *.zip* file path to be extracted and deployed to the *staging* slot of the *mywebapp<unique_number>* web app.

Clicking the slot swap task reveals the following task configuration, as shown in Figure 2-39:

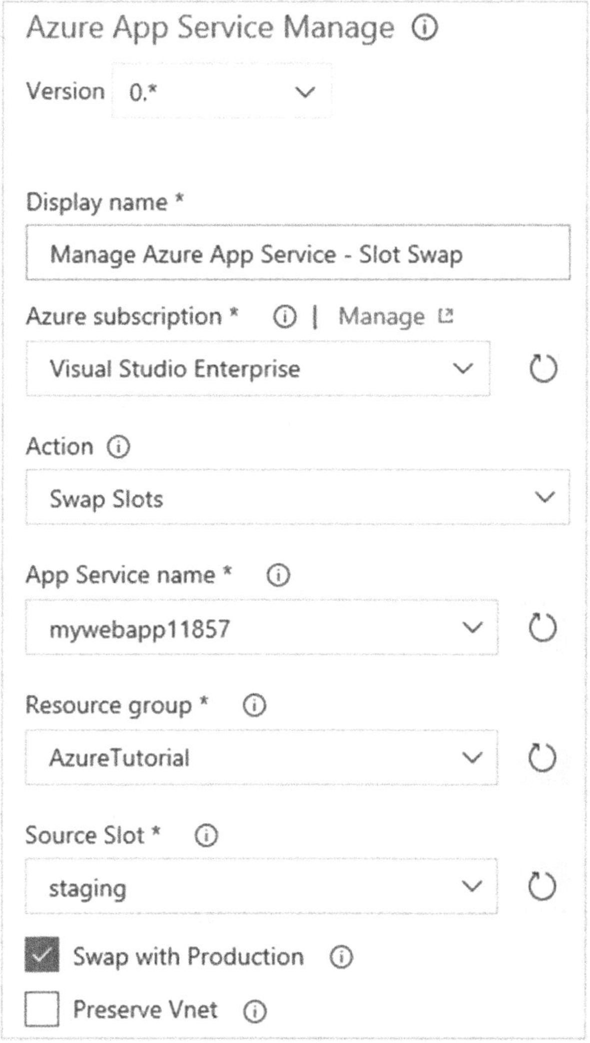

Figure 2-39. *Release pipeline slot swap task*

The subscription, resource group, service type, web app name, and deployment slot details are provided. The **Swap with Production** check box is checked. Consequently, the bits deployed to the *staging* slot are swapped into the production environment.

Additional Reading

- Create your first pipeline with Azure Pipelines

- Build and .NET Core project

- Deploy a web app with Azure Pipelines

Monitor and Debug

Having deployed the app and built a DevOps pipeline, it's important to understand how to monitor and troubleshoot the app.

In this section, you'll complete the following tasks:

- Find basic monitoring and troubleshooting data in the Azure portal.

- Learn how Azure Monitor provides a deeper look at metrics across all Azure services.

- Connect the web app with Application Insights for app profiling.

- Turn on logging and learn where to download logs.

- Stream logs in real time.

- Learn where to set up alerts.

- Learn about remote debugging Azure App Service web apps.

Basic Monitoring and Troubleshooting

App Service web apps are easily monitored in real time. The Azure portal renders metrics in easy-to-understand charts and graphs.

1. Open the Azure portal, and then navigate to the *mywebapp<unique_number>* App Service.

2. The **Overview** tab displays useful "at-a-glance" information, including graphs displaying recent metrics, as shown in Figure 2-40.

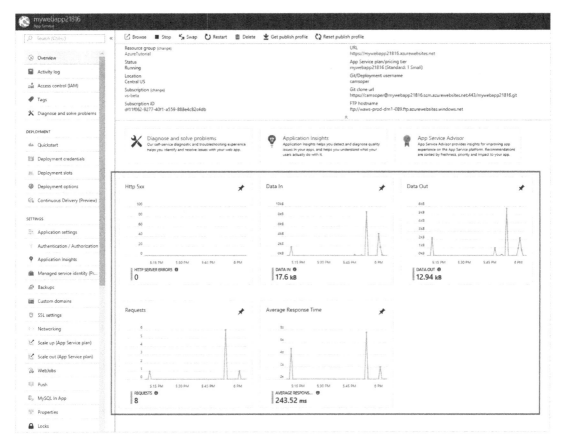

Figure 2-40. *Overview panel*

– **Http 5xx**: Count of server-side errors, usually exceptions in ASP.NET Core code.

– **Data In**: Data ingress coming into your web app.

– **Data Out**: Data egress from your web app to clients.

– **Requests**: Count of HTTP requests.

– **Average Response Time**: Average time for the web app to respond to HTTP requests.

Several self-service tools for troubleshooting and optimization are also found on this page, as shown in Figure 2-41.

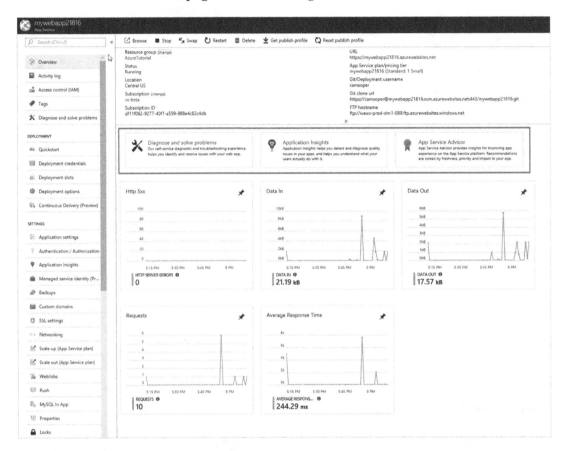

Figure 2-41. *Self-service tools*

- **Diagnose and solve problems** is a self-service troubleshooter.

- **Application Insights** is for profiling performance and app behavior, and is discussed later in this section.

- **App Service Advisor** makes recommendations to tune your app experience.

Advanced Monitoring

Azure Monitor is the centralized service for monitoring all metrics and setting alerts across Azure services. Within Azure Monitor, administrators can granularly track performance and identify trends. Each Azure service offers its own set of metrics to Azure Monitor.

Profile with Application Insights

Application Insights is an Azure service for analyzing the performance and stability of web apps and how users use them. The data from Application Insights is broader and deeper than that of Azure Monitor. The data can provide developers and administrators with key information for improving apps. Application Insights can be added to an Azure App Service resource without code changes.

1. Open the Azure portal, and then navigate to the *mywebapp<unique_number>* App Service.

2. From the **Overview** tab, click the **Application Insights** tile, as shown in Figure 2-42.

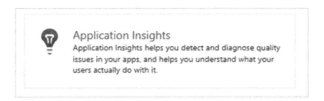

Figure 2-42. *Application Insights tile*

3. Select the **Create new resource** radio button. Use the default resource name and select the location for the Application Insights resource. The location doesn't need to match that of your web app, as shown in Figure 2-43.

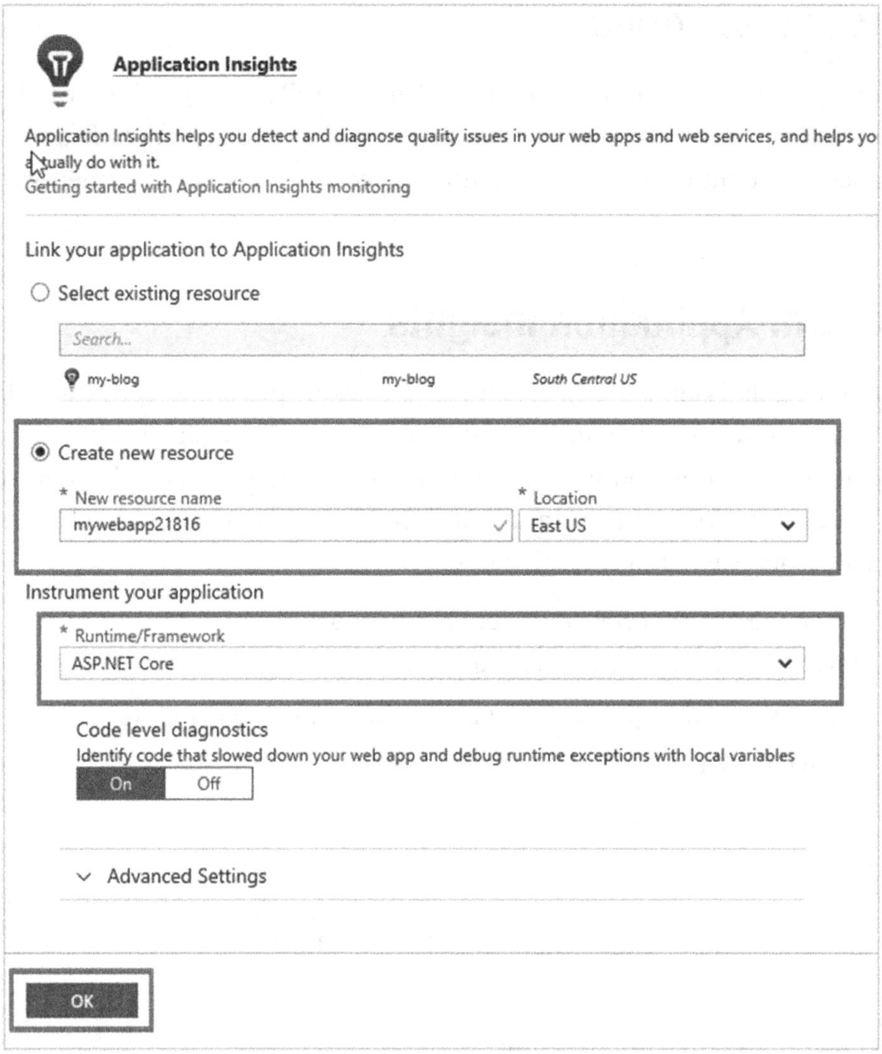

Figure 2-43. *Application Insights setup*

4. For **Runtime/Framework**, select **ASP.NET Core**. Accept the default settings.

5. Select **OK**. If prompted to confirm, select **Continue**.

6. After the resource has been created, click the name of Application Insights resource to navigate directly to the Application Insights page, as shown in Figure 2-44.

Figure 2-44. *New Application Insights resource is ready*

As the app is used, data accumulates. Select **Refresh** to reload the blade with new data, as shown in Figure 2-45.

Figure 2-45. *Application Insights overview tab*

Application Insights provides useful server-side information with no additional configuration. To get the most value from Application Insights, instrument your app with the Application Insights SDK. When properly configured, the service provides end-to-end monitoring across the web server and browser, including client-side performance. For more information, see the Application Insights documentation.

Logging

Web server and app logs are disabled by default in Azure App Service. Enable the logs with the following steps:

1. Open the Azure portal, and navigate to the *mywebapp<unique_number>* App Service.

2. In the menu to the left, scroll down to the **Monitoring** section. Select **Diagnostics logs**, as shown in Figure 2-46.

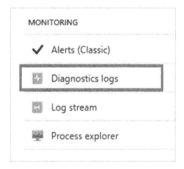

Figure 2-46. Diagnostic logs link

3. Turn on **Application Logging (Filesystem)**. If prompted, click the box to install the extensions to enable app logging in the web app.

4. Set **Web server logging** to **File System**.

5. Enter the **Retention Period** in days. For example, 30.

6. Click **Save**.

ASP.NET Core and web server (App Service) logs are generated for the web app. They can be downloaded using the FTP/FTPS information displayed. The password is the same as the deployment credentials created earlier in this guide. The logs can be streamed directly to your local machine with PowerShell or Azure CLI. Logs can also be viewed in Application Insights.

Log Streaming

App and web server logs can be streamed in real time through the portal.

1. Open the Azure portal, and navigate to the *mywebapp<unique_ number>* App Service.

2. In the menu to the left, scroll down to the **Monitoring** section and select **Log stream**, as shown in Figure 2-47.

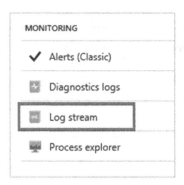

Figure 2-47. Log stream link

   Logs can also be streamed via Azure CLI or Azure PowerShell, including through the Cloud Shell.

Alerts

Azure Monitor also provides real-time alerts based on metrics, administrative events, and other criteria.

Note   Currently alerting on web app metrics is only available in the Alerts (classic) service.

The Alerts (classic) service can be found in Azure Monitor or under the **Monitoring** section of the App Service settings, as shown in Figure 2-48.

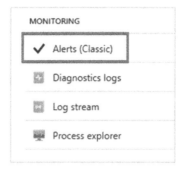

Figure 2-48. *Alerts (classic) link*

Live Debugging

Azure App Service can be debugged remotely with Visual Studio when logs don't provide enough information. However, remote debugging requires the app to be compiled with debug symbols. Debugging shouldn't be done in production, except as a last resort.

Conclusion

In this section, you completed the following tasks:

- Find basic monitoring and troubleshooting data in the Azure portal.

- Learn how Azure Monitor provides a deeper look at metrics across all Azure services.

- Connect the web app with Application Insights for app profiling.

- Turn on logging and learn where to download logs.

- Stream logs in real time.

- Learn where to set up alerts.

- Learn about remote debugging Azure App Service web apps.

Additional Reading

- Troubleshoot ASP.NET Core on Azure App Service

- Common errors reference for Azure App Service and IIS with ASP. NET Core

- Monitor Azure web app performance with Application Insights

- Enable diagnostics logging for web apps in Azure App Service

- Troubleshoot a web app in Azure App Service using Visual Studio

- Create classic metric alerts in Azure Monitor for Azure services – Azure portal

Wrap Up

With Azure App Service and Azure DevOps, ASP.NET Core developers have powerful, professional-grade tools to build business-critical application.

CHAPTER 3

The Professional-Grade DevOps Environment

As we equip our team with a professional-grade environment, we need a model by which we can know what we are missing. This model is a depiction of a complete environment set up for DevOps success. The name for this model is Onion DevOps Architecture, as shown in Figure 3-1.

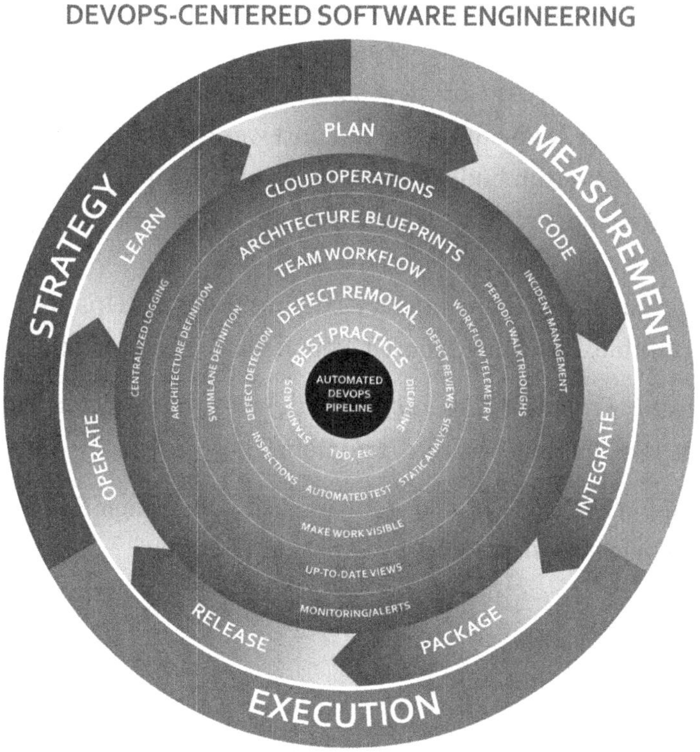

Figure 3-1. *The Onion DevOps Architecture model for a complete DevOps environment*

© Jeffrey Palermo 2019
J. Palermo, *.NET DevOps for Azure*, https://doi.org/10.1007/978-1-4842-5343-4_3

You can see that the automated DevOps pipeline is at the center of the onion – the center of the model. The layers surrounding it are successive capabilities with which the team is equipped. Each capability has a strategy, method of execution, and method of measurement. Once equipped with all the capabilities, the process happens in very short cycles, and is expected to accelerate with maturity. We will dive deeper into Onion DevOps Architecture later in this book. To continue defining the professional-grade DevOps environment, it's interesting to reflect on the current state of DevOps in the industry.

The State of DevOps

Several organizations are performing ongoing research into the advancement of DevOps methods across the industry. Puppet and DORA are two that stand out. Microsoft has sponsored the DORA State of DevOps Report. Sam Guckenheimer is the product owner for all Azure DevOps products at Microsoft and contributed to the report. He also spoke about that on his recent interview with the Azure DevOps Podcast, which can be found at `http://azuredevopspodcast.clear-measure.com/sam-guckenheimer-on-testing-data-collection-and-the-state-of-devops-report-episode-003`.

A key finding of DORA's State of DevOps Report was that elite performers take full advantage of automation. From builds to testing to deployments and even security configuration changes, elite performers have a seven times lower change failure rate and over 2,000 times faster time to recover from incidents.

Other key texts that have led the industry's definition of DevOps are a series of books, all including Jez Humble. The progression in which you should read them is

- *The Phoenix Project: A Novel about IT, DevOps, and Helping Your Business Win*, by Kim, Spafford, and Behr[I]

- *Continuous Delivery: Reliable Software Releases through Build, Test, and Deployment Automation*, by Farley and Humble[II]

[I]Kim, Behr, & Spafford, The Phoenix Project: A Novel About IT, DevOps, and Helping Your Business Win, 2013

[II]Humble, 2010

- *The DevOps Handbook: How to Create World-Class Agility, Reliability, and Security in Technology Organizations*, by Kim, Humble, and Debois[III]

If you are just getting into DevOps, don't be discouraged. The industry is still figuring out what it is too, but there are now plenty of success stories to learn from.

Removing the Ambiguity from DevOps

In the community of large enterprise software organizations, many define DevOps as development and operations coming together and working together from development through operations. This is likely the case in many organizations, but I want to propose what DevOps will likely be as you look back on this era 20 years from now from a time when your worldview isn't colored by the problems of today.

In the 1950s there were no operating systems. Therefore, there was no opportunity for multiple programs to run at the same time on a computer. There was no opportunity for one programmer to have a program that interfered with the program of another. There was no need for this notion of operations. The human who wrote the program also loaded the program. That person also ran the program and evaluated its output.

Fast-forward to the era of the terminal mainframe server. In this era, a programmer could load a program, and it had the potential of causing problems for the other users of the mainframe. In this era, it became someone's job to keep the mainframe operating for the growing pool of mainframe users. Even if you have never programmed for a mainframe, you might remember using Pine for email. This was popular at universities in the 1990s. If this predates you, you can see it in Figure 3-2.

[III]Kim, Debois, Willis, & Humble, 2016

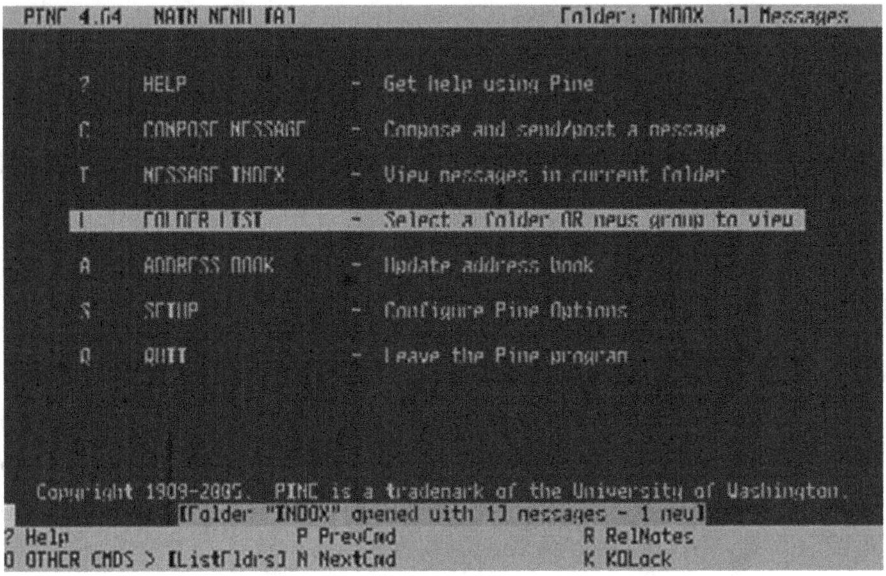

Figure 3-2. *Pine was a popular Unix mainframe email client in the 1990s (Photo credit: Wikipedia* `https://upload.wikimedia.org/wikipedia/en/c/ce/` `PineScreenShot.png`*)*

I believe that the DevOps movement is the correction of a software culture problem that began with the mainframe era. Because multiuser computers, soon to be called servers, became relied upon by an increasing number of people, companies had to ensure that they remained operational. This transformed data processing departments into IT departments. All of the IT assets need to run smoothly. Groups that sought to change what was running on them became known as developers, although I still call myself a computer programmer. Those who're responsible for stable operations of the software in production environments are known as operations, filled with IT professionals, systems engineers, etc.

I believe you're going to look back at the DevOps era and see that it's not a new thing you're creating but an undoing of a big, costly mistake over two or three decades. Instead of bringing together two departments so that they work together, you'll have eliminated these two distinct departments and will have emerged with one type of persona: the software engineer. Smaller companies, by the way, don't identify with all the talk of development and operations working together because they never made this split in the first place. There are thousands upon thousands of software organizations that have always been responsible for operating what they build. And with the Azure cloud, any infrastructure operation becomes like electricity and telephone service, which companies have always relied on outside parties to provide.

74

Microsoft has already reorganized their Azure DevOps department in this fashion. There is no notion of two departments working together. They eliminated the divide by making one department staffed with two roles:

- Program manager

- Engineer

I believe this type of consolidation will happen all across the industry. Although there's always room for specialists in very narrow disciplines, software organizations will require the computer programmer to be able to perform all of the tasks necessary to deliver something they envisioned as it's built and operated.

A Professional-Grade DevOps Vision

When you look at your own organization, you're probably in the camp where you want better quality and better speed. Your form of quality may be fewer bugs. It may be fewer problems in production. It may be more uptime or better handling of user load spikes. When you think of speed, you may be thinking about developing new features. But business executives may be thinking about reducing the lead time between when they fund a strategic initiative and when they're able to launch the software to support it. Regardless of the specific issues, it seems to always come down to quality and speed. That's when you need Capers Jones, your industry's leading software research statistician. In his recent book, *Software Engineering Best Practices*, he demonstrates research that proves two points:

- Prioritizing speed causes shortcuts, which causes defects, which causes rework, which depletes speed. Therefore, prioritizing speed achieves neither speed nor quality.

- Prioritizing quality reduces defects, which reduces rework, which directs all work capacity to the next feature. Therefore, prioritizing quality achieves speed as well.

You want to design a DevOps environment that squeezes out defects all along the way. You can do this by automating the repetitive tasks and taking them away from the human. Humans are not good at repetitive tasks. Computers are much better at such things. But humans are very good at solving problems. Computers are not good at "thinking outside the box." The following capabilities are my vision for a professional-grade DevOps environment:

- Private build

- Continuous integration build

- Static code analysis

- Release candidate versioning and packaging

- Environment provisioning and configuration

- Minimum of a three-tier deployment pipeline

- Production diagnostics managed by development team

- Insanely short cycle time through the previous steps

You don't need an infrastructure like Netflix in order to accomplish this. In fact, you can set this up with a skeleton architecture even before you've written your first feature or screen for a new application. And you can retrofit your current software into an environment like this as well. You want to keep in mind the 80/20 rule and gain these new capabilities without adding to much scope or trying to "boil the ocean" in your first iteration.

DevOps Architecture

Let's walk through the process that a DevOps environment manages. Figure 3-3 shows the logical structure of a DevOps environment. The full-sized image can be downloaded from `https://jeffreypalermo.com/2018/08/applying-41-architecture-blueprints-to-continuous-delivery/`.

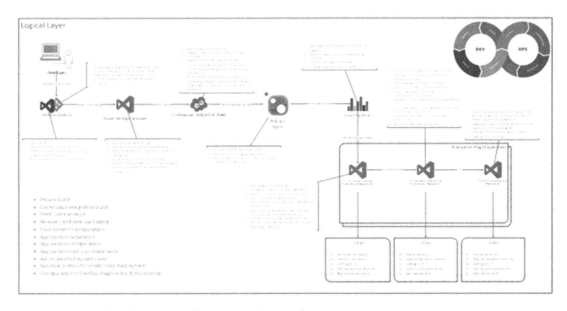

Figure 3-3. *The logical architecture layer of a DevOps environment*

As I walk through this, I'll take the stages one at a time.

Version Control

First, you must structure your version control system properly. In today's world, you're using Git. Everything that belongs to the application should be stored in source control. That's the guiding principle. Database schema scripts should be there. PowerShell scripts to configure environments should go there. Documents that outline how to get started developing the application should go there. Once you embrace that principle, you'll step back and determine what exceptions might apply to your situation. For instance, because Git doesn't handle differences in binary files very well, you may elect not to store lots and lots of versions of very big Visio files. And if you move to .NET core, where even the framework has become NuGet packages, you may elect to not store your /packages folder like you might have with .NET Framework applications. But the Git repository is the unit of versioning, so if you have to go back in time to last month, you want to ensure that everything from last month is correct when you pull it from the Git repository.

Everything that belongs to the application should be stored in source control. That's the guiding principle. Database schema scripts should be there.

Private Build

The next step to configure properly is the private build. This should run automated unit tests and component-level integration tests on a local workstation. Only if this private build works properly and passes should you commit and push your changes to the Git server. This private build is the basis of the continuous integration build, so you want it to run in as short a period of time as possible. No more than 10 minutes is widely accepted industry guidance. For new applications that are just getting started, 45 seconds is normal and will show that you're on the right track. This time should include running two levels of automated test suites: your unit tests and component-level integration tests.

Continuous Integration Build

The continuous integration build is often abbreviated "CI Build." This build runs all the steps in the private build, for starters. It's a separate server, away from the nuances of configuration on your local developer workstation. It runs on a server that has the team-determined configuration necessary for your software application. If it breaks at this stage, a team member knows that they need to back out their change and try again. Some teams have a standard to allow for "I forgot to commit a file" build breaks. In this case, the developer has one shot to commit again and fix the build. If this isn't achieved immediately, the commit is reverted so that the build works again. There's no downside to this because in Git, you never actually lose a commit. The developer who broke the build can check out the commit they were last working on and try again once the problem is fixed.

The continuous integration build is the first centralized quality gate. Capers Jones' research,[IV] referenced earlier, also concludes that three quality control techniques can reliably elevate a team's defect removal efficiency (DRE) up to 95%. The three quality control techniques are testing, static code analysis, and inspections. Inspections are covered later in a discussion of pull requests, but static code analysis should be included in the continuous integration build. Plenty of options exist, and these options integrate with Azure DevOps Services very easily.

[IV]Jones, 2016

STATIC CODE ANALYSIS

Static code analysis is the technique of running an automated analyzer across compiled code or code in source form in order to find defects. These defects could be noncompliance to established standards. These defects could be patterns known in the industry to result in runtime errors. Security defects can also be found by analyzing known patterns of code or the usage of the library versions with published vulnerabilities. Some of the more popular static code analysis tools are

Visual Studio Code Analysis (`https://docs.microsoft.com/en-us/visualstudio/code-quality/code-analysis-for-managed-code-overview?view=vs-2017`

ReSharper command-line tools (`www.jetbrains.com/resharper/download/index.html#section=resharper-clt`)

Ndepend (`https://marketplace.visualstudio.com/items?itemName=ndepend.ndependextension`)

SonarQube (`https://marketplace.visualstudio.com/items?itemName=SonarSyource.sonarqube`)

The CI build also runs as many automated tests as possible in 10 minutes. Frequently, all of the unit tests and component-level integration tests can be included. These integration tests are not full-system tests but are tests and that validate the functionality of one or two components of the application that require code that calls outside of the .NET AppDomain. Examples are code that relies on round trips to the database or code that pushes data onto a queue or file system. This code that crosses an AppDomain or process boundary is orders of magnitude slower than code that keeps only to the AppDomain memory space. This type of test organization heavily impacts CI build times.

The CI build is also responsible for producing the versioned release candidate package. Whether you package your application components in NuGet packages or zip files, you need organized packaging. Each package needs to be named and numbered with the build version. Because you're only building this once, regardless of how many environments you deploy to, it's important that this package contains everything necessary to provision, configure, and install the application component on downstream environments. Note that this doesn't include credentials or environment-specific settings. Every assembly inside this package must be stamped with the build number. Make sure you use the right command-line arguments when you compile so that all produced assemblies receive the build number. The following snippet shows an example of this with parameters configured as PowerShell variables:

```
dotnet build $syource_dir\$projectName.sln -nologo
        --no-restore -v $verbosity -maxcpucount
        --configuration $projectConfig --no-incremental
        /p:Version=$version
```

Package Management

Because you're producing release candidate packages, you need a good place to store them. You could use a file system or the simple artifacts capability of Azure DevOps, but using the rock-solid package management infrastructure of NuGet is the best current method for storing these. This method offers the API surface area for downstream deployments and other tools, like Octopus Deploy.

Azure DevOps Services offers a built-in NuGet server as Azure Artifacts. With your MSDN or Visual Studio Enterprise subscription, you already have the license configuration for this service, and I recommend that you use it. It allows you to use the standard *.nupkg (pronounced nup-keg) package format, which has a place for the name and a version that can be read programmatically by other tools. It also retains release candidates, so they are always available for deployment. And when you need to go back in time for a hotfix deployment or reproduction of a customer issue, you always have every version.

Test-Driven Development Environment (TDD Environment)

The first of the three types of environments in a DevOps pipeline is the TDD environment. You might also call it the ATTD environment if you have adopted acceptance test-driven development. This is the environment where no humans are allowed. Once your pipeline deploys the latest release candidate, your suites of automated full-systems tests are unleashed on this environment. Some examples of full-system tests might be

- Web UI tests using Selenium

- Long-running full-system tests that rely on queues

- ADA accessibility tests

- Load tests

- Endurance tests

- Security scanning tests

The TDD environment can be a single instance, or you can create parallel instances in order to run multiple types of test suites at the same time. This is a distinct type of environment, and builds are automatically deployed to this environment type. It's not meant for humans because it automatically destroys and recreates itself for every successive build, including the SQL Server database and other data stores. This type of environment gives us confidence that you can recreate an environment for your application at any time you need to. That confidence is a big boost when performing disaster recovery planning.

The TDD environment is a distinct type of environment, and builds are automatically deployed to this environment type. It's not meant for humans.

Manual Test Environment

This is an environment type, not a single environment. Organizations typically have many of these. QA, UAT, and staging are all common names for this environment type, which exists for the manual verification of the release candidate. You provision and deploy to this environment automatically, but you rely on a human to check something and give a report that either the release candidate has issues or that it passed the validations. This type of environment is the first environment available for human testing, and if you need a Demo environment, it would be of this type. It uses a full-size production-like set of data. Note that it should not use production data because doing so likely increases the risk of data breach by exposing sensitive data to an increased pool of personnel. The size and complexity of the data should be similar in scale to production. During deployments of this environment type, data is not reloaded every time, and automated database schema migrations run against the existing database and preserve the data. This configuration ensures that the database deployment process will work against production when deployed there. And because of the nature of this environment's configuration, it can be appropriate for running some nonfunctional test suites in the background. For instance, it can be useful to run an ongoing set of load tests on this environment as team members are doing their normal manual validation.

This can create an anecdotal experience to give the humans involved a sense of whether or not the system feels sluggish from a perception point of view. Finally, this environment type should be configured with similar scale specs as production, including monitoring and alerting. Especially in Azure, it's not quite affordable to scale up the environment just like production because environments can be turned off on a moment's notice. The computing resources account for the vast majority of Azure costs; data sets can be preserved for pennies even while the rest of the environment is torn down.

Production Environment

Everyone is familiar with this environment type. It's the one that's received all the attention in the past. This environment uses the exact same deployment steps as the manual environment type. Obviously, you preserve all data sets and don't create them from scratch. The configuration of monitoring alert thresholds will have its own tuning, and alerts from this environment will flow through all communication channels; previous environments wouldn't have sent out "wake-up call" alerts in the middle of the night if an application component went down. And in this environment, you want to make sure that you're not doing any new. You don't want to do anything for the first time on a release candidate. If your software requires a zero-downtime deployment, the previous environment should have also used this method so that nothing is tested for the first time in production. If an off-line job is taken down and transactions need to queue up for a while until that process is back up, a previous environment should include that scenario so that your design for that process has been proven before it runs on production. In short, the deployment to production should be completely boring if all needed capabilities have been tested in upstream environments. That's the goal.

Deployment to production should be completely boring if all needed capabilities have been tested in upstream environments.

Production Monitoring and Diagnostics

Production monitoring and diagnostics is not an independent state but is a topic that needs to apply to all environments. Monitoring and operating your software in Azure isn't just a single topic. There is a taxonomy of methods that you need in order to prevent incidents. Recently, Eric Hexter made a presentation on this topic to the Azure DevOps User Group,[v] and that video recording can be found at `https://youtu.be/6O-17phQMJo`. Eric goes through the different types of diagnostics including metrics, centralized logs, error conditions, alerts, and heartbeats.

Tools of the Professional DevOps Environment

Now that you've covered the capabilities that need to be a part of a professional DevOps environment, let's discuss how to use what Microsoft and the marketplace have to offer. Figure 3-4 shows the physical (runtime) environment view of this environment.

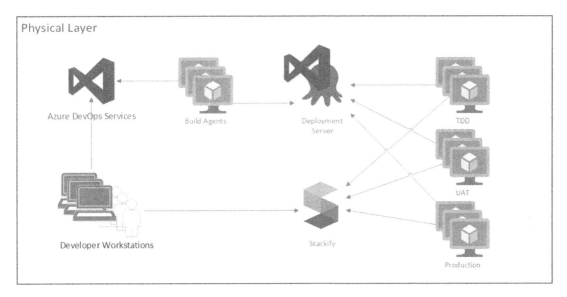

Figure 3-4. *This view shows what runs where the pieces of DevOps infrastructure run*

In Figure 3-4, you make a sample selection of marketplace tools that complement Azure DevOps Services. The Visual Studio and Azure marketplaces offer a tremendous array of capable products, and you'll want to select and integrate the ones that fit your software architecture. In this configuration, you see that Azure DevOps Services will be what developers interact with by committing code from their workstations, making changes to work items, and executing pull requests. You are specifying that you'll

---

[v]Hexter

have your own virtual machines as build agents in order to provide more speed to the build process. You'll also use the Release Hub in Azure DevOps in conjunction with Octopus Deploy as your deployment capability. Although Azure Pipeline is increasing its breadth of support for all kinds of deployment architectures, Octopus Deploy was the original deployment server for the .NET ecosystem, and its support is unparalleled in the industry at the moment. You show that you have deployment agents at the servers that represent each of your environments, and that they call back to the deployment server rather than having the deployment server call through the firewall directly into each server. Then you have specified Stackify as an APM tool collecting logs, telemetry, and metrics from each environment. Your developers can then access this information. Obviously, this architecture shows an environment very light on PaaS. Although new applications can easily make heavy use of PaaS, and we encourage it, most of you readers also have an existing system that would require a great deal of work in order to shift the architecture to free itself from VM-based environments. Professional DevOps is not only for greenfield applications. It can be applied to all applications.

Azure DevOps Services

On September 10, 2018, Microsoft pulled the trigger on a major release that included the segmentation of its popular product, Visual Studio Team Services (VSTS). It broke the product into five products and has named this family of products Azure DevOps. The new five products are

- Azure Pipelines: Supports continuous integration builds and automated deployments

- Azure Repos: Provides source code hosting for a TFVC repository and any number of Git repositories

- Azure Boards: Organizes work and project scope using a combination of backlogs, Kanban boards, and dashboards

- Azure Test Plans: Integrates tightly with Azure Boards and Azure Pipelines by providing support for automated and manual full-system testing, along with some very interesting stakeholder feedback tools

- Azure Artifacts: Provides the capability to provision your team's own package feeds using NuGet, Maven, or npm

The independent services that has been receiving lightning-fast adoption since early September is Azure Pipelines. Especially with the acquisition of GitHub, the experience to set up a build for a code base stored in GitHub is simple and quick.

Azure Subscription

In order to set up your DevOps environment, you need an Azure subscription. Even if all your servers are in a local data center, Azure DevOps Services runs connected to your Azure subscription, even if only for billing and Azure Active Directory. Using your Visual Studio Enterprise subscription, you also have a monthly budget for trying out Azure features, so you might as well use it.

The Azure subscription is a significant boundary. If you are putting your application in Azure, you really want to think about the architecture of your subscriptions and your resource groups. There will never be only one. In fact, even if you attempt to put all your applications in a single subscription, you'll quickly find out that the subscription wasn't designed to be used that way. The subscription is a strong boundary of security, billing, and environment segmentation. Some rules of thumb when it comes to deciding on when to create a new subscription or resource group are

- A subscription that houses the production environment of a system should not also house an environment with lesser security controls. The subscription will only be as secure as its least secure resource group and access control list.

- Pre-production environments may be grouped together in a single subscription but placed in separate resource groups.

- A single team may own and use many Azure subscriptions, but a single subscription should not be used by multiple teams.

- Resource groups should be created and destroyed rather than individual resources within a resource group.

- Just because you're in the cloud doesn't mean that you can't accidentally end up with "pet" resource groups; only create resources through the Azure portal in your own personal subscription that you use as a temporary playground. See Jeffrey Snover's Pets vs. Cattle at `http://cloudscaling.com/blog/cloud-computing/the-history-of-pets-vs-cattle/`.

- Resource groups are good for grouping resources that are created and destroyed together. Resources should not be created through handcrafting. The analogy of pets vs. cattle can be applied to Pet Azure subscriptions where things are named and cared for by a person rather by a process or automated system.

The Azure subscription is a significant boundary. If you are putting your application in Azure, you really want to think about the architecture of your subscriptions and your resource groups. There will never be only one subscription for all your applications.

Visual Studio 2019

You can certainly start with Visual Studio Community, but Visual Studio Enterprise will be what you want to use in a professional DevOps environment. You will need to do more than just write C# code. You'll need to have a holistic tool set for managing your software. As an example, the industry-leading database automation tool SQL Change Automation from Redgate installs right into Visual Studio Enterprise. This makes it a breeze to create automated database migration scripts. You'll also want to equip your IDE with some extensions from the Visual Studio marketplace. Of course, ReSharper from JetBrains is a favorite.

A DevOps-Centered Application

Once we have created the environment of tools and practices for our team, we must turn our attention to our application. You likely have many existing applications that will need to be modernized, but we will build up an application throughout this book so that you can see how we apply all the concepts in the real world. We start with architecture and how to structure any .NET application conceptually, regardless if the application is to be the only application in the system or whether the application will be one of many in a microservices-based system.

Using Onion Architecture to Enable DevOps

You've seen how the Azure DevOps family of products can enable a professional DevOps environment. You have seen how to use Azure Repos to properly store the source for an application. You've made all your work visible using Azure Boards, and you've modeled your process for tracking work and building quality into each step by designing quality control checks with every stage. You've created a quick cycle of automation using Azure Pipelines so that you have a single build deployed to any number of environments, deploying both application components as well as your database. You've packaged your release candidates using Azure Artifacts. And you've enabled your stakeholders to test the working software as well as providing exploratory feedback using Azure Test Plans.

Each of these areas has required new versioned artifacts that aren't necessary if DevOps automation isn't part of the process. For example, you have a build script. You have Azure ARM templates. You have new PowerShell scripts. Architecturally, you have to determine where these live. What owns these new artifacts?

What is Onion Architecture?

Onion Architecture is an architectural pattern I first wrote about in 2008. You can find the original writing at `https://jeffreypalermo.com/2008/07/the-onion-architecture-part-1/`. There are four key tenets of Onion Architecture:

- The application is built around an independent object model.

- Inner layers define interfaces. Outer layers implement interfaces.

- The direction of coupling is toward the center.

- All application core code can be compiled and run separately from the infrastructure.

Figure 3-5 shows an extended model of Onion Architecture that represents the pattern extended for the DevOps world.

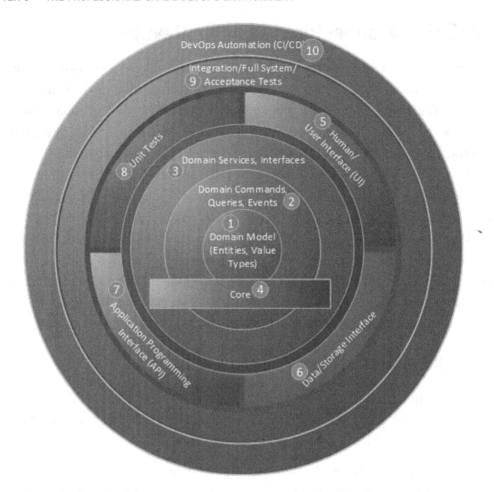

Figure 3-5. *Onion Architecture can be extended for the DevOps world*

The core is familiar, with entities, value types, commands, queries, events, and domain services. The core also defines interfaces that must be fulfilled by types of infrastructure. The interfaces in the core are C# interfaces or abstract types. The parts of this model are as follows:

- Domain model objects are at the very center. They represent real things in the business world. They should be very rich and sophisticated but should be void of any notions of outside layers.

- Commands, queries, and events can be defined around the core domain model. These are often convenient to implement using CQRS patterns.

- Domain services and interfaces are often the edge of the core in Onion Architecture. These services and interfaces are aware of all objects and commands that the domain model supports, but they still have no notion of interfacing with humans or storage infrastructure.

- The core is the notion that most of the application should exist in a cohesive manner with no knowledge of external interfacing technologies. In Visual Studio, this is represented by a projected called "Core." This project can grow to be quite large, but it remains entirely manageable because no references to infrastructure are allowed. Very strictly, no references to data access or user interface technology is tolerated. The core of the Onion Architecture should be perfectly usable in many different technology stacks and should be mostly portable between technology such as web applications, Windows applications, and even Xamarin mobile apps. Because the project is free from most dependencies, it can be developed targeting .NET Standard (netstandard2.x).

- Human interfaces reside in the layer outside the core. This includes web technology and any UI. It's a sibling layer to data access, and it can know about the layers toward the center but not code that shares its layer. That is, it can't reference data access technology. That's a violation of the Onion Architecture. More specifically, an ASP. NET MVC controller isn't allowed to directly use a DbContext in a controller action. This would require a direct reference, which is a violation of Onion Architecture.

- Data interfaces implement abstract types in the core and be injected via IoC (Inversion of Control) or a provider. Often, code in the data interfacing layer has the capability to handle a query that's defined in the Core. This code depends on SQL Server or ORM types to fulfill the needs of the query and return the appropriate objects.

- APIs are yet another interfacing technology that often require heavy framework dependencies. They call types in the core and expose that functionality to other applications that call.

- Unit tests exercise all the capabilities of the core and do so without allowing the call stack to venture out of the immediate AppDomain. Because of the dependency-free nature of the core, unit tests in Onion Architecture are very fast and cover a surprisingly high percentage of application functionality.

- Integration tests and other full-system tests can integrate multiple outer layers for the purpose of exercising the application with its dependencies fully configured. This layer of tests effectively exercises the complete application.

- DevOps automation. This code or sets of scripts knows about the application as a whole, including its test suites, and orchestrates the application code as well as routines in the test suites that are used to set up configuration or data sets for specific purposes. Code in this layer is responsible for the set up and execution of full-system tests. Full-system tests, on the other hand, know nothing of the environment in which they execute and, therefore, have to be orchestrated in order to run and produce test reports.

The preceding is an update on Onion Architecture and how it has fared over the past decade. The tenets have been proven, and teams all over the world have implemented it. It works well for applications in professional DevOps environments, and the preceding model demonstrates how DevOps assets are organized in relation to the rest of the code.

Implementing Onion Architecture in .NET Core

The Visual Studio solution that implements Onion Architecture in .NET Core looks quite similar to the structure used for .NET Framework applications. Figure 3-6 shows the Solution Explorer within Visual Studio.

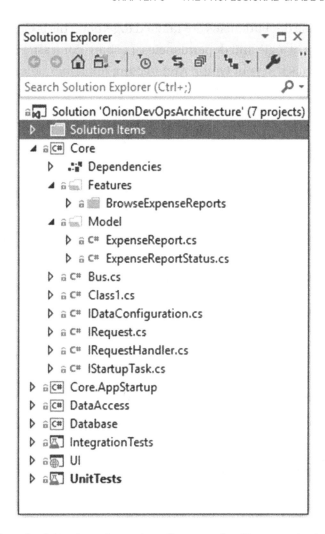

Figure 3-6. *Onion Architecture is centered around a Core project*

The biggest project in the Visual Studio solution should be the Core project. This project will have most of your classes and most of your business logic. By strictly preventing extra framework dependencies from being referenced by this project, you keep your code safe for the long run. You prevent your business logic and domain model from becoming tangled in code specific to web frameworks, ORMs, or reading and writing files or queue messages. All of the latter tend to change at a rapid clip. If you let your code become coupled to them, your application will have a short shelf-life. You, dear reader, have probably been exposed to an application where if they were to remove all of the user interface and data access code, there would be no code left.

This is because of these dependencies are tangled together. This is called spaghetti code—a tangled mess of logic and dependencies. In sharp contrast, Figure 3-7 shows the direction of dependencies in your Onion Architecture implementation.

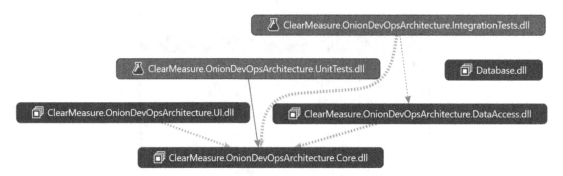

Figure 3-7. *The Core project references no others*

Pay special attention to the DataAccess assembly. Notice that it depends on the core assembly rather than the other way around. Too often, transitive dependencies encourage spaghetti code when user access code references a domain model and the domain model directly references data access code. With this structure, there are no abstractions possible, and only the most disciplined superhuman software engineers have a chance at keeping dependencies from invading the domain model.

Integrating DevOps Assets

There are some new files that need to exist in order to facilitate automated builds and deployments. These need to be versioned right along with the application. Let's discuss what they are and convenient places for them. You've already covered the build script, **build.ps1**. Let's go through each new DevOps asset and the path of each:

- /build.ps1: Contains your private build script

- /src/Database/DatabaseARM.json: Contains the ARM template to create your SQL Server database in Azure

- /src/Database/UpdateAzureSQL.ps1: Contains your automated database migrations command

- /src/Database/scripts/Update/*.sql: Contains a series of database schema change scripts that run in order to produce the correct database schema on any environment

- /src/UI/WebsiteARM.json: Contains the ARM template to create your app service and web site in Azure

For the full source of any of these files, you can find them at the included code link for this article. In a professional DevOps environment, each pre-production and production environment must be created and updated from code. These DevOps assets enable the build and environment automation necessary in a professional DevOps environment.

NEED FOR DEVOPS

DevOps arose as a response to dysfunction ingrained within the software development life cycle (SDLC), even within teams using agile methodologies. Since the first multiuser mainframes with networked terminals, organizations have struggled with balancing keeping systems running in a stable fashion with continually changing them to meet additional business scenarios. Over the following decades, the industry formalized a division of roles for people who held these responsibilities. The original computer programmers were split into software developers and systems administrators. As an example of this divide, Microsoft flagship technology conferences were (and sometimes still are) split into sessions designed for "developers" and those designed for "IT professionals." Today, separate job descriptions and even departments exist for each role. Many large companies have consolidated their IT professionals in order to maintain standards, consistency, and cost efficiency as they strive to operate stable, reliable computing systems. They've learned along the way that this imperative is inherently in conflict with the goals and objectives of the developers, whose job it is to move fast, change the systems, and provide new capabilities to users. As modern companies use custom software applications to connect directly with their customers, this makes software a part of strategic revenue generation. Accordingly, speed is more important now than ever.

Wrap Up

Now that you are up to speed with the technology that will be leveraged in this book along with the elements of a complete, professional DevOps environment, the next chapter will dive into the beginning of the process in more detail, starting with tracking work in a way that feeds a high performance DevOps cycle.

Bibliography

Hexter, E. (n.d.). *DevOps Diagnostics w/ Eric Hexter (Azure DevOps User Group)*. Retrieved from www.youtube.com/watch?v=60-17phQMJo

Humble, J. a. (2010). *Continuous Delivery: Reliable Software Releases through Build, Test, and Deployment Automation*. Addison-Wesley.

Jones, C. (2016). *Exceeding 99% in Defect Removal Efficiency (DRE) for Software*. Retrieved from www.ifpug.org/Documents/Toppin99percentDRE2016.pdf

Kim, G., Behr, K., & Spafford, G. (2013). *The Phoenix Project: A Novel About IT, DevOps, and Helping Your Business Win*. Retrieved February 18, 2019, from https://amazon.com/phoenix-project-devops-helping-business/dp/0988262592

Kim, G., Debois, P., Willis, J., & Humble, J. (2016). *The DevOps Handbook: How to Create World-Class Agility, Reliability, and Security in Technology Organizations*. Retrieved April 19, 2019, from https://amazon.com/devops-handbook-world-class-reliability-organizations/dp/1942788002

Palermo, J. (n.d.). *The Onion Architecture*. Retrieved March 21, 2019, from http://jeffreypalermo.com/blog/the-onion-architecture-part-1/

CHAPTER 4

Tracking Work

Now that you've looked at the capabilities of the professional DevOps environment and a mix of tools that can be a part of it, we'll drill down into each product within the Azure DevOps family and set it up in the proper way. You'll certainly want to customize the configuration, but your suggested configuration works great in 80% of the cases. If you've already read the book *The Phoenix Project* by Kim, Spafford, and Behr, you'll recognize the principles we implement in this chapter. You might want to create a new project so that you can test different configurations as you read. Once you have your Azure DevOps project created, take a glance at your project settings, and select the products that you'd like enabled.

In Figure 4-1, you can see that I have all of the products enabled. For your team, you'll want to equip them with the Visual Studio Enterprise subscription (formerly called MSDN Premium) so that they have licensing for all of the products. You'll need them. Packages is the first one you'll miss if you are using a free or lower license. And as we move through the book, you'll make use of all the products in the Azure DevOps family.

© Jeffrey Palermo 2019
J. Palermo, *.NET DevOps for Azure*, https://doi.org/10.1007/978-1-4842-5343-4_4

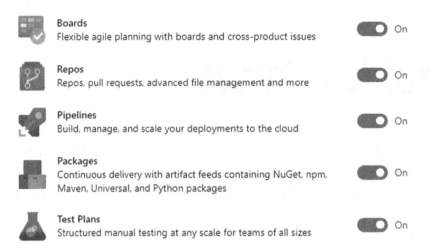

Azure DevOps services

Boards
Flexible agile planning with boards and cross-product issues — On

Repos
Repos, pull requests, advanced file management and more — On

Pipelines
Build, manage, and scale your deployments to the cloud — On

Packages
Continuous delivery with artifact feeds containing NuGet, npm, Maven, Universal, and Python packages — On

Test Plans
Structured manual testing at any scale for teams of all sizes — On

Figure 4-1.   You can enable or disable any of the products in the Azure DevOps family

Change your Process Template

The title of this section is not "choose your process template." You will do that, but your organization has a workflow, and you must capture it and make the process template faithfully model that workflow. Within the first way of DevOps is the principle of "make work visible." Azure Boards is the tool of choice for modeling the shape of your work. Azure Boards uses work items to track a unit of work. A work item can be of any type and has a status as well as any number of other fields you'd like. As you think about your hierarchy of work, don't immediately start creating work items using the built-in sample hierarchy. Instead, think about the work that you already do and the parent-child relationships between some of the types of work. For example, in a marketing department, the structure in Figure 4-2 may be appropriate.

All processes > Scrum for Marketing

Work item types   Backlog levels   Projects

Portfolio backlogs
Portfolio backlogs provide a way to group related items into a hierarchical structure. You can rename a

+ New top level portfolio backlog

Backlog	Work item types
▒▀ Epics	👑 Epic (disabled)
▒▀ Campaigns	📣 Campaign (default)
	🏆 Feature (disabled)
	🏆 Project

Requirement backlog
The requirement backlog level contains your base level work items. There is only one requirement bac

Backlog	Work item types
▒▀ Execution	🗒 Campaign Item (default)
	📋 Product Backlog Item

Iteration backlog
The iteration backlog contains your task work items. There is only one level of iteration backlog and it

Backlog	Work item types
Tasks	🗒 Task

Figure 4-2. *A marketing department has Campaigns that are broken down into individual items*

This marketing department has decided that they only need three levels of work. A Campaign can have multiple Campaign Items or Product Backlog Items. A Campaign Item and a Product Backlog Item can have multiple tasks. At the top level, they can track at the Campaigns level or the Execution level. An individual iteration or sprint is tracked with tasks. You can have any number of higher-level portfolio backlogs if you need higher levels of groupings. Even while the built-in process template includes Epic ➤ Feature ➤ Product Backlog Item, you'll quickly outgrow this because it won't match your organization. You need to disable most of the built-in work item types and create your own so that you can name them and put only the fields and the progression of statuses that make sense in your teams' environments.

You may think of the following work types to get the creative juices flowing in order to capture the model of your organization's world. Notice that I didn't say "design the model." Your model already exists. You need to capture the nouns and the verbs of your existing reality and make Azure Boards represent what's already there. If you capture the wrong model, it won't fit, and your coworkers will have a hard time tracking their work because it just won't make sense. So, consider the following types:

- Business initiatives

- Marketable features

- Plannable work to budget, schedule, and fund

- Individual tasks to get done

This becomes the foundation of your usage of Azure Boards going forward. You'd never think of starting a new application with the Northwind or AdventureWorks database schema. Those tables were chosen by someone else. That model just doesn't fit the nature of the data you're trying to store. In this same way, the schema of the built-in process templates won't fit your organization. You need to load your own model. Once you have your model, you need to specify the process of each major entity (work item). For example, if you were writing an article or a book, you might create a chapter work item and specify the status progression on the Kanban board like that shown in Figure 4-3.

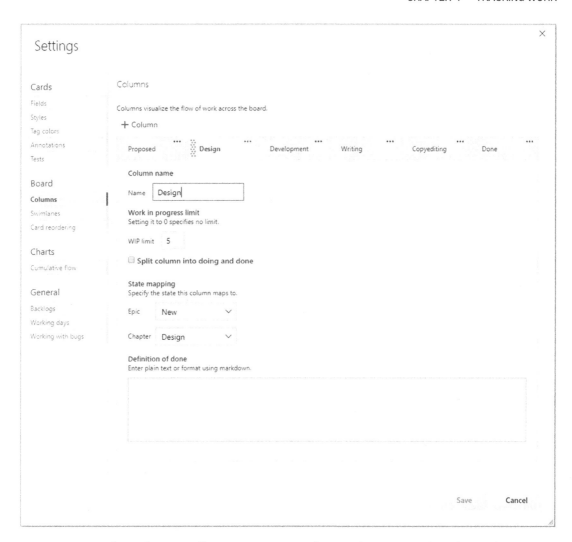

Figure 4-3. *The columns all map to a state of a work item, and each can be assigned a definition of Done*

By determining ahead of time what the process is to take a certain level of work item from creation to done, you organize your team. Each state, or board lane, should be owned by a type of role. For example, if you have a stakeholder designated as the person who'll give the go ahead on the sketch of a screen before it's developed, that stakeholder should have a column where they own the work within it. Each work item is represented by a visual card on the Kanban board, and the cards in their column are theirs to work. If the stakeholder does nothing, cards pile up in that column, and nothing is developed because of the bottleneck in that column. A dashboard report can bring this to light on a daily basis so that no column has too much work in it. The stakeholder's job would be to

99

either approve the sketch of the screen or initiate a conversation to fix it. In no case would you want a bad screen to be coded. That would be worse. By creating a good number of columns, mapped to the states of the work item, you can move the work through a known process where every column has a type of role responsible for performing a known set of work and then forwarding the work in process WIP to the next column. From a quality control perspective, every person starting on work has the obligation for inspecting the WIP to see if the work is ready for them yet. If something is missing, you stop the line and get it corrected before propagating the error further downstream.

For the purposes of software teams, the level of backlog that is prepopulated with Product Backlog Items in the case of the Scrum process template, or User Stories in the case of the Agile process template, is the appropriate level for doing branches and pull requests as well as designed test cases, as you'll see a bit later in the article. Iterations or sprints can be planned with work items from this level. Then, tasks can be organically created, completed, or destroyed day by day. It's often good to make plans based on the lowest backlog level and then break those down into tasks as needed on an ad hoc basis during the sprint.

Types of Work Items

Depending on the process template you choose when you create your project, you'll start with a predefined set of work item types, statuses, and swim lanes in your boards. You should change these because there are only three process templates built in, and they are all very basic. Don't expect to use them without customization except for very simple projects. You have three process templates to choose from when starting a project. If you have already created a project, and you want to choose a different process template, you are out of luck. Create a new project. If that ship sailed long ago, don't fret. You can morph any of the project templates into just about anything you want.

The choices for project template are CMMI, Agile, and Scrum. The Scrum template is probably the most widely used at the writing of this book, and it is the template that is maintained the most. But the Basic template is new, and has been simplified down to just the basics. If you don't know what process template to use, and you don't know the difference between these, **choose the Basic template**,[1] and modify it from there. It is the least prespecified, and you'll be able to add anything you like.

---

[1]Pit of success: start new process templates inheriting from Basic

You will see some similarities and differences in the built-in process templates, but they all share more than they differ. The table in Figure 4-4 illustrates the configurations of the templates.

Backlogs	CMMI	Agile	Scrum	Basic
Portfolio	Epic Feature	Epic Feature	Epic Feature	Epic
Requirements	Requirement	User Story	Product Backlog Item	Issue
Iteration	Task	Task	Task	Task
Others	Bug Issue Change Request Review Risk	Bug Issue	Bug Impediment	n/a

Figure 4-4. *Built-in process templates come with a set of work item types that are meant to be customized*

You can see how similar the process templates are, and you should examine each one to gain some ideas because each work item is configured with a certain number of fields, and the fields of each are likely not going to fit your needs. As with a database schema if you go forward with tables and columns that are not used, your data set ends up with many null values. This causes confusion with reporting. If you are not going to use a field, customize your template and remove it or hide it from a work item. Simple is better.

You may think that the preceding processes are so similar that it doesn't matter which one you start with, but the requirements level work item type will probably help you make your decision. Here are the fields in this key work item type out of the box, as shown in Figure 4-5.

	CMMI	Agile	Scrum	Basic
Name	Requirement	User Story	Product Backlog Item	Issue
Main Section	Description (multi-line text)	Description (multi-line text)	Description (multi-line text)	Description (multi-line text)
Secondary Section	Impact Assessment (multi-line text)	Acceptance Criteria (multi-line text)	Acceptance Criteria (multi-line text)	n/a
Development Section	Development (links)	Development (links)	Development (links)	Development (links)
Related Work Section	Related Work (links)	Related Work (links)	Related Work (links)	Related Work (links)
Planning Section	Planning •Size •Priority •Triage •Blocked •Committed	Planning •Story Points •Priority •Risk	Details •Priority •Effort •Business Value •Value area	Planning •Priority •Effort
Classification Section	Classification •Type •Value area	Classification •Value area	n/a	
Other	Effort •Original Estimate Schedule •Start Date •Finish Date Build and test •Integrated In •User Acceptance Test Subject Matter Experts •Subject matter expert 1 •Subject matter expert 2 •Subject matter expert 3	n/a	n/a	

Figure 4-5. *Structure of the main work item type per process template*

As you can see, the process templates start to diverge at this point. You can hide fields of the built-in work item types, but you can't remove them. It's a cleaner work tracking data model to add custom fields rather than hide most of the built-in fields.

Customizing your Process

With Azure DevOps, as with any project management tool, you can customize the states of the work. The task before you here is to make sure to model all of the states the work needs to go through in order to be finished. Many tools provide a board similar to this, as shown in Figure 4-6.

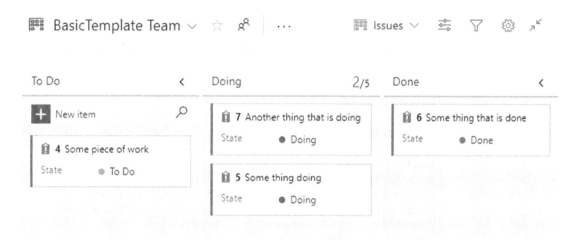

Figure 4-6. *Each board starts out with simple states*

This process is fine with a to-do list around the house, but it will not support any kind of serious software development project. There is much more activity inherent in the software development life cycle. Regardless if your team would like to use Scrum or Kanban, or some other methodology, you will need to decide on the unique states that work can be in at any given time. Here is a very common list of states you might choose. Each of which would show up as a column on your board. Note that I use the generic term "card" in place of Work Item, Issue, Product Backlog Item, User Story, and so on. When modeling your board, each item of work will be manifested as a digital index card on a digital board. We suggest the typical owner of the card while it is in the corresponding state. Note that for the most part, the ownership cycles back and forth between product management and engineering. We are not being any more specific than that regarding roles. For teams who have adopted the DevOps ways as outlined in *The Phoenix Project*,[II] there are only those who commission the work and those who deliver the work. Any more organization beyond that is up to the team, which is consistent with the Manifesto for Agile Software Development.[III]

[II]Kim, Behr, & Spafford, 2013

[III]Beck, et al., 2001

State	Activity	Done Criteria	Defects Types	Typical Owner
Idea/Backlog	Envision a software capability. Come up with and track the idea while contemplating priority. Create a card (work item) on the board.	An idea is deemed to be worth pursuing.	n/a	Product Management
Definition	Analyze the needed software behavior and capability and determine the user's experience when exercising this new capability. Add this information to the card.	The software capability can be fully described from a user's perspective.	Card is hard to describe. What the software should do in certain cases is unknown. Concept is not concrete enough to be workable	Product Management
Design	Make technical decisions needed to enable this capability. Diagrams, wire-frames, library, technology selection, logging levels, telemetry, etc. Break up the card into multiple cards of the right size for the team.	All key decisions on how to implement new capability have been determined. Cards are at the right size to proceed.	Design activity uncovers analysis gaps. Card's scope is not concrete or understood.	Engineering
Test Spec	With a good understanding of the new capability, bullet list out the steps one would execute in order to test this card	Card has test scenarios listed in a concrete, understandable fashion.	Unclear test procedures/ interface. Behavior combinations too many to simplify.	Product Management

Figure 4-7. *Representative board structure for common states in a software development project*

The preceding Figure 4-7 might seem like too many states if you are working by yourself, but by the time you have three or more developers on your team, you'll be glad you are able to see where the work is. Without this structure, you will forget what is holding up each card of work. Let's simplify these states so that we can see a different view:

Plan

- Idea/Backlog

- Definition

- Design

- Test Spec

Build

- Implement

Check

- Inspect

- Test

- Stabilize

- Release

Interestingly, we are sandwiching the state that represents building with four states on either side. If you jump right into building without proper planning, there are four categories of decisions that will trip you up:

1. Idea: Faulty concept of what to build

2. Definition: Analysis gaps or unclear scope of what to build

3. Design: Technology/architecture/pattern decisions needed in order to build

4. Test Spec: How to know when you've build everything you need to build

Again, if you are building the software as a team of one or two, you can simplify this down because you communicate frequently and take care of these things as they come. For teams larger than that, you need these concepts in some form, regardless of what you decide to name the states or columns.

Working with the Process

Now that you have determined for your organization how many stages, or swim lanes, are appropriate, you'll need to integrate your version control system with Azure Boards in order to be able to track every code or asset change that is associated with a card (or work item, within Azure Boards).

While organizing our version control system is covered later in the book, we will now cover the basic things to do in order to integrate those changes. GitHub, acquired by Microsoft[IV] in 2018, is strategically meant to be the premium Git source control offering for Microsoft going forward. The work is happening this year to enable that: Microsoft AD sign-in, automatic pull request linking, and so on. If your code is already inside GitHub, you can do some linking today at the time of writing. Inside your Azure DevOps project settings, you can connect your GitHub account. Refer to Figure 4-8.

Connect GitHub with Azure Boards

Link commits and pull requests to work items, and see the status of your development from within Azure Boards. Learn more

Connect your GitHub account

Want to use a Personal Access Token? Click here

Figure 4-8. *Navigate to Project Settings ➤ Boards ➤ GitHub connections, in order to begin the process*

Linking Commits

If you are not already a GitHub user, you can work with Git source control right within Azure Repos. In Figure 4-9, we are performing a commit right from within Visual Studio to our Azure Repos Git repository.

[IV]Microsoft to acquire GitHub for $7.5 billion, n.d.

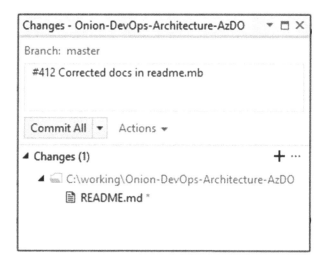

Figure 4-9. *A commit from Visual Studio can auto-link with the work item by including #{work item id}*

All it takes to link a commit with your work items in Azure Boards is to start the commit message with the work item number. You should do this every time, even if you are working by yourself. Along with better traceability on what changes a work item required, it will encourage the team to control scope and stay on track by only making changes for the work item in front of them.

STAYING IN FLOW

As a developer, it is easy to get distracted when browsing code because you will see refactoring opportunities and you will want to make the code better. It is not uncommon to look up after an hour of coding work to realize that you aren't even working on the item you set out to complete. By setting a team rule that you will always link commits with a work item, you can keep yourself and your teammates on the most productive path every day.

Regardless of the Git tool you elect to use, starting your commit message with the number of the current work item will cause Azure Boards to make the link.

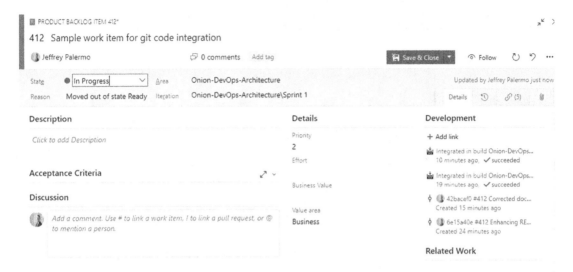

Figure 4-10. *Azure Boards automatically links work items with git commits and builds that are related*

In Figure 4-10, you can see that work item #412 has been linked with two git commits and the two resulting builds that contained these commits. If you tag your commits but don't see this automatically, check in the Azure Repos settings that a teammate hasn't turned this off. It is on by default for new projects but may not be on by default for repositories that were imported from outside sources. In that case, you'll need to enable it for the new repository.

Branching from Azure Boards

When working with work items of any type in Azure Boards. you'll want to build them up throughout the process. As you analyze the needed change and create screen mockups or any other document, either attach the document or include it inside the Git repository itself. When you are ready to begin coding, create a branch. If you know how to organize your branches, then you are ahead of the game. If you are wondering what branching strategy to choose, then keep it simple and use plain feature branches instead of a "features" namespace. For more research on available branching strategies, see the Branch Organization docs from Microsoft.[V]

When starting to code on a work item, let Azure Boards do the work for you. In Figure 4-11, you can see that we can create our feature branch right from the board.

[V]Adopt a Git branching strategy, n.d.

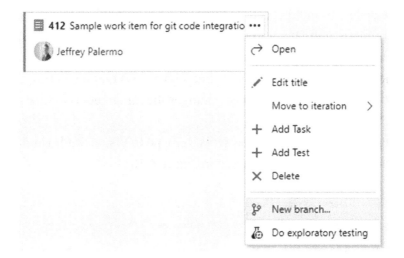

Figure 4-11. *By clicking the menu icon, we can create a new branch for development on the work item*

From here, we'll want to maintain our team's branching convention.

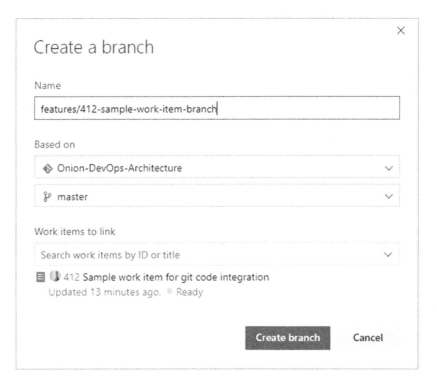

Figure 4-12. *Place the work item number in the branch name to keep them organized*

You can create any branching scheme that you can imagine, so keep it simple. Place the work item number at the beginning so that you'll be able to find your branch. Then, use all lower case with dashes. You can't use spaces in a branch name. An added benefit of including the work item number in your branch name is that it will be a **constant reminder to stay on track** and only make changes that are needed for the current work in front of you.

Now that you have a branch for your work item, go to Visual Studio and check out the new branch from Team Explorer, as shown in Figure 4-13.

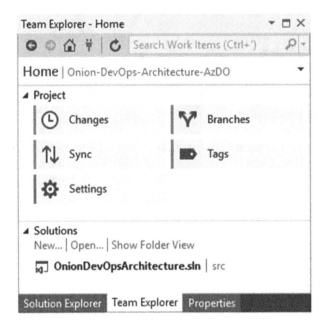

Figure 4-13. *View the branches using Team Explorer*

Any commits you make with then stay on the new branch. If you break down features into user stories and tasks, remember to tag the commit message to the most specific work item you are working on. For record-keeping, you'll have a branch that corresponds to your feature (or issue, or user story), and then you'll have individual commits tagged to it or any of the children that you've worked on.

When you have completed the work and are ready to merge your branch back in, you can create a pull request.

Merging Using Pull Requests

Within Azure DevOps, there are a few places where you can create a pull request. And while you can perform a Git merge without a pull request, using one allows your team to integrate a formal inspection process, which is a proven way to find and prevent defects from being shipped to your customers.

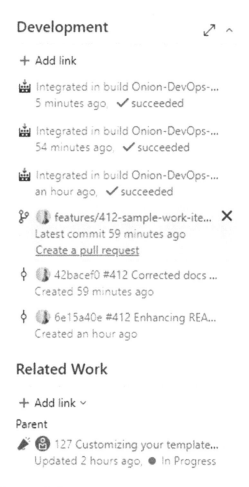

Figure 4-14. *Within the work item screen, you can create a pull request*

In Figure 4-14, we can see the branch that was created for the work item. When we are finished building the feature that the work item represents, we can create a pull request so that our team can bring in the changes back to the master branch.

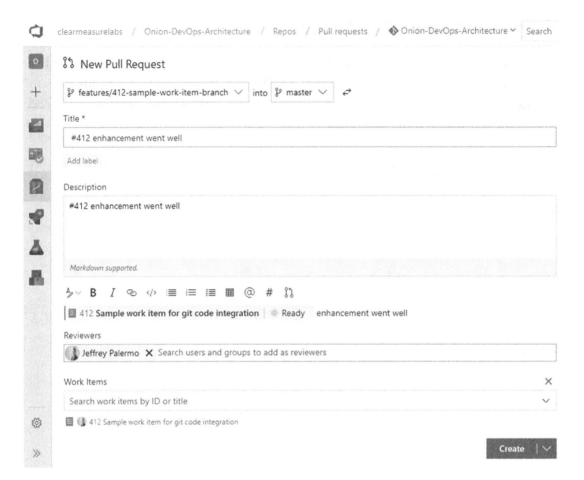

Figure 4-15. *You can choose individuals or groups to be pull request reviewers*

After you've created your pull request, your team will be notified. They will be able to see and browse the changes you are bringing in. They will be able to comment on the changes and even have a back and forth conversation if necessary. This provides an opportunity to make any changes before the code is merged into master. If any changes are needed, simply make the changes on the branch. The pull request will update itself automatically. The pull request operates at the branch level, not the commit level. Therefore, if you need to do more work and make more commits, your pull request will not be invalidated. When approved, you can complete your pull request and monitor the automated merge, as shown in Figure 4-16.

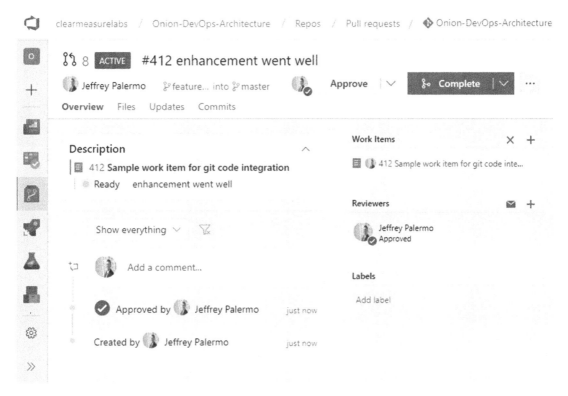

Figure 4-16.   *Complete the pull request after approvers have marked it as approved*

Wrap Up

When using Azure Boards to manage your software project, you benefit from the automatic integration with the rest of the Azure DevOps family. This chapter, while showing some fantastic capabilities, only scratches the surface on the power of Azure Boards. The purpose of this book is not to be a comprehensive feature guide for Azure DevOps. For more reading on Azure Boards, visit the official documentation.[VI]

We have taken you through a micro-workflow of customizing your board and working with a software change through your customized process. Figure 4-17 shows the level of details captured in just this small example. Your work items will be even richer with information as you track your work through your board.

[VI]Azure Boards Documentation, n.d.

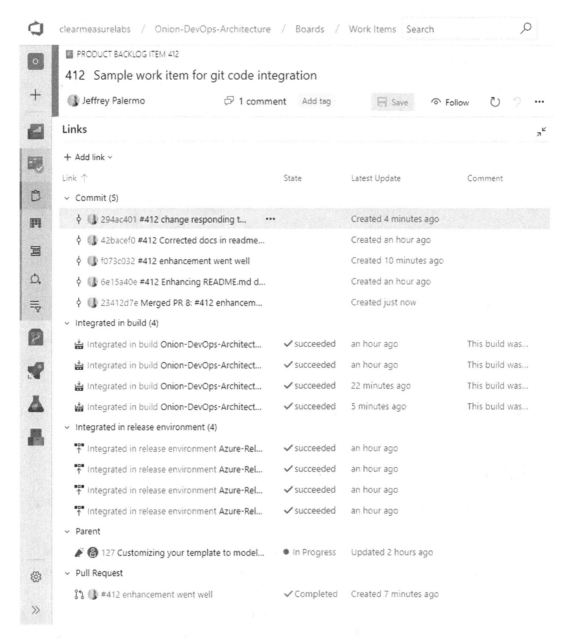

Figure 4-17. *Your work item will become rich with information just by tracking it on Azure Boards*

Armed with this tool, you have a world-class project tracking capability, enabling you to focus on your code. In the next chapter, we'll look at Azure Repos, but more importantly, how to set up your Git repository for success.

Bibliography

Adopt a Git branching strategy. (n.d.). Retrieved February 18, 2019, from `https://docs.microsoft.com/en-us/azure/devops/repos/git/git-branching-guidance?view=azure-devops`

Azure Boards Documentation. (n.d.). Retrieved from `https://docs.microsoft.com/en-us/azure/devops/boards/?view=azure-devops`

Beck, K., Grenning, J., Martin, R. C., Beedle, M., Highsmith, J., Mellor, S., . . . Marick, B. (2001). *Manifesto for Agile Software Development.* Retrieved February 18, 2019, from Agile Alliance: `http://agilemanifesto.org/`

Kim, G., Behr, K., & Spafford, G. (2013). *The Phoenix Project: A Novel About IT, DevOps, and Helping Your Business Win.* Retrieved February 18, 2019, from `https://amazon.com/phoenix-project-devops-helping-business/dp/0988262592`

Microsoft to acquire GitHub for $7.5 billion. (n.d.). Retrieved February 18, 2019, from `https://news.microsoft.com/2018/06/04/microsoft-to-acquire-github-for-7-5-billion/`

CHAPTER 5

Tracking Code

Version control systems (VCS) have fully matured over the last 20 years, and the Git version control system has become the de facto standard in the software world. In fact, the largest active source control repository on the planet, the Microsoft Windows source code, has been converted to Git. Centralized source control systems like Subversion and Team Foundation Version Control (TFVC) have given way to Mercurial and Git. Of those two, Git has become the version control tool of choice for developers on all the modern platforms. Tracking your code in Git version control is part of a modern DevOps process. Throughout the industry, practitioners use version control, source control, VCS, and SCM interchangeably as synonyms.

Azure Repos is the version control system in the Azure DevOps family. It supports the old TFVC format of source control as well as an unlimited number of private or public Git repositories. There are import tools for migrating existing code repositories into Azure Repos, so regardless of where your code is now, you can move it in. Azure Repos not only works with Visual Studio, but it also works with any other Git client, such as TortoiseGit, which is one of my favorites for Windows Explorer "right click" integration. For the purposes of this chapter, and much of the book, we will equate Azure Repos with Git version control. While TFVC will be supported for well over another decade, any new investment you make should use the Git technology.

How Many Repositories?

In setting up your Git repository in the professional way, there are some principles to keep in mind. First, your team will likely have multiple repositories, unless you ship only one product. The architecture of your software will have something to do with the granularity of your repository design. For example, if you deploy your entire system together and the architecture doesn't support deploying only a subset of the system, it's likely that you will put the entire system into a single Git repository. As an

117

J. Palermo, *.NET DevOps for Azure*, https://doi.org/10.1007/978-1-4842-5343-4_5

organization, you may have multiple software teams. Figure 5-1 is an entity relationship diagram to help you understand how to factor your system into Git repositories.

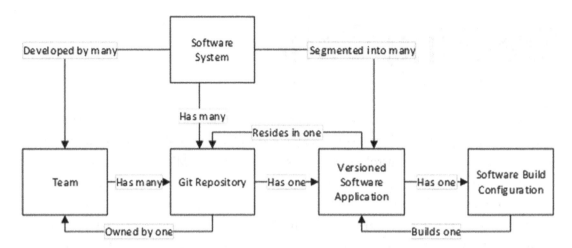

Figure 5-1. *Relationship rules when designing Git repositories*

Your team will own your Git repositories. A single Git repository cannot be owned or developed by multiple teams. With centralized version control systems of years past, this was possible only because these systems supported child-level branching. These systems hosted a repository of a different type. The reuse of the term "repository" has led to some confusion among users of TFVC and Subversion, which happily hosted multiple software systems while allowing branching at the child level. While merging was difficult much of the time, these tools did support it. Git's repository design is different. Cloning and branching are done at the top level only. Therefore, to manage multiple pieces of software, you create multiple Git repositories. In Azure Repos, a single project can have an unlimited number of Git repositories, so you do have a way to maintain groupings of related Git repositories.

Now that we understand that a team must have a dedicated Git repository, our next relationship is the software application itself. Regardless of the size of the software application, there should be only one. Your application can be a small microservice with nothing more than an Azure Function, or it can be a very sizable application. If it maintains independent versioning and can be deployed independently, it must reside in its own Git repository, which owns the concept of versioning. If you are a Git and build expert reading this, you may be able to invent a custom paradigm that can violate this rule, but for the rest of us, this rule holds true. Let's consider some examples of this:

1. You have a very large Visual Studio solution for a software
    system that is over 10 years old. It has a few web applications,
    some Windows services, some schedule jobs, and a SQL Server
    database. The question to ask is "do any parts of it build or
    version independently of the rest?" If the answer is no, then all
    of it belongs in the same Git repository. Don't fret if sometimes
    you make changes to the web site and then decide not to deploy
    the rest to production. That's not the same as being versioned
    independently.

2. You have designed a system with independent applications or
    microservices. Each of these applications owns its own small
    database, and the parts communicate asynchronously via queues.
    Each can change and deploy at a completely different cadence.
    In this scenario, you would segment each into its own Git
    repository in order to preserve the ability to maintain version
    independence.

There are some examples where you might have a system decomposed into mostly
independent applications but want to keep them in the same Git repositories. Azure
DevOps itself is a perfect example of this. The segmentation is to benefit the deployment
architecture rather than version independence. There are dozens of services that make
up the Azure DevOps product, but they all reside in a single Git repository, and a single
(but large) team develops the system in Git. The whole system is built together and
deployed together with a single version number. You can read more about how the Azure
DevOps team does DevOps online.[1] To drive to a rule of thumb: put your current Visual
Studio solution in its own Git repository.

---

[1] DevOps at Microsoft, n.d.

What Should be in Your Git Repository

There's often a discussion about what to store in the application's Git repository. The short answer is "store everything you can." Absolutes are never right. (Except for the previous sentence.) However, you do store almost everything in your Git repository, including

- Database schema migration scripts

- Azure Resource Manager (ARM) JSON files

- PowerShell scripts

- Tests

- Build scripts

- Images

- Content assets

- Visio architecture blueprints

- Documentation

- Dependencies, including libraries and tools that don't come from a package manager

Given that there are some exceptions that cannot be committed to VCS, I'll go through a few of the items required for developing software that you do not store in your Git repository. You can see that the items on this list are already impractical to store. Although it may be technically possible to store some of these items, the pain starts to become a losing trade-off in risk.

- Windows, the obvious one.

- Visual Studio or VSCode, even if it's possible to run it straight from disk.

- Environment-specific data and configuration; this doesn't belong to the software, it belongs to the environment.

- Secrets; they are secret, so you shouldn't know them anyway.

- Large binary files that change very frequently, such as files from Autodesk products like AutoCAD and Revit.

I want to address .NET Core specifically because the architecture of the .NET Framework has some fundamental differences here. With .NET Framework applications, the framework versions are installed on the computer as a component of the operating system itself. So, it's obvious that you don't check it in. You check in only your libraries that your application depends on. If you need 7Zip or Log4Net, you obtain those libraries and check them into your Git repository because you depend on a particular version of them. With the advent of package managers, the debate has raged over when to not check in packages from npm or NuGet. That argument isn't settled, but for .NET Framework applications, my advice has been to check in all your dependencies, including packages.

This fundamentally changes with the architecture of .NET Core. With .NET Core, the framework isn't installed as a component of the operation system. The framework is delivered by NuGet to the computer running the build process. Furthermore, .NET Core libraries that are packaged as NuGet components have been elevated to framework status and are delivered in the same way as .NET Core SDK components are. Therefore, my advice for .NET Core applications is to leave the defaults in place and do not commit the results of the dotnet.exe restore process into your Git repository. Under active development, this mix of SDK components and other NuGet packages will change quite a bit. Once the system reaches maturity and the rate of change slows, it may be appropriate to move and commit the **packages** folder in order to lock in that mix of dependencies given that package managers do not absolutely guarantee that the same mix of dependencies will be restored next month or next year. If you want to evaluate this for yourself and determine your risk tolerance, you can examine the packages easily by application by adding a Nuget.config file to your solution with the following configuration:

```xml
<?xml version="1.0" encoding="utf-8"?>
<configuration>
  <config>
    <add key="globalPackagesFolder"
        value=".\packages" />
  </config>
</configuration>
```

The Structure of the Git Repository

We have discussed how to determine how many Git repositories we need for our system. Now we need to factor an individual application appropriately. Regardless of the architecture of the application, our relationship with the VCS comes from the Visual Studio solution. That solution can contain a large code base you call an application or a tiny code base that you might call a microservice. For the purposes of this guidance, these are the same.

If you are an experienced developer, you might be able to design a different structure that works for laying out a Git repository; however, if you would like prescriptive guidance in where everything should go within Git, consider the following advice. Shown within Azure Repos, Figure 5-2 depicts the top level of a well-factored Git repository.

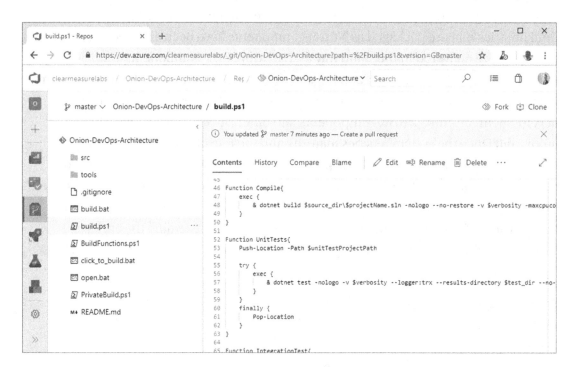

Figure 5-2. *The top level of a Git repository can be quite standard regardless of the type of Visual Studio software you're developing*

You can see some directories and some script files at the top level. Notice that you don't see a Visual Studio solution at the top level. That's intentional. Let's take the directories and files that you need in a properly organized Git repository:

- /src/: The application code is in this directory, beginning with the solution file. This is a common convention in multiple programming platforms.

- /tools/: Any tools needed for the build process go in this directory. Common needs are 7Zip, Octo.exe, and the like.

- /build.ps1: This is the private build script. Whether you name it this or not, you need your private build script in the top-level directory.

- /click_to_build.bat: A mouse/keyboard-friendly helper that adds an "& pause" to the build script so that the console window remains open for examination of the build output.

- /open.bat: A mouse/keyboard-friendly helper that opens the Visual Studio solution via a double-click or Enter.

- /build/: This directory is automatically created and destroyed by the build script. It shouldn't be committed to source control. This is the destination for test/publish output that is temporary in nature.

The preceding implementation is our example application for this book. More generally, the structure should be as shown to the left. This structure works for small microservices as well as very large applications with hundreds of screens and functions. Notice that this structure only goes down to the Visual Studio solution level and the folders within that solution. The separation within Visual Studio projects will vary.

Here are the rules:

1. The top of the Git repository will contain your private build assets. This includes the actual private build script, helper functions, and any assets/shortcuts in order to very run a private build on a local workstation.

2. The Git repository needs some basic documentation about what it contains and how to build what it contains. This is where the Readme.md comes in. You can use .txt or .docx, but Azure Repos, GitHub, and many other tools work well with the markdown format and can show this file as a dashboard page.

3. The "build" directory is a temporary directory that will contain things generated by your build scripts. Call it what you like but this folder does not get committed to Git. Make sure to add it to your .gitignore file. Whether it is test output or artifacts created through running a "publish" command, use this folder for generated output both locally in the private build process and online in the continuous integration build.

4. The "tools" directory can contain any tools needed by the build process including a build framework if you choose to use one. With .NET Core, the process for building has been simplified. Many developers enjoy build tools like psake and others.

5. The "src" directory (source) contains the visual studio solution and all the code of the application. The Visual Studio solution file should be inside this folder

6. Each project/assembly within the Visual Studio solution will have its own folder. Take care to keep these folders at the same directory level as the Visual Studio solution.

Regardless of application type, nest your code in the /src folder. .NET Framework, .NET Core, Xamarin, TypeScript, etc. Reserve the top level of the repository for build assets, as shown in Figure 5-3.

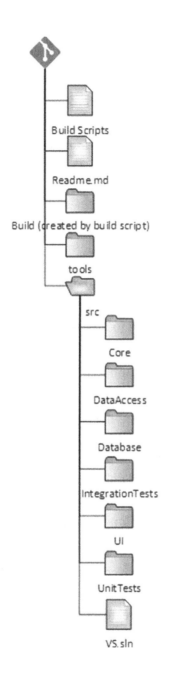

Figure 5-3.

Choosing a Branching Pattern

If you are reading these chapters out of order, we discussed branching and merging while working on work items in Chapter 4. Since branching is a means by which related code changes can be grouped, make sure to use branching for every change to the application. This rule of thumb can raise additional questions. Google, Facebook, and the Microsoft team responsible for the Azure DevOps family of products all use "trunk-based development."[II] You can also research other available branching strategies on Microsoft's branching documentation.[III]

Use trunk-based development. In trunk-based development, the main branch (master) is build up like the trunk of a tree, thicker than branches and always getting longer. Branches are very short-lived and small and exist to facilitate a reviewed pull request process. Aim to merge branches every day.

The sound of "trunk-based development" may cause you to think that adopting it means that you don't branch. Not at all. Every branching strategy includes branches. Branches are a very effective way to group commits that are destined for the main code line (master in Git). As covered in Chapter 4, a pull request is your method for reviewing with the team a group of changes to the product. When a pull request is approved, the branch is merged into master and deleted. Until the pull request for the branch is approved, these commits stay on the branch, guaranteed not to destabilize master. Through this process of review, the team together keeps the master branch stable. Here are some rules for working effectively with branches:

- Make them insanely short-lived: Don't try to add large new capabilities on a single branch. If your user stories are small and discreet, you'll be able to create/pull request/merge/delete a branch in a 24-hour period. Branches living into their second day are a red flag that should generate a team discussion.

- Tie them to a work item so that every change on the branch is related to the work item.

[II]Hammant

[III]Adopt a Git branching strategy, n.d.

- Avoid large application refactorings while others have open branches – expect painful merge conflicts if you break this rule.

- Configure your DevOps pipeline to operate on all branches in order to get the benefit of the build and first deployment. If the first time your changes are deployed is after a pull request, you will be passing through more bugs onto master.

Useful Tips in Azure Repos Configuration

Because Azure Repos is integrated within an Azure DevOps project, you need to be aware of how names and URLs are built. A project is meant to house multiple Git repositories. Because of this, the project name is included in the Git URL. Consider this same project name.

```
My Clunky Project
```

Azure Repos will produce a URL for initial cloning like this:

```
https://clearmeasurelabs@dev.azure.com/clearmeasurelabs/My%20Clunky%20
Project/_git/My%20Clunky%20Project
```

Notice that the spaces in the project name are transformed into %20 in the URL. While this can function just fine, there are some automation scenarios and tools some have run into that don't properly handle the %20 in the URLs. If it is within your control when creating the project, simply avoid spaces in the project name. The public Azure DevOps project used for this book is a good example of this technique:

```
https://dev.azure.com/clearmeasurelabs/Onion-DevOps-Architecture
```

This yields a GIT URL as follows:

```
https://clearmeasurelabs@dev.azure.com/clearmeasurelabs/Onion-DevOps-
Architecture/_git/Onion-DevOps-Architecture
```

When you create your second Git repository within the same project, take care to avoid spaces so that you have a clean URL:

```
https://clearmeasurelabs@dev.azure.com/clearmeasurelabs/Onion-DevOps-
Architecture/_git/My-New-Repository
```

How does GitHub Fit in?

Microsoft acquired GitHub in 2018.[IV] GitHub is intended to be the premiere offering for Git VCS hosting within the Microsoft ecosystem. At the time of this writing, Azure Repos is the fully integrated Git hosting offering. As such, it supports all the enterprise scenarios needed across customers including seamless identity management and logins with Office 365 and Active Directory accounts. GitHub has this integration on the roadmap and will become just as seamlessly integrated as Azure Repos, but as of this writing, that work has not been completed. If your code is already on GitHub, don't move it. Keep it where it is, and integrate the capabilities of the Azure DevOps family of products. If your code is already in Azure Repos, don't move it.

Wrap Up

In this chapter we covered how to properly track your code when implementing a proper DevOps environment. We covered how to determine the size and scope of a Git repository and how many you should have. We discussed what should and should not be committed to your VCS. We analyzed the structure within the repository as well as how to think about and use branches. As you create or modernize source code, follow this guidance, and you won't go wrong. As you encounter complex scenarios, plan adjustments while keeping the core principles in mind.

Now that we understand how to properly organize and track our code in our .NET DevOps environment, continue with Chapter 6 where you will learn how to design and configure your build process.

Bibliography

(n.d.). Retrieved from DevOps at Microsoft: https://docs.microsoft.com/en-us/azure/devops/learn/devops-at-microsoft/

Adopt a Git branching strategy. (n.d.). Retrieved February 18, 2019, from https://docs.microsoft.com/en-us/azure/devops/repos/git/git-branching-guidance?view=azure-devops

---

[IV]Microsoft to acquire GitHub for $7.5 billion, n.d.

Hammant, P. (n.d.). Retrieved from Trunk Based Development: `https://trunkbaseddevelopment.com/`

Microsoft to acquire GitHub for $7.5 billion. (n.d.). Retrieved February 18, 2019, from `https://news.microsoft.com/2018/06/04/microsoft-to-acquire-github-for-7-5-billion/`

CHAPTER 6

Building Code

In Chapter 5, you learned how to properly organize your Git repository in preparation of DevOps automation. In this chapter, you will learn how to build the code. You will learn the difference in a private build and an integration build, often called a continuous integration build or CI build. And you will learn how to configure your CI build in Azure DevOps Services. If you are following along in the code, make sure you have cloned the sample application.

```
https://clearmeasurelabs@dev.azure.com/clearmeasurelabs/
    Onion-DevOps-Architecture/_git/
    Onion-DevOps-Architecture
```

Structure of a Build

In 2007, Paul Duvall, Steve Matyas, and Andrew Glover published a book called *Continuous Integration: Improving Software Quality and Reducing Risk.*[1] At the time, continuous integration was a new topic, and the industry was conducting a far-reaching conversation. This book documented the proven structure for the practice of continuous integration. In it, the two types of builds were clearly defined:

- Private build

- Integration build

The private build only runs on a single developer workstation, and it is a tool to know that immediate changes did not destabilize the application. The integration build runs on a shared server and belongs to the team. It builds code from many developers. With the rise in popularity of branching models, the integration build has been adapted

---

[1]Duvall, 2007

to run on feature branches as well as the master branch. Before we move on to how to implement our builds, let's review the structure and flow of a build process.

Flow of a Build on a Feature Branch

Before we discuss the steps of a private build or a CI build, let's look at it from a high level. When you start work on a user story or software change, regardless of branching strategy, you will create a branch. Remember in Chapter 4, you learned that even those using trunk-based development still use short-lived branches. Figure 6-1 shows the flow of build activities that happen when you are working on a feature branch.

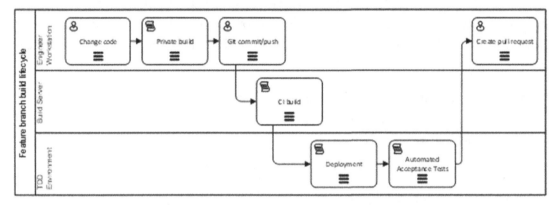

Figure 6-1. *The build process for code on a feature branch flows across three environments*

When you change code, you will run your private build at every stopping point. This keeps you safe. You will learn right away if you accidentally broke something. Because you at working in Git, a decentralized version control system, you'll make many, short commits. This enables you to undo changes very easily. Based on your judgment, you'll run the private build locally. In our application, it is a PowerShell script and is described in more detail later in this chapter. When you decide to push changes to your team's Git server, the CI build will detect those changes and run the integration build process on the team's build server. Upon success, the build will archive the built artifacts, most likely in Azure Artifacts, a NuGet repository. Then an automated deployment script will trigger and deploy those built artifacts to an environment dedicated to the continuous integration process. The best name for this environment is the "TDD environment." The purpose of this environment is to validate that (1) the new version of the software can be deployed and (2) the new version of the software still passes all its acceptance tests.

This does require that you have full-system acceptance tests in your code base. If you don't, they are easy to start developing. After the acceptance tests succeed and you determine your changes are complete, you, as the developer, will create a pull request so that your team knows that you believe the work on your branch is complete and that the code is ready to be inspected for inclusion in the master branch.

Flow of a Build on the Master Branch

Once a pull request has been approved, your branch is automatically merged into master. This is true whether you are using GitHub or Azure Repos. The CI build, which is monitoring for changes, will initiate. Upon success, the build artifacts will be stored in Azure Artifacts as NuGet packages. Then the build will be deployed to the TDD environment for validation of deployability and for the running of the automated full-system acceptance tests. Once these acceptance tests complete successfully, the build is considered a valid release candidate. That is, it is a numbered candidate for potential release and can be validated further in manual testing environments (or even additional automated testing environments) and deployed along the pipeline toward production. Figure 6-2 shows the life cycle of a master branch build.

The deployable package for a software build can be as simple as a zip file, but in .NET, the NuGet package is the standard, and these are meant to be archived in Azure Artifacts.

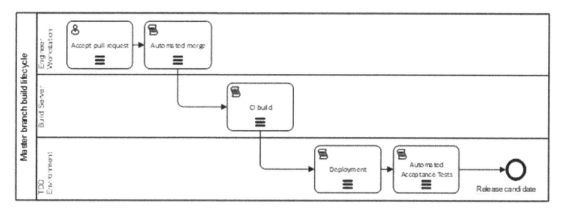

Figure 6-2. *The build process for changes on master end with a new release candidate*

Steps of a Build

Before we walk through how to configure a build on your own workstation and in Azure
Pipelines, let's review the steps a private build and a CI build must have.

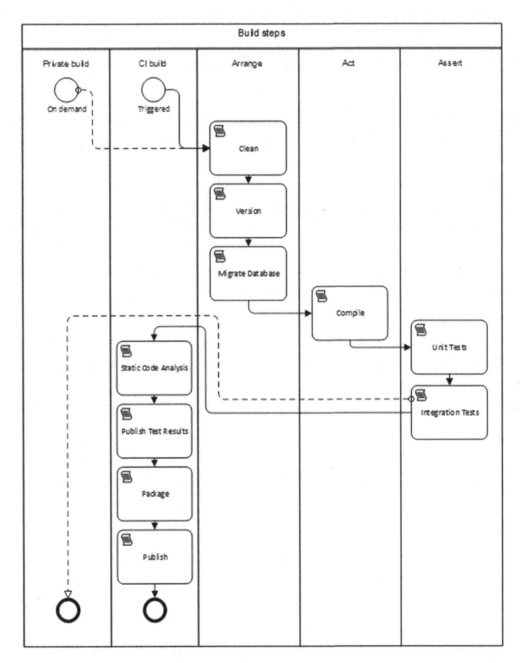

Figure 6-3. *The private and CI build have many steps in common*

The private build runs on a developer workstation. The CI build runs on shared team build infrastructure, whether a full server or in Azure Pipelines. Test-driven development[II] (TDD) introduced the validation concept of Arrange, Act, Assert. Here is the flow:

1. Arrange: In any validation, whether an automated test, a manual test, a static analysis run, or a CI build, the validation process is responsible for setting up an environment in which it can run.

2. Act: In this step, you execute a process, run some code, kick off a procedure, and so on.

3. Assert: Finally, you see how things went. You check to make sure that what did happen was in line with what you expected to happen. If what happened met expectations, your validation has succeeded. If it didn't meet expectations, your validation has failed.

Just like in TDD, a build process is a formal validation. You will need to add steps to your build script to set up the environment for the build to run (Arrange), run the transition from source files to executable form (Act), and check as many things as you can (Assert). In Figure 6-3, you can see the types of activities that are in both our private build and our CI build. Let's go through them one by one:

•   Start: The private build will be triggered on demand by a developer. The CI build will be triggered by a watcher on the Git repository – when a new commit occurs.

•   Clean: Any temporary directories or files are deleted, and any remnants of previous builds are expunged.

•   Version: The build number is pushed into any areas of input needed for the resulting executable software to be stamped with the version number of the build. It's common for a private build to have a hard-coded version such as 0.0.0 or 9.9.9 so that anyone observing can immediately tell that a build is from a private build. In Azure Pipelines, the build number will come in from an environment variable, and the build script should push this number into relevant

---

[II]Beck, 2002

places, such as an AssemblyInfo.cs file for .NET Framework or the dotnet.exe command line for .NET Core. If this step is omitted, resulting .NET assemblies will not be properly labeled with the build number.

- Migrate Database: This step represents anything environmental that the application needs in order to function. Most applications store data, so a database needs to be created and migrated to the current schema in preparation for the subsequent build steps. In this book, we show examples using a SQL Server relational database schema.

- Compile: This step transforms source files into assemblies, and performs any encoding, transpiling,[III] minification, and so on to turn source code into a form suitable for execution in the intended runtime environment.

- Unit Tests: This is the first step that falls into the Assert category. Now that we have a form of the software that can be validated, presuming the compile step succeeded, we start with the fastest type of validations. Unit tests execute classes and methods that do not call out of process. In .NET, this is the AppDomain, which is the boundary for a space of memory. Therefore, unit tests are blazing fast.

- Integration Tests: These tests ensure that various components of the application can integrate with each other. The most common is that our data access code can integrate with the SQL Server database schema. These tests execute code that traverses across processes (.NET AppDomain, through the networking stack, to the SQL Server process) in order to validate functionality. These tests are important, but they are orders of magnitude slower than unit tests. As an application grows, expect about a 10:1 ratio of unit tests to integration tests.

- Private Build Success: After these steps, a private build is done. Nothing further is necessary to run on a developer workstation.

- Static Code Analysis: Whether it be the FxCop family of analyzers, products like Ndepend or SonarQube, or JavaScript linters, a CI build

---

[III]TypeScript in Visual Studio Code, n.d.

should include static code analysis in its list of validations. They are easy to run and find bugs that automated tests will not. Capers Jones includes them in the top 3 defect detection methods from his research.[IV]

- Publish Test Results: At this point, the CI build has succeeded and needs to output the build artifacts. Each application type has a process that outputs the artifacts in a way that is suitable for packaging, which is the next step.

- Package: In .NET, this is the act of taking each deployable application component and compressing it into a named and versioned NuGet package, for example, UI (ASP.NET web site), database (SQL Server schema migration assets), BatchJob (Windows service, Azure Function, etc.), and acceptance tests (deployable tests to be run in further down the DevOps pipeline). These NuGet packages are to be pushed to Azure Artifacts. While it is possible to use zip files, NuGet is the standard package format for .NET.

- Publish: Pushing the packaged NuGet files to Azure Artifacts so they are available through the NuGet feed.

- CI Build Success: The continuous integration build has now completed and can report success.

Your implementation of a private build and a CI build can vary from the examples shown in this book but take care to include each of the preceding steps in a fashion that is suitable for your application. Now that you know the structure of the builds, let's cover how to configure and run them in a .NET environment.

Using Builds with .NET Core and Azure Pipelines

Azure Pipelines is gaining wide adoption because of the compatibility and ease with which an automated continuous delivery pipeline can be set up with a software application residing anywhere. Whether GitHub or Azure Repos, or your own Git repository, Azure Pipelines can provide the build and deploy pipeline. There are four

---

[IV]Jones, 2012

stages to continuous delivery, as described by the 2010 book *Continuous Delivery: Reliable Software Releases through Build, Test, and Deployment Automation.*[V] These stages are

- Commit

- Automated acceptance tests

- Manual validations

- Release

The commit stage includes the private build and continuous integration build. The automated acceptance test stage includes your TDD environment with the test suites that represent acceptance tests. The UAT environment, or whatever name you choose, represents the deployed environment suitable for manual validations. Then, the final release stage goes to production where your marketplace provides feedback on the value you created for it. Let's look at the configuration of the private build and of Azure Pipelines and see how to enable the commit stage of continuous delivery.

Enabling Continuous Delivery's Commit Stage

Before you configure Azure Pipelines, you must have your private build. Attempting to create a CI build without this foundation is a recipe for lost time and later rework. In the source code that accompanies this book, you will find a PowerShell build script named "./build.ps1". The full listing for this file is at the end of this chapter. Feel free to use it as a build script for your own .NET Core applications. It contains all the necessary steps narrated earlier and will serve as a good jump start for your CI build. This build scripts contains steps to restore, compile, create a local database, and run tests. The first time you clone the repository, you'll see quite a bit of NuGet restore activity that you won't see on subsequent builds because these packages are cached. Figure 6-4 shows the dotnet. exe restore output that you'll only see the first time after clicking click_to_build.bat.

[V]Humble, 2010

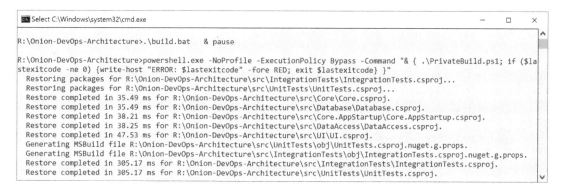

Figure 6-4. *The first time the private build runs, you'll see more output than normal from the Restore step*

Click_to_build.bat is a simple helper file that makes running a private build easy and convenient by adding a "& pause" so that the command window remains open when invoked by the keyboard or mouse from Windows Explorer. In the normal course of development, you'll run the private build repeatedly to make sure that every change you've made is a solid, stable step forward. You'll be using a local SQL Server instance, and the build script will destroy and recreate your local database every time you run the script. Unit tests will run against your code. Component-level integration tests will ensure that the database schema and ORM configuration work in unison to persist and hydrate objects in your domain model. Figure 6-5 shows the full build script executive with "quiet" verbosity level enabled.

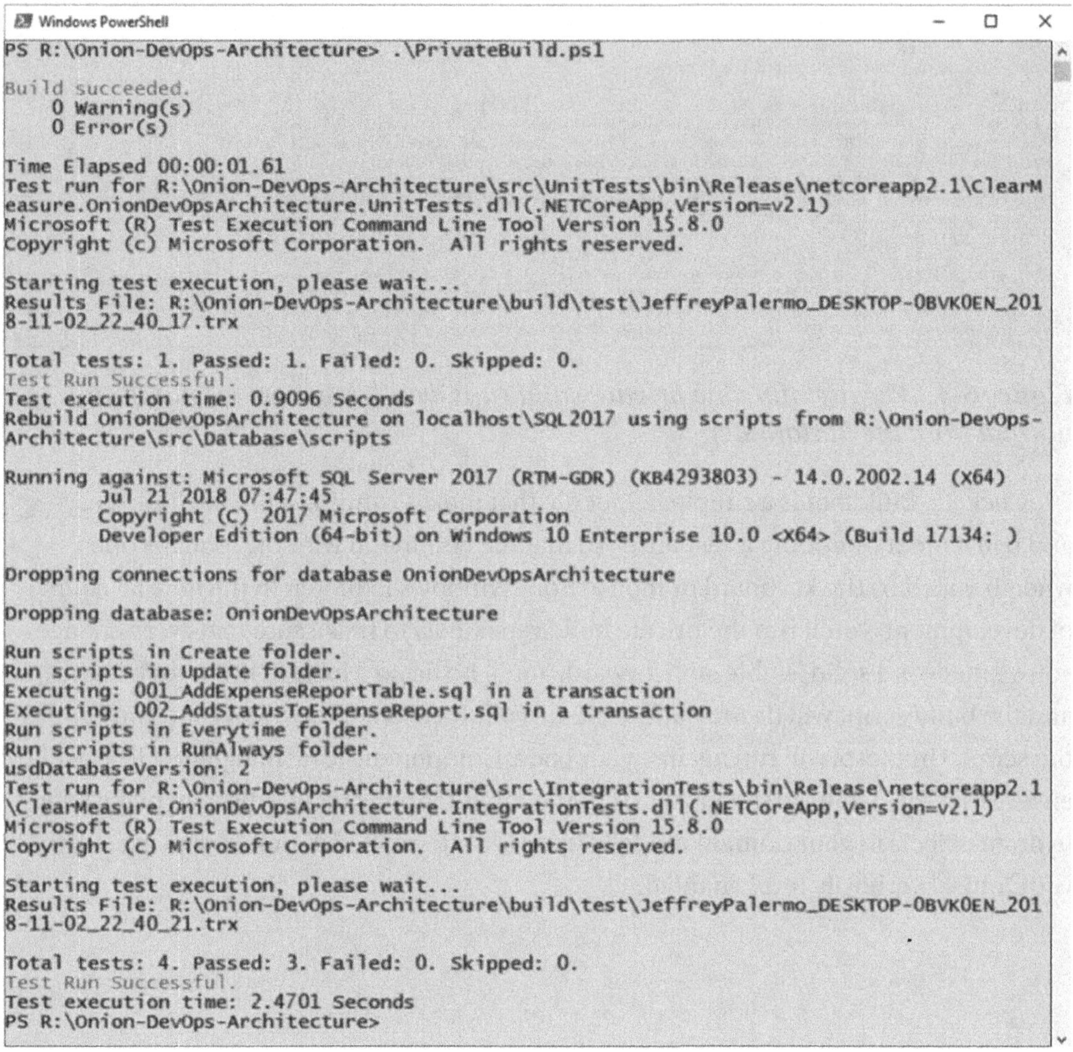

Figure 6-5. *The output from the private build can fit on one screen and run in less than 1 minute*

This is a simple private build script, but it scales with you no matter how much code you add to the solution and how many tests you add to these test suites. In fact, this build script doesn't have to change even as you add table after table to your SQL Server database. This build script pattern has been tested thoroughly over the last 13 years across multiple teams, hundreds of clients, and a build server journey from CruiseControl.NET to Jenkins to Bamboo to TeamCity to VSTS to Azure Pipelines. Although parts and bits might change a little, use this build script to model your own. The structure is proven.

Now that you have your foundational build script, you're ready to create your Azure Pipeline CI build. As an overview, Figure 6-6 shows the steps you use, including pushing your release candidate packages to Azure Artifacts.

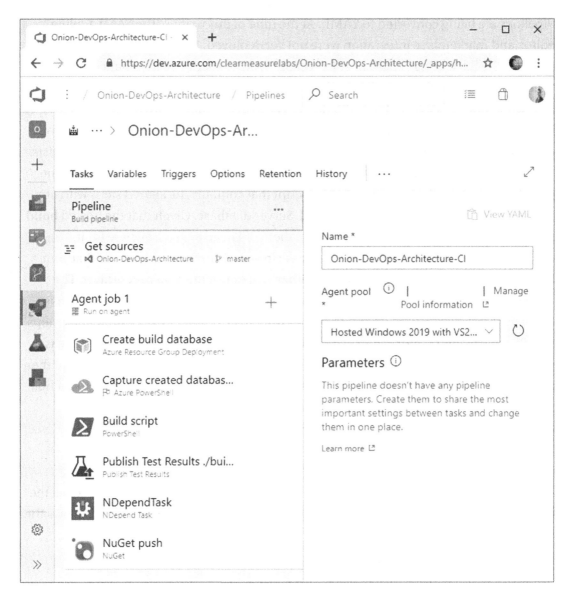

Figure 6-6. *Azure Pipelines build configuration is quite simple when you start with the foundation of a private build script*

Many of the defaults are suitable for CI builds and don't have to be customized. Let's go through the parts that are important. First, you'll choose your agent pool. I've chosen hosted agent for Visual Studio 2019. For the purposes of illustration, I'm using the build designer rather than the YAML option. All the builds and release definitions in Azure Pipelines are being converted to YAML. At the time of this writing, the YAML tooling, editor, and marketplace integration were not yet deployed. Because of this, the designer provides the full editing experience. Expect the YAML experience to enhanced quickly. When it is fully complete, you'll be able to save your CI build configuration as a YAML file in your Git repository right next to your application. You will want to do this because any logic not versioned with your code could break your pipeline since it is inherently not compatible with branching given that only one version of the build configuration exists.

To continue down the CI build configuration, you need to set up the environment for the execution of the PowerShell build script that contains the shared steps with our private build. This means that I need a SQL Server database. Given that the hosted build agents don't have a SQL Server installed on them, I'll need to go elsewhere for it. You can use an ARM script to provision a database in your Azure subscription so that your integration tests have the infrastructure with which to test the data access layer. The ARM scripts for this are part of the sample application. After the creation of a database that can be used by the integration tests, you want to ensure that your compilation steps handle the versioning properly. After all, the purpose of this build is to create a release candidate. The candidate for release must be versioned and packaged properly and then run through a gauntlet of validations before you would ever trust it to run in production. As you call your PowerShell build script, you call the command with the following arguments:

```
./build.ps1 ; CIBuild
```

Even though there is only one explicit parameter in the preceding command, all the build variables are available to any script as environment variables. Figure 6-7 shows the variables that are configured for this build.

Name ↑	Value	🔒
BuildConfiguration	Release	
BuildPlatform	any cpu	
ConnectionString	Server=$(DatabaseServer);Database=$(DatabaseName);Persist Security ...	
DatabaseAction	Update	
DatabaseName	build-$(Build.BuildNumber)-$(Build.BuildId)	
DatabasePassword	********	
DatabaseResourceGroupName	BuildDatabases-$(System.TeamProject)-$(Build.DefinitionName)	
DatabaseServer	databaseserver$(resourceGroupUniqueString).database.windows.net	
DatabaseUser	dbuser	
system.collectionId	2a617deb-3284-4138-8ccd-d08a0593369f	
system.debug	false	
system.definitionId	7	
system.teamProject	DevOps-Architecture-Pro-Sample	
Version	$(Build.BuildNumber)	

Figure 6-7. *The build variables are available to the build steps as environment variables*

As variables are defined, make use of other variables in order to build up the appropriate values. You will find that once you create a few CI build configurations and variable sets, the patterns are very portable from one application to the next. Make sure to vary values so that multiple builds can run in parallel. In the following you will see how to configure the build to support parallel builds on feature branches. Another very important configuration is the build number, which provides the version for our build. In the build script shown at the end of the chapter, we have some PowerShell variables that pull in variables from the CI build configuration. The build configuration and version are captured here:

```
$projectConfig = $env:BuildConfiguration
$version = $env:Version
```

In this way, you can call dotnet.exe so that every DLL is labeled properly. See the command-line arguments used as you compile the solution:

```
Function Compile{
  exec {
    & dotnet build $syource_dir\$projectName.sln
    -nologo --no-restore -v $verbosity
    -maxcpucount --configuration $projectConfig
    --no-incremental /p:Version=$version
    /p:Authors="Clear Measure"
    /p:Product="Onion DevOps Architecture"
  }
}
```

The build script also runs tests that output *.trx files so that Azure Pipelines can show and track the results of tests as they repeatedly run over time:

```
Function UnitTests{
  Push-Location -Path $unitTestProjectPath
  try {
    exec {
      & dotnet test -nologo -v $verbosity --logger:trx
        --results-directory $test_dir --no-build
        --no-restore --configuration $projectConfig
    }
  }
  finally {
    Pop-Location
  }
}
```

We are using NUnit as our automated testing framework for this application. Notice that we hard-code very little in formulating our commands. This is to make our build script more maintainable. It can also be standardized someone across our teams and other applications given that the variances occur in the properties at the top of the file. Pay special attention to the arguments –no-restore and –no-build. By default, any call to dotnet.exe will recompile your code and perform a NuGet restore. You do not want to do this, as it is precious time wasted and creates new assemblies just before they are tested.

After the build script finishes, we can run our static analysis tools and then push the application with its various components to Azure Artifacts as *.nupkg files, which are essentially *.zip files with some specific differences.

Besides the steps of the build configuration, there are a few other options that should be changed from their defaults. The first is the build number. By default, you have the date embedded as the version number. This can certainly be the default, but to use the SemVer,[VI] or Semantic Versioning, pattern (`https://semver.org/`), you must change the "Build number format" to the following:

`1.0.$(Rev:r).0`

Additionally, as you enable continuous integration, you're asked what branches should be watched. The default is the master branch, but you'll want to change that to any branch. As you create a branch to develop a backlog item or user story, you'll want commits on that branch to initiate the pipeline as well. A successful build, deployment, and the full battery of automated tests will give you the confidence that it's time to put in your pull request. This setting is tricky and not obvious. As you click in the "Branch specification," you'll type an asterisk (*) and hit the Enter key. Figure 6-8 shows what you should see.

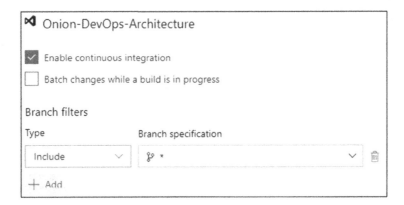

Figure 6-8. *Configure the continuous integration build to trigger on commits to every branch*

[VI]Preston Werner, n.d.

Once your CI build is up and running, add the Build History widget shown in Figure 6-9 to your project dashboard.

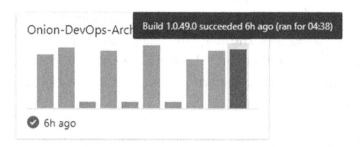

Figure 6-9. *Seeing the builds on the dashboard can alert you to increasing build times*

Notice that the build time is over 4 minutes. This is a simple application, but your build time is already up to 4 minutes and 38 seconds. Yet, your private build runs in about 1 minute locally. This is because of the hosted build agent architecture. As soon as you have your build stable, you'll want to start tuning it. One of the first performance optimizations you can make is to attach your own build agent so that you can control the processing power as well as the levels of caching you'd like your build environment to use. Although hosted build agents will certainly improve over time, you must use private build agents in order to achieve the short cycle time necessary to move quickly. And the 3 minutes overhead you incur at the time of this writing for hosted agents is not what you want for short cycle times across your team.

At the time of this writing, internal Microsoft teams use private build agents in order to achieve the performance and control necessary for complex projects. Use the hosted agents to stabilize new build configurations. Then measure and tune them to decide if you need to provision your own private agents.

Wrap Up

In this chapter, you've learned how to build your code. You've learned the structure of a build, the types, and how to set up each. You've seen the flow of a build on a feature branch as well as on a master branch and how the steps differ. You've also seen how to implement a build on Azure Pipelines for a .NET Core solution, as shown in Listing 6-1.

Listing 6-1. ./build.ps1

```powershell
. .\BuildFunctions.ps1
$startTime =
$projectName = "OnionDevOpsArchitecture"
$base_dir = resolve-path .\
$source_dir = "$base_dir\src"
$unitTestProjectPath = "$source_dir\UnitTests"
$integrationTestProjectPath = "$source_dir\IntegrationTests"
$acceptanceTestProjectPath = "$source_dir\AcceptanceTests"
$uiProjectPath = "$source_dir\UI"
$jobProjectPath = "$source_dir\Job"
$databaseProjectPath = "$source_dir\Database"
$projectConfig = $env:BuildConfiguration
$framework = "netcoreapp2.2"
$version = $env:Version
$verbosity = "m"

$build_dir = "$base_dir\build"
$test_dir = "$build_dir\test"

$aliaSql = "$source_dir\Database\scripts\AliaSql.exe"
$databaseAction = $env:DatabaseAction
if ([string]::IsNullOrEmpty($databaseAction)) { $databaseAction =
"Rebuild"}
$databaseName = $env:DatabaseName
if ([string]::IsNullOrEmpty($databaseName)) { $databaseName = $projectName}
$databaseServer = $env:DatabaseServer
if ([string]::IsNullOrEmpty($databaseServer)) { $databaseServer =
"localhost\SQL2017"}
$databaseScripts = "$source_dir\Database\scripts"

if ([string]::IsNullOrEmpty($version)) { $version = "9.9.9"}
if ([string]::IsNullOrEmpty($projectConfig)) {$projectConfig = "Release"}

Function Init {
    rd $build_dir -recurse -force  -ErrorAction Ignore
        md $build_dir > $null
```

```
        exec {
                & dotnet clean $source_dir\$projectName.sln -nologo -v
                $verbosity
                }
        exec {
                & dotnet restore $source_dir\$projectName.sln -nologo
                --interactive
                 -v $verbosity
                }

    Write-Host $projectConfig
    Write-Host $version
}

Function Compile{
        exec {
                & dotnet build $source_dir\$projectName.sln -nologo --no-
                restore
                 -v $verbosity -maxcpucount --configuration $projectConfig
                --no-incremental /p:Version=$version
                /p:Authors="Clear Measure" /p:Product="Onion DevOps
                Architecture"
        }
}

Function UnitTests{
        Push-Location -Path $unitTestProjectPath

        try {
                exec {
                        & dotnet test -nologo -v $verbosity --logger:trx `
                        --results-directory $test_dir --no-build `
                        --no-restore --configuration $projectConfig `
                        --collect:"Code Coverage"
                }
        }
```

```
        finally {
                Pop-Location
        }
}

Function IntegrationTest{
        Push-Location -Path $integrationTestProjectPath

        try {
                exec {
                        & dotnet test -nologo -v $verbosity --logger:trx `
                        --results-directory $test_dir --no-build `
                        --no-restore --configuration $projectConfig `
                        --collect:"Code Coverage"
                }
        }
        finally {
                Pop-Location
        }
}

Function MigrateDatabaseLocal {
        exec{
                & $aliaSql $databaseAction $databaseServer $databaseName
                  $databaseScripts
        }
}

Function MigrateDatabaseRemote{
    $appConfig = "$integrationTestProjectPath\app.config"
    $injectedConnectionString = "Server=tcp:$databaseServer,1433;Initial
        Catalog=$databaseName;Persist Security Info=False;
        User ID=$env:DatabaseUser;Password=$env:DatabasePassword;
        MultipleActiveResultSets=False;Encrypt=True;TrustServerCertificate=
        False;
        Connection Timeout=30;"
```

```
    write-host "Using connection string: $injectedConnectionString"
    if ( Test-Path "$appConfig" ) {
        poke-xml $appConfig "//add[@key='ConnectionString']/@value"
        $injectedConnectionString
    }

    exec {
        & $aliaSql $databaseAction $databaseServer $databaseName
        $databaseScripts
            $env:DatabaseUser $env:DatabasePassword
    }
}

Function Pack{
    Write-Output "Packaging nuget packages"
    exec{
        & dotnet publish $uiProjectPath -nologo --no-restore --no-build -v
        $verbosity
            --configuration $projectConfig
    }
    exec{
        & .\tools\octopack\Octo.exe pack --id "$projectName.UI" --version
        $version
            --basePath $uiProjectPath\bin\$projectConfig\$framework\publish
            --outFolder $build_dir --overwrite
    }

    exec{
        & .\tools\octopack\Octo.exe pack --id "$projectName.Database"
            --version $version --basePath $databaseProjectPath --outFolder
            $build_dir
            --overwrite
    }

    exec{
        & dotnet publish $jobProjectPath -nologo --no-restore --no-build -v
        $verbosity
```

```
            --configuration $projectConfig
    }
    exec{
        & .\tools\octopack\Octo.exe pack --id "$projectName.Job" --version
        $version
            --basePath $jobProjectPath\bin\$projectConfig\$framework\publish
            --outFolder $build_dir --overwrite
        }

    exec{
        & dotnet publish $acceptanceTestProjectPath -nologo --no-restore
        --no-build
            -v $verbosity --configuration $projectConfig
    }
    exec{
        & .\tools\octopack\Octo.exe pack --id "$projectName.AcceptanceTests"
            --version $version
            --basePath $acceptanceTestProjectPath\
            bin\$projectConfig\$framework\publish
            --outFolder $build_dir --overwrite
        }
}

Function PrivateBuild{
        $sw = [Diagnostics.Stopwatch]::StartNew()
        Init
        Compile
        UnitTests
        MigrateDatabaseLocal
        IntegrationTest
        $sw.Stop()
        write-host "Build time: " $sw.Elapsed.ToString()
}

Function CIBuild{
        Init
        MigrateDatabaseRemote
```

```
        Compile
        UnitTests
        IntegrationTest
        Pack
}
```

Bibliography

Beck, K. (2002). *Test Driven Development: By Example.* Addison-Wesley Professional.

Duvall, P. M. (2007). *Continuous Integration: Improving Software Quality and Reducing Risk.* Addison Wesley.

Humble, J. a. (2010). *Continuous Delivery: Reliable Software Releases through Build, Test, and Deployment Automation.* Addison-Wesley.

Jones, C. (2012). Retrieved from SOFTWARE DEFECT ORIGINS AND REMOVAL METHODS: www.ifpug.org/Documents/Jones-SoftwareDefectOriginsAndRemovalMethodsDraft5.pdf

Preston-Werner, T. (n.d.). Retrieved from Semantic Versioning 2.0.0: https://semver.org/

TypeScript in Visual Studio Code. (n.d.). Retrieved from https://code.visualstudio.com/docs/languages/typescript

CHAPTER 7

Validating the Code

Now that you are working with code, tracking changes against work items, and building the code, you need to squeeze out defects. In Chapter 4, we discussed how to configure Azure Boards to shed light on every type of work that must be done for a work item to make its way from an idea to the customer. In this way, you are baking defect detection into every part of your process. You can certainly have code that performs perfectly while doing the wrong thing because of poor design or poor analysis. But this chapter is about ensuring that the code is working properly. Since the code is what the software is built from, you want to ensure that your DevOps process and infrastructure are set up to be able to validate it all comprehensively and quickly. You will likely accumulate a volume of code that is impossible to keep in your head. Significant software systems have so many code files that the only way the code can be validated in a manageable way is to automate most of it and create a process for manual review of just the recent changes. This chapter will span steps that will be automated through the continuous integration build, the first deployed environment, and the pull request.

Strategy for Defect Detection

From the research that our industry has available, and summarized by Capers Jones, "the cost of finding and fixing bugs or defects is the largest single expense element in the history of software."[I] Mr. Jones goes on to report that for the expected 25-year life span of a 500,000 line-of-code .NET system (estimated at 52 LOC C# to 1 Function Point[II]), almost $0.50 of our of every dollar will be spent on finding and fixing bugs. A review of the available quality research would be beneficial to anyone looking to put together a high-performing DevOps environment.

[I]Jones, SOFTWARE DEFECT ORIGINS AND REMOVAL METHODS, 2012
[II]Jones, Software Economics and Function Point Metrics: Thirty years of IFPUG Progress, 2017

© Jeffrey Palermo 2019
J. Palermo, *.NET DevOps for Azure*, https://doi.org/10.1007/978-1-4842-5343-4_7

To summarize, defect removal efficiency (DRE) is a metric that has a basic in industry research. Among all of the methods and techniques that are available for maximizing DRE, three emerge as a good balance of investment while together having a track record of achieving the range of 85%-95% DRE. This should be considered the minimal starting point. Excluding any of these techniques will almost certainly yield poor quality given that other techniques are not shown to make up for the lack of these. Use these as an essential starting point and evaluate what your standard should be. The three essential defect removal techniques are

- Static analysis

- Testing

- Inspections

Discussing 85% isn't worthwhile without knowing how many defects we should expect to be generated in a given software project. Only then would we know how many defects would have to be caught and fixed in order to arrive at the 85% DRE level. And after this, what number of defects are shipped to production if 15% of them escape? Capers Jones summarizes this research as well in his 2016 article "Exceeding 99% in Defect Removal Efficiency (DRE) for Software."[III] The table in Figure 7-1 shows the average defects potentials by phase of work. These are the average rate of defects generated by each type of work from software projects studies through 2016.

Phase of work	Defects per 100 lines of C# (1 FP = ~52 C#)
Requirements	1.35
Architecture	0.19
Design	1.83
Code	2.21
Security code flaws	0.48
Documents	0.87
Bad fixes	1.25

Figure 7-1. *Defects that should be expected by phase of work per 100 lines of resulting C# code*

[III]Jones, Exceeding 99% in Defect Removal Efficiency DRE for Software, 2016

The research community uses Function Points to normalize projects and make them comparable. We can convert averages into comparable lines of code by using a technique called backfiring. This is where we take that the average function point of software functionality can be implemented in 52 lines of C#. We use this conversation ratio to determine what range of defect potentials might be relevant for our own software system. If our system is 10,000 lines of C# (HTML, VB, SQL all have very similar conversion ratios), we should expect a ballpark defect potential in the neighborhood of 800 defects, from all sources. At minimum quality bar, 85% DRE would catch 680 defects before releasing to the customer and would release to production 120. Research shows that around 25% of these released defects can be caught and fixed each year after release. This is why for systems that have been in production usage for many years can become quite stable – and why new changes tend to break things in a visible way, especially when users have been used to stability.

If our system is much larger, say 500,000 lines of code, we should expect around 41,000 defects to be generated from all phases of work. These number can become quite scary. If we achieve 95% DRE, we are still releasing over 6,000 defects to our customers. 99% DRE would bring the number of defects released to customers to around 400. These numbers are sobering. It is tempting to think that even with industry averages like this, certainly your team is above average. One would hope so, and one should be able to articulate why. If you were to speculate to beat the averages by a factor of 2, feel free to cut these numbers in half. Even there, we can see the importance of a clear defect detection and defect removal strategy if we are to have any hope of producing a quality software system. A highly automated DevOps environment is an enabler of quality and speed, but it must be a rich pipeline, full of quality controls.

Consider the analogy of a water treatment system for a town. We can think of this as a pipeline where water from available sources comes in to the pipeline. Through a series of treatment steps, water that is prone to cause disease and sickness is cleaned, filtered, and treated so that good drinking water is produced as an output. The drinking water is not perfect, but it is good enough for the community. This series of treatments and filters in this water pipeline is what we must create in our DevOps pipeline. The raw ideas that come from business initiatives are not suitable for working software. We translate the ideas into requirements (features), and then we break those down into units that can be implemented (user stories). We translate these into code, then into a deployable release candidate, then into a deployed environment, and then into a working production system. Each step of the way, the work in process coming from the left, as visualized by our swim lanes in Azure Boards, has more hidden defects that we want promoted

155

to stages to the right of our project board. It is up to us to ensure that every time the work moves from one swim lane to the next that there is a filter or a "treatment" that find the defects that are hiding at that point in time and removes them. For the rest of this chapter, we'll focus on the quality control techniques that are the minimum bar for detecting and removing defects that are produced in the code that our teams write.

Strategy and Execution of Defect Detection

While this chapter, or book, could not comprehensively cover all of the defect detection techniques you may want to implement, it will cover the three essential techniques. Omitting any of these could be considered malpractices given the documented effectiveness and affordability of each of the three.

PAIR PROGRAMMING AS DEFECT DETECTION

Pair programming does have a good track record for defect detection. Read the texts cited in this chapter in order to dive into the actual numbers. Pair programming is the act of having two developers create and change the code together, each trading off at the keyboard and swapping roles of coder and navigator. Those who partake in these exercises report anecdotally what the research shows: for tough problems, it helps push through quicker, but for normal to easy code, it creates overhead. The reason this technique isn't one of the first you should reach for is the high cost as a defect detection method. The rate of return is not as high as static analysis, testing, and inspections because it does double the cost of labor for the same scope of software created. The software is of very high quality, but the ROI does not translate into an economic advantage. This technique is best used for the smaller number of more risky or difficult software features.

Let's briefly define each of three essential defect removal methods.

Static Analysis

Static analysis is the automated examination of a source file in order to predict defects. More broadly, static analysis can be used as a technique against documents and other artifacts as well as source code. The spelling and grammar check in Microsoft Word is a very valuable static analyzer, without which this book might sound very unprofessional, indeed. While the copy editor performs testing on each chapter by reading every word, and the chapter layout proofer inspects images, tables, and margins, the static analyzer in Microsoft Word is run many times, often after every change to the document. Because it is automated, it can be run essentially for free frequently. For our source code, we will implement a number of static analysis tools. These will run automatically as part of our DevOps pipeline. These tools will emit warnings and errors. We may choose to fail a step in our pipeline when errors occur – or choose to fail on new warnings.

Testing

Since the dawn of software, testing has been part of the workflow. A programmer has always run the written code to see if it works as intended. In 2002, Kent Beck published a very influential book that has shifted the testing methods of scores of teams. This book is *Test Driven Development: By Example.*[IV] James Newkirk, coauthor of NUnit 2 and XUnit testing frameworks, illustrated TDD for .NET in his 2004 book, *Test-Driven Development in Microsoft .NET.*[V] The technique of test-driven development shifts the developer from either manual desk checking or custom test harnesses to a standard pattern for creating executable tests. This standard format, and the method of creation, allows for test suites that continually grow as the software grows. In many cases, the best format for Scrum's acceptance criteria for a backlog item is a written down test scenario whose steps are coded into an automated test that exercises the system in that fashion.

Inspections

Anything that is built is inspected. We value home inspectors that can use a formal checklist to inspect a house or apartment before purchase or move-in. These inspectors are experts. They know what to look for, and they are equipped with a checklist to ensure they don't forget to inspect all of the necessary items. Laypeople cannot be inspectors. They lack the training or knowledge of what to inspect. The author would likewise be unqualified to inspect a house being purchased. In software, one can craft an inspection at several stages in the value chain. The DevOps process includes more than just the pipeline and begins once an idea has been crafted and placed on the project board. Take care to evaluate what steps should include a formal inspection, who should perform it, and what the checklist should be.

[IV]Beck, 2002
[V]Newkirk & Vorontsov, 2004

Code Validation in the DevOps Pipeline

We have seen that work moves through our process according to our swim lane progression, as shown in Figure 7-2.

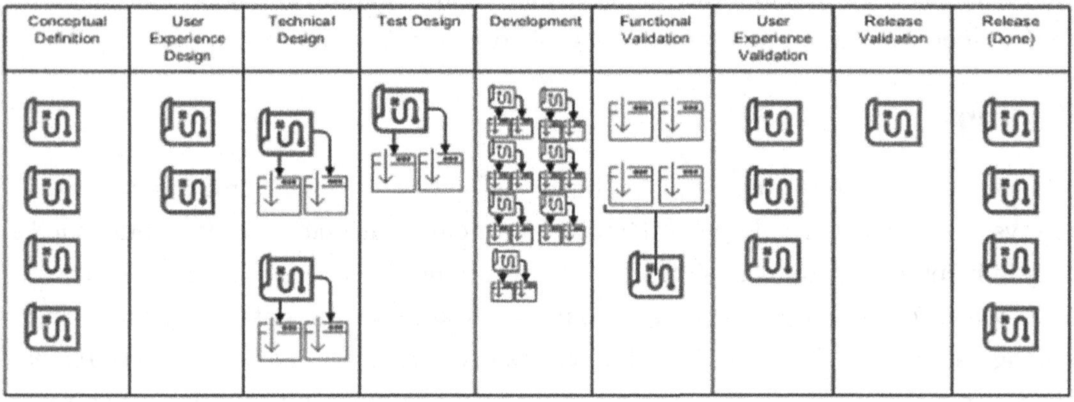

Figure 7-2. *Standard swim lanes for a measurable DevOps process*

For the purposes of this chapter, we will focus on just the following:

- Test design

- Development

- Functional validation

These three phases of work surround the code and produce a release candidate that can be further evaluated. So our scope of focus is narrowed to just these three columns, as shown in Figure 7-3.

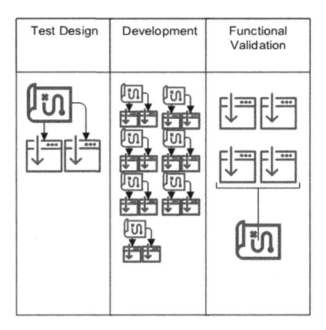

Figure 7-3. *Validating the code focuses on these three swim lanes in our process*

For simplicity, here is the part of our automated DevOps pipeline that will be impacted by the implemented of our defect removal methods.

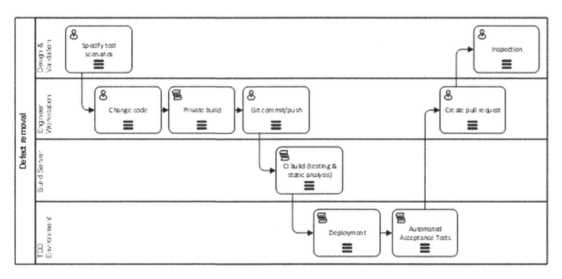

Figure 7-4. *Validating the code starts a few steps before coding and includes some critical steps after*

Figure 7-4 is a snapshot of the DevOps process surrounding making code changes. Static analysis, testing, and inspections go in specific places in this process. Each method integrates well into Azure DevOps Services, Visual Studio, and .NET. Let's take them one at a time.

Static Analysis

Once you have decided what static analysis tools you should use, you will configure them in the continuous integration build. It is often unnecessary to have them run every time as part of the private build, but developers may run them frequently on their own. Any static analysis tool will be able to be run locally on demand, but you will want to make it an automated part of your pipeline. Placing it before release candidate packaging is important. If the revision doesn't pass static analysis checks, there may be little point in archiving the packages from the build given that the revision has no chance of ever becoming a release candidate.

In Visual Studio, FxCop has long been an available static analysis tool for .NET. It fully supports .NET Framework. With recent changes in the C# compiler, Roslyn-based analyzers have been replacing FxCop and are the preferred method. These analyzers become part of the Visual Studio solution and can run both in the IDE as well as command line. This chapter will not duplicate the documentation, which can be found online.[VI] Other popular static analysis tools include

- ReSharper Command Line: For code style conventions

- Ndepend: For code metrics, warnings, and high-level quality gradings

- SonarQube: For code metrics, warnings, and high-level quality gradings

- TSLint: For readability, maintainability, and functionality errors

- WAVE: Web Accessibility Evaluation Tool for statically analyzing web pages for screen reader compatibility errors

This is not meant to be a comprehensive list of static analysis tools. There are many, many more. Static analysis is a method for which there are many implementations. Evaluate your software and include as many as you can.

[VI]Microsoft, n.d.

Testing

Manual testing will always occur. For some validation, only a human eye can uncover a defect that may affect customers. Certainly if there was a defect in colors or a CSS spreadsheet that made all text white on a white background, your software may function just fine, but few customers would be able to use it. The majority of system functionality can be covered by forms of automated testing, and this section will focus on that. By applying levels of automated testing, we minimize the load needed on manual testers and ensure that people performing usability testing do not encounter functional defects. Further, those performing exploratory testing will be able to focus on that task rather than using time to report functional defects preventable by automated testing.

When we consider automated testing, one can group them into four categories.

- Unit tests

- Integration tests

- Full-system tests

- Specialized tests

Rather than create an exhaustive listing, specialized tests include types of testing that do not have a short enough cycle time to reliably include in an automated DevOps pipeline in any comprehensive fashion. Load testing and security testing fall into this category. While you may include some spot checks of these types of tests in your full-system tests, these types of specialized test cases often require special environments and human assistance in order to run. They are valuable, but they will be outside the scope of this chapter. For the first three types of tests, Microsoft provides some documentation[VII] and guidance on how they separate these test types within their Azure DevOps product team. They correlate tests in four different categories, L0-L3, and match nicely the preceding list. All of these tests can be run with popular testing frameworks like NUnit and XUnit.

Unit Tests (L0)

These tests are very fast. The call stack stays in memory. The average execution time for these tests should hover around 50-70ms. Because of these, code that includes out-of-process dependencies is disqualified. Any of these would make the tests too slow.

[VII]Microsoft/Azure, n.d.

These tests can test a single method or many classes together, but they should be testing some logical unit of software logic. The watchwords for these tests are small and fast. These tests should be able to be run on each developer's workstation as well as on the build server. These tests should be included in the Visual Studio solution with the production code. Some antipatterns for unit tests are

- Use of global or threading resources like Mutexes, file I/O, registry, and so on

- Any dependencies between a test and another

- High consumption of CPU or memory for a single test

- Including code that calls out of the current process

Integration Tests (L1)

Microsoft's guidance is that L1 tests should run under 2 seconds. The vast majority of these tests should run within 1 second. Consider 2 seconds to be an upper bound. When the code is covered with unit tests, we are left with a code base where the individual classes do the right thing, but we have not yet proven that all of the modules or layers work together. The best example of this is the database schema, the data layer, and the domain model entities. Entity Framework Core is a very good choice for working with relational data in .NET Core, but without executing tests that round-trip from the domain model entities to the database and back, we cannot know that those components will work when integrated together on a downstream environment. Unit tests will not test this capability because any call to the database is an out-of-process call. Integration tests are run with the continuous integration build as well as within the private build script on the developers' workstation. These tests should be included in the Visual Studio solution with the production code. Some antipatterns for integration tests are

- Requirement for large amounts of data setup.

- Any functional dependency on any other test.

- Validating more than one logical behavior between layers (being too large).

- Requiring external test state or data setup: Every test is responsible for its own setup.

Full-System Tests (L2)

These tests are a superset of the designed test scenarios for each developed feature and defect fix proofs created when the root cause of a defect is identified. Full-system tests require a fully deployed environment in order to execute. They often will execute through the same interfaces as other interactors of the software. In a web page, Selenium may be used to type in text boxes and push buttons. All layers of the application or service are online as these tests execute. They are responsible for their own setup and are often responsible for reliably running in any order even as other tests continually change the state of the system. These tests should assume the context of an identity and execute the full application just as a normal user would. These tests should be included in the Visual Studio solution with the production code. Some antipatterns for integration tests are

- Unnecessarily Slow: While these tests will be a few orders of magnitude slower than unit tests, the aggregate of them will determine the cycle time of a release branch.

- Modify global state.

- The use of shared resources that prevent parallelization.

- Requirement of third-party services that are outside of the team's control, that is, Office 365 login, PayPal, and the like.

For these three types of automated testing, you will see a decline in the numbers of each. Let's consider a code base that is 300,000 lines of code. Some averages this author has seen (not backed at all by research) is around a unit test for every 50 lines of code. For covered code, the average should be lower, but some production code will not be covered, especially code that is on the edge, hopelessly coupled to third-party libraries and frameworks and wrapped in isolation layers. Beyond this, drop an order of magnitude for your expectation of integration tests. This would be an integration test for every 500 lines of code. Then for full-system tests, one of these for every 5000 lines of code. Giving concrete numbers like these is fraught with peril because inadequate research exists for one to give any numbers at all. Given the uselessness of the "it depends" answer, anecdotal experience has seen ratios such as 100:10:1 when looking at unit tests to integration tests to full-system tests. Don't expect the drop in order of magnitude to be exact, but do expect each smaller scope of tests to include a greater number. Your ratio is certain to vary, but take alarm if you end up with more full-system tests than integration tests and more integration tests than unit tests. Take alarm if the numbers are similar. You should see a significant difference in numbers. For example, full-system tests are testing user scenarios with the fully deployed system online. Each branch of business logic can be tested as a unit test, and each branch of database or queue behavior can be tested with an integration test. So take care that you pick the type of test with the smallest scope when determining how to test an aspect of code behavior.

ACCEPTANCE TEST-DRIVEN DEVELOPMENT

Before coding, we have a swim lane called test design. In this column, test scenarios are to be added to the work item definition. Scrum calls for clear acceptance criteria to be added to backlog items. Scripted test scenarios are an implementation of Scrum's acceptance test concept that creates a test name and a set of test steps that can be programmed into an executable full-system test. In this fashion, acceptance criteria are added to an executable regression tests suite so that all accumulated acceptance criteria are validated with every successive build of the software. This puts the product owner, or other leader, in control of this aspect of verifiable quality.

Inspections

Inspections are a manual process. But it is different than manual testing. An inspection is a consistent process whereby a human checks some work product using the same checklist and criteria as every other work product. In software, we can implement inspections in several places across the broader process. For example, a good precode inspection would be after all four elements of design are complete and before the feature or user story is cleared for development. The checklist for this type of inspection might have high-level items to verify completeness:

- Feature includes conceptual definition and vision description along with objectives.

- Feature includes detailed user experience design such as wireframes, screen mockups, and the like.

- Feature includes changes to architecture layers, new libraries needed, and other key technology decisions.

- Feature includes written test scenarios complete with test steps suitable for manual execution as well as test automation.

Without this inspection, it would likely be common for features to make it to developers and lack a critical part of the design. Faced with an incomplete design, developers will have to stop developing and backtrack with the right conversations in order to complete the work that was left incomplete upstream in the process. Without catching this design rework, it may appear that the development phase of work is dropping in productivity (throughput) when the developers are actually finding upstream design defects and working to fix them before continuing with coding.

For the purposes of finding coding defects, a good implementation of an inspection would be integrated with the pull request process. If every feature/user story is developed using a feature branch, a pull request can govern and document the process of accepting the changes on the branch back into the master branch. In Azure Repos or GitHub, the pull request experience is rich enough to accommodate a formal, documented inspection. When the pull request fails inspection, which is not to be feared given that this would indicate a defect being found, the branch can continue to be worked in order to resolve the defect. Once the defect is fixed, the branch can be inspected again, and upon passing inspection, the pull request can then be approved, and the branch merged into master. In this example, we would use an expert inspector – another member of the engineering team. For this type of inspection, a power user or product owner would not be a qualified inspector because the target of the inspection is source code. But a product owner/product manager would likely be very interested in the results of the inspection, reports that they are happening, and the number of defects that are found and fixed through executing inspections.

Along with other items, a pull request code inspection might have steps from the following list:

- The application works after a Git pull and private build.

- The changes conform to the approved architecture of system.

- The changes implement the design decisions called out in the feature.

- The changes conform to existing norms of the code base.

- No unapproved packages or libraries were introduced to the code base.

- The code is accompanied by right balance of tests.

- All test scenarios in acceptance criteria of the feature have been implemented as full-system L2 tests.

- Logging is implemented properly and of sufficient detail.

- Performance Considerations: Application specific.

- Security Considerations: Application specific and conforming to organizational standards.

- Readability Considerations: Code is scannable – factored and named so that it is self-documenting and quickly reveals what it does.

When the inspector (pull request approver) approves the pull request, that individual is affirming that they have faithfully inspected the changes on the branch according to the inspection checklist and that in their professional opinion, the branch meets all the demands of the inspection and does not contain any defects that can be seen or suspected at this time. With this large responsibility, code reviews become a thing of the past. Quick glances at the code and subjective comments in the pull request record cease. In its place, we gain a rigorous and comprehensive inspection of each set of changes as branches are created and merged back into master. Using trunk-based development, branches are very short-lived, so inspections remain quick to perform. And because the standards for passing inspection are well-known, developers understand exactly what is expected and submit pull requests fully expecting to pass inspection.

Implementing Defect Detection

Armed with these defect removal methods and where they should reside in the process, let's look at how each one of them looks in .NET and implementing them using Azure DevOps Services.

Static Analysis

Microsoft provides very good documentation on FxCop analyzers for Visual Studio, and those instructions can be found in the footnotes.[VIII] After adding FxCop analyzers to a .NET Framework application, we can customize the built-in Microsoft rulesets right from within Visual Studio.

[VIII]Install FxCop analyzers in Visual Studio, 2018

Figure 7-5. *Visual Studio will save a project-specific ruleset file if you modify any of the settings of the Microsoft ruleset*

In your build script, you can add the following command-line arguments so that the analyzers are run when you want them run. Make sure to fail the build on a rule failure:

```
msbuild.exe
/t:Clean`;Rebuild /v:m /maxcpucount:1 /nologo
/p:RunCodeAnalysis=true
/p:ActiveRulesets=MinimumRecommendedRules.ruleset
/p:Configuration=Release
src\MySolution.sln
```

When you add the NuGet package

`Microsoft.CodeAnalysis.FxCopAnalyzers`

To your project in .NET Core, you'll see the analyzers appear in your Solution
Explorer, and warnings will start to show when you build your code inside Visual Studio,
as shown in Figure 7-6.

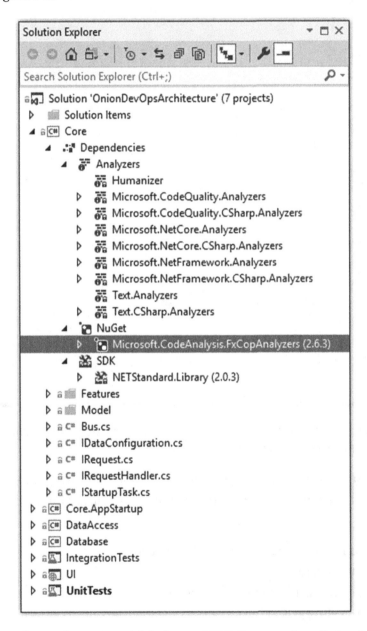

Figure 7-6.   *Code analyzers are added to a .NET Core project through NuGet*

There is no need to add a command-line argument to your call to dotnet.exe in your build script. When analyzers are added to your project, they will automatically run and generate the appropriate warnings or errors.

Each static analysis product has its own instructions for integrating it with your code, but in order to keep your Azure Pipelines build configuration simple, make sure to add your static analysis tools to your build script so that the configuration is stored in your Git repository. If you convert your Azure Pipelines build to YAML, you'll be storing more build logic in Git.

Testing

Implementing automated tests could fill a volume of its own, and there are plenty of books on the topic. If you are new to test automation, you would spend some time well reading James Newkirk's book mentioned earlier. For brevity, here are some examples of the various types of tests that are mentioned in this chapter.

Unit Tests

In our example application, we have an entity which serves as an aggregate root, in domain-driven design terms. It has a number of properties and methods. The code for this short class is as follows:

```
using System;

namespace ClearMeasure.OnionDevOpsArchitecture.Core.Model
{
    public class ExpenseReport
    {
        public Guid Id { get; set; }
        public string Title { get; set; }
        public string Description { get; set; }
        public ExpenseReportStatus Status { get; set; }
        public string Number { get; set; }
```

```
public ExpenseReport()
{
    Status = ExpenseReportStatus.Draft;
    Description = "";
    Title = "";
}

public string FriendlyStatus
{
    get { return GetTextForStatus(); }
}

protected string GetTextForStatus()
{
    return Status.ToString();
}

public override string ToString()
{
    return "ExpenseReport " + Number;
}

protected bool Equals(ExpenseReport other)
{
    return Id.Equals(other.Id);
}

public override bool Equals(object obj)
{
    if (ReferenceEquals(null, obj)) return false;
    if (ReferenceEquals(this, obj)) return true;
    if (obj.GetType() != this.GetType()) return false;
    return Equals((ExpenseReport) obj);
}
```

```
    public override int GetHashCode()
    {
        return Id.GetHashCode();
    }
    }
}
```

There is quite a bit of logic here that could fail. This logic can be tested inside a single memory space without needed to call out of process to any application dependencies; therefore, we can write some unit tests. In a code base where entities are placed into collections, sorted, and compared, some methods are used by the base class library (BCL) and show a diminished return on investment for explicit unit tests. These methods are Equals() and GetHashCode(). Any entity in a domain model that doesn't implement these will force other logic to know what property represents its identity in order to see if two objects represent the same record. Most of these objects have data that is pulled from a database of some sort. Full coverage on Equals() and GetHashCode() normally happens automatically as tests of business logic are written. And some tools such as JetBrains ReSharper will generate these methods automatically, so the likelihood of defects is low unless you handwrite them.

A unit test class for ExpenseReport is shown here:

```
using System;
using ClearMeasure.OnionDevOpsArchitecture.Core.Model;
using NUnit.Framework;

namespace ClearMeasure.OnionDevOpsArchitecture.UnitTests
{
    public class ExpenseReportTester
    {
        [Test]
        public void PropertiesShouldInitializeToProperDefaults()
        {
            var report = new ExpenseReport();
            Assert.That(report.Id, Is.EqualTo(Guid.Empty));
            Assert.That(report.Title, Is.EqualTo(string.Empty));
            Assert.That(report.Description, Is.EqualTo(string.Empty));
```

```
    Assert.That(report.Status, Is.EqualTo(ExpenseReportStatus.
    Draft));
    Assert.That(report.Number, Is.EqualTo(null));
}

[Test]
public void ToStringShouldReturnNumber()
{
    var report = new ExpenseReport();
    report.Number = "456";
    Assert.That(report.ToString(), Is.EqualTo("ExpenseReport 456"));
}

[Test]
public void PropertiesShouldGetAndSetValuesProperly()
{
    var report = new ExpenseReport();
    Guid guid = Guid.NewGuid();
    report.Id = guid;
    report.Title = "Title";
    report.Description = "Description";
    report.Status = ExpenseReportStatus.Approved;
    report.Number = "Number";

    Assert.That(report.Id, Is.EqualTo(guid));
    Assert.That(report.Title, Is.EqualTo("Title"));
    Assert.That(report.Description, Is.EqualTo("Description"));
    Assert.That(report.Status,
        Is.EqualTo(ExpenseReportStatus.Approved));
    Assert.That(report.Number, Is.EqualTo("Number"));
}

[Test]
public void ShouldShowFriendlyStatusValuesAsStrings()
{
    var report = new ExpenseReport();
    report.Status = ExpenseReportStatus.Submitted;
```

```
        Assert.That(report.FriendlyStatus, Is.EqualTo("Submitted"));
    }
  }
}
```

As you read this code file, you see that each test validates that a piece of logic works correctly while keeping all the executing code in process. Unit tests written in this fashion run very fast, and thousands of them can execute in seconds.

Integration Tests

Our ExpenseReport object is persisted, through Entity Framework Core, to a SQL Server database. In order to validate that the expense report class can be hydrated from data in SQL Server, we need a test that puts several layers together:

- The domain model itself, containing the expense report class

- The Entity Framework Core mapping configuration

- The data access logic, specifying the query to run

- The SQL Server schema, which contains the DDL (data definition language) for the ExpenseReport table

In most cases, these tests are easy to write, but they are very important. Without them, you will encounter defects, and you will spend valuable time debugging through these four layers in order to find the problem. If all of your database-backed classes are equipped with persistence-level integration tests, you will seldom find yourself in a debugging session for a problem in this area.

We have seen the expense report class. The next class to examine is the Entity Framework Core mapping configuration, which is comprised of the data context class and a mapping class. The data context class is as follows:

```
using ClearMeasure.OnionDevOpsArchitecture.Core;
using Microsoft.EntityFrameworkCore;
using Microsoft.EntityFrameworkCore.Diagnostics;
```

```
namespace ClearMeasure.OnionDevOpsArchitecture.DataAccess.Mappings
{
    public class DataContext : DbContext
    {
        private readonly IDataConfiguration _config;

        public DataContext(IDataConfiguration config)
        {
            _config = config;
        }

        protected override void OnConfiguring(DbContextOptionsBuilder
            optionsBuilder)
        {
            optionsBuilder.EnableSensitiveDataLogging();
            var connectionString = _config.GetConnectionString();
            optionsBuilder
                .UseSqlServer(connectionString)
                .ConfigureWarnings(warnings =>
                    warnings.
                    Throw(RelationalEventId.QueryClientEvaluationWarning));

            base.OnConfiguring(optionsBuilder);
        }

        protected override void OnModelCreating(ModelBuilder modelBuilder)
        {
            new ExpenseReportMap().Map(modelBuilder);
        }
    }
}
```

In our example application, we have one aggregate root, so in our OnModelCreating class, we include one "Map" class. We use this pattern so that as we accumulate hundreds of mapped entities, each has it's own class rather than bloating the single DataContext class:

```
using System;
using ClearMeasure.OnionDevOpsArchitecture.Core.Model;
using Microsoft.EntityFrameworkCore;
using Microsoft.EntityFrameworkCore.Metadata.Builders;
using Microsoft.EntityFrameworkCore.ValueGeneration;

namespace ClearMeasure.OnionDevOpsArchitecture.DataAccess.Mappings
{
    public class ExpenseReportMap : IEntityFrameworkMapping
    {
        public EntityTypeBuilder Map(ModelBuilder modelBuilder)
        {
            var mapping = modelBuilder.Entity<ExpenseReport>();
            mapping.UsePropertyAccessMode(PropertyAccessMode.Field);
            mapping.HasKey(x => x.Id);
            mapping.Property(x => x.Id).IsRequired()
                .HasValueGenerator<SequentialGuidValueGenerator>()
                .ValueGeneratedOnAdd()
                .HasDefaultValue(Guid.Empty);
            mapping.Property(x => x.Number).IsRequired().HasMaxLength(10);
            mapping.Property(x => x.Title).HasMaxLength(200);
            mapping.Property(x => x.Description).HasMaxLength(4000);
            mapping.Property(x => x.Status).HasMaxLength(3)
                .HasConversion(status => status.Code
                    , s => ExpenseReportStatus.FromCode(s));

            return mapping;
        }
    }
}
```

Rather than rely on defaults, which tend to change, our map class specifies how to map each property. Choosing to be explicit in this fashion also lowers the bar for developers understanding what is going on. Each developer will have a different level of memorization for what Entity Framework Core's default behavior is. Our ExpenseReport table looks like the following:

```
CREATE TABLE [dbo].[ExpenseReport] (
    [Id]          UNIQUEIDENTIFIER NOT NULL,
    [Number]      NVARCHAR (10)    NOT NULL,
    [Title]       NVARCHAR (200)   NULL,
    [Description] NVARCHAR (4000)  NULL,
    [Status]      NCHAR (3)        NOT NULL
);
```

With four different layers of code running across two different processes, most of the time across a network on different servers, you should see the importance of an automated test ensuring the stability of the integration of these layers. Our integration test to validate persistence logic is here:

```
using ClearMeasure.OnionDevOpsArchitecture.Core.Model;
using NUnit.Framework;
using Shouldly;

namespace ClearMeasure.OnionDevOpsArchitecture.IntegrationTests.DataAccess.
Mappings
{
    public class ExpenseReportMappingTester
    {
        [Test]
        public void ShouldPersist()
        {
            new DatabaseTester().Clean();
            var report = new ExpenseReport
            {
                Title = "TestExpense",
                Description = "This is an expense",
                Number = "123",
                Status = ExpenseReportStatus.Cancelled
            };
```

```
using (var context = new StubbedDataContextFactory().
GetContext())
{
    context.Add(report);
    context.SaveChanges();
}

ExpenseReport rehydratedExpenseReport;
using (var context = new StubbedDataContextFactory().
GetContext())
{
    rehydratedExpenseReport = context
        .Find<ExpenseReport>(report.Id);
}

rehydratedExpenseReport.Title.ShouldBe(report.Title);
rehydratedExpenseReport.Description.ShouldBe(report.
Description);
rehydratedExpenseReport.Number.ShouldBe(report.Number);
rehydratedExpenseReport.Status.ShouldBe(report.Status);
        }
    }
}
```

This pattern for an integration test can be repeated across all classes that must be persisted to a database through an object-relational mapper. The base case is to send an object through the ORM to the database, clear memory, and then query again to build up the object. We have our first test helper illustrated in this case. The call to DatabaseTester.Clean() represents a helper that can remove all records from all tables in the database in the order of foreign key dependencies. It contains a bit too much code than can be printed in this book. If you are interested in it, clone the Git repository that accompanies this book. In integration tests involving a database, each test is responsible for putting the database in a known state. In many cases, it can be appropriate to run a test starting with no records in the database. Certainly, this case works that way. In other cases, you may want a small known set of data to be loaded into the database before the test suite executes. Maintaining a data test set for build purposes can become time-consuming, so don't make that your first solution.

Full-System Tests

Full-system tests, implementing acceptance criteria should begin at external interfaces of the application. If the feature in question is a web service, then the test should perform setup and call the web service. If the interface is a user interface screen, the test should navigate to the screen and use it. If the interface is file ingestion of a custom Excel file for data import, the test should build up an Excel file and place it in the right file path to be process. You get the pattern.

Since web applications are so popular, you will definitely have Selenium tests running in your .NET DevOps pipeline. You can see how to implement Selenium tests in Microsoft's docs.[IX] For a simple form-based login screen, a Selenium test might look similar to the following:

```
[Test]
public void ShouldLoginAndLogOut()
{
    Driver.Navigate().GoToUrl(AppUrl);
    var login = Driver.FindElement(
        By.XPath("//button[contains(text(), 'Log In')]"));
    login.Click();

    Driver.Title.ShouldStartWith("Home Page");

    var logout = Driver.FindElement(By.LinkText("Logout"));
    logout.Click();

    Driver.Title.ShouldStartWith("Login");
}
```

In this case, Driver is a property that is the Selenium Driver class that wraps a model of the web page being viewed by the browser. These tests can execute from any machine where the executing identity can actually start up and control an instance of a web browser. And since full-system tests are run against a fully deployed environment, it is important that the CI build process packages up the test suite and deploys it along with the application components in the TDD environment. We will cover more about packaging and deploying in later chapters.

[IX]UI test with Selenium, n.d.

Inspections

A pull request in Azure Repos or GitHub is the perfect place to facilitate a code inspection. Here is a flow in Azure Repos. We start with a feature branch ready for merging. The developer creates the pull request. By policy, the developer initializes the description with a markdown task list that includes all the steps of the inspection. This can be pulled from a wiki or markdown file stored with the application, as shown in Figure 7-7.

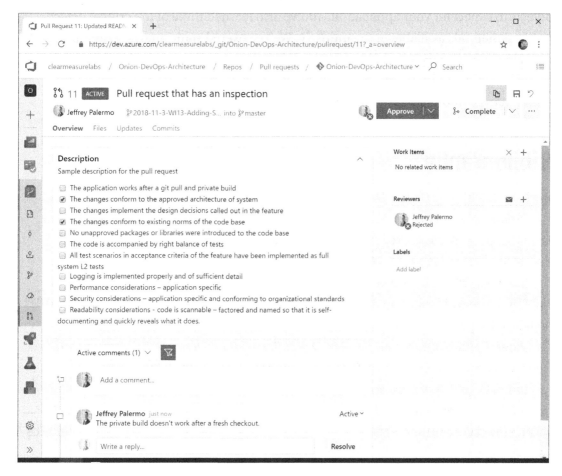

Figure 7-7.   *Pull request that executes a multistep inspection*

The approver can check off the items as they are inspected. When an item fails, the comments can be used and the pull request rejected. More commits can be added to the branch to fix the issue. Then, using the comments in the pull request, the submitter can request that the inspector have another look. Once the branch meets all criteria in the inspection, the inspector approves the pull request and merges the branch. The checklist, and the complete dialog used to resolve any issues, is fully documented in Azure Repos.

Wrap Up

In this chapter, you've learned how to use some available research to predict how many defects to expect for your application. You've also learned three of the critical defect removal methods available in the industry. We've covered static analysis, multiple levels of testing, and the concept and implementation of inspections. Armed with these defect removal methods, your teams will quickly remove defects even within development rather than promoting them to downstream phases.

Bibliography

Beck, K. (2002). *Test Driven Development: By Example.* Addison-Wesley Professional.

Install FxCop analyzers in Visual Studio. (2018, 8 2). Retrieved from Visual Studio Docs: https://docs.microsoft.com/en-us/visualstudio/code-quality/install-fxcop-analyzers?view=vs-2017

Jones, C. (2012). Retrieved from SOFTWARE DEFECT ORIGINS AND REMOVAL METHODS: www.ifpug.org/Documents/Jones-SoftwareDefectOriginsAndRemovalMethodsDraft5.pdf

Jones, C. (2016). *Exceeding 99% in Defect Removal Efficiency (DRE) for Software.* Retrieved from www.ifpug.org/Documents/Toppin99percentDRE2016.pdf

Jones, C. (2017). *Software Economics and Function Point Metrics: Thirty years of IFPUG Progress.* Retrieved from www.ifpug.org/wp-content/uploads/2017/04/IYSM.-Thirty-years-of-IFPUG.-Software-Economics-and-Function-Point-Metrics-Capers-Jones.pdf

Microsoft. (n.d.). *Get started with Roslyn analyzers.* Retrieved from Visual Studio Docs: https://docs.microsoft.com/en-us/visualstudio/extensibility/getting-started-with-roslyn-analyzers?view=vs-2017

Microsoft/Azure. (n.d.). *Shift Left to Make Testing Fast and Reliable.* Retrieved from Azure DevOps Docs: `https://docs.microsoft.com/en-us/azure/devops/learn/devops-at-microsoft/shift-left-make-testing-fast-reliable#test-taxonomy`

Newkirk, J. W., & Vorontsov, A. A. (2004). *Test-Driven Development in Microsoft .NET.* Microsoft Press.

UI test with Selenium. (n.d.). Retrieved from `https://docs.microsoft.com/en-us/azure/devops/pipelines/test/continuous-test-selenium?view=azure-devops`

CHAPTER 8

Release Candidate Creation

You have previously learned how to code, build, and validate a build of software. In order for that build to become a release candidate, you must package the build in a format that is suitable for a production release. In addition, in order to make our continuous integration "Commit Stage"[I] more robust, you will have to package the build for release to a TDD (test-driven development) environment. This environment was covered in previous chapters as a deployed environment dedicated solely to the execution of automated tests. The type of tests executed in this environment is acceptance tests.[II] For a web application, you would commonly use Selenium[III] for tests through the user interface. You can also create other test suites that would require a fully deployed instance of the software system to be deployed. This chapter will focus on the essential elements you will design and configure in order to convert a build to a versioned release candidate suitable for deployment to downstream environments. The chapter will cover the principles involved, the model and relationships of packages to the software architecture, and the process for storing the packages and using them.

Designing Your Release Candidate Architecture

In order to specify the architecture for your release candidate packages, you will need to analyze the logical and physical layers of your 4+1 architecture[IV] and determine the unit of deployment. Keep in mind these rules of thumb for release candidate packages:

[I]Duvall, 2007

[II]Wells, n.d.

[III]Microsoft Docs: Testing with Selenium, n.d.

[IV]Kruchten

© Jeffrey Palermo 2019

J. Palermo, *.NET DevOps for Azure*, https://doi.org/10.1007/978-1-4842-5343-4_8

- **Build/package once, deploy many**

  A continuous integration build that succeeds will package a set of release candidate packages. These packages should be suitable for deployment to any environment, including production. Do not configure branches or builds so that each environment is built separately. We build and package once so that every subsequent activity performed in our DevOps pipeline further proves the suitability of the release candidate for release to our users of the production environment. When a problem is found, the release candidate is no longer qualified for release. When a release candidate makes its way through our entire pipeline, we can be confident that it is ready for our users.

- **One package per runtime component**

  Generally, a release candidate is made up of a set of packages (NuGet packages for our .NET applications). Each runtime component in our physical architecture layer makes up a package. That is, our web site is packaged entirely in a NuGet package. Our SQL Server database schema and migration scripts are packaged in a separate NuGet package, and so on.

- **Use the NuGet package format**

  While anyone can invent a new package format, it's best to use an industry standard format that has tooling such as viewers. The .NET package format is a *.nupkg file (pronounced NUPKEG). While you could technically put your files in a *.zip file, you are better served using a more specific format for your platform. Likewise, if you were developing a NodeJS application, you would use the *.npm package format.

- **Embed the build number as the release candidate version**

  Build numbers are automatically assigned according to the format you specify. Flow the build number all the way through to each package of your release candidate. If you have build 3.4.352, then your NuGet packages for the release candidate should all be marked 3.4.352. This ensures that regardless of environment, you always know the release candidate being tested and the build that created the release candidate.

- **Package only application artifacts**

  Take care that you do not package up any environment-specific files or
  configuration. What is put into each application component package should
  be suitable for deployment to any environment. Global configuration is
  appropriate, but any configuration that changes from environment to
  environment should be pushed in at deploy time, not package time. Be wary of
  any contents of packages that include reference to an environment name.

Creating and Using Release Candidate Packages

Let's first look at the part of the process where release candidates fit. Figure 8-1 illustrates
the sequence of events in our DevOps pipeline.

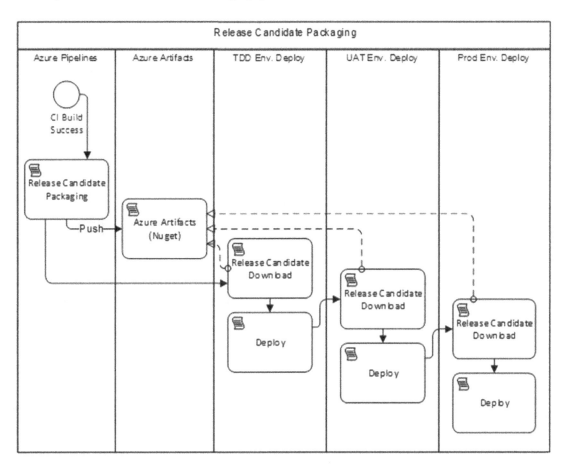

Figure 8-1. *Release candidate packages are the bridge between a build and*
deployment

The release candidate packages are created by the CI build and are used by the deployment configuration. In Azure Pipelines, you will have a single continuous integration build for your application, regardless of the number of runtime components. For a single Git repository containing a Visual Studio solution, you will have one build. That build, upon success of all its steps, should package your application for deployment into a set of NuGet packages. We will cover how to determine the number of packages shortly.

Once the release candidate (the results of the build that is about to succeed) is packaged, the build configuration should push them into Azure Artifacts. Azure Artifacts provides a built-in NuGet feed for your team. Unless you have a specific reason to use something else, use this. Once the release candidate packages have been pushed, the CI build finishes and reports success. If the release candidate cannot be packaged or stored, then the build should fail.

While we have not yet covered release configurations or deployments (that will be covered in a later chapter), let's cover the process that packages are used for. Each of the downstream environments (TDD, UAT, and Prod) will have a deployment process starting with the retrieval of the NuGet packages for the release candidate. This process will access the NuGet feed hosted in Azure Artifacts and retrieve the packages, extract them, and use the contents to deploy your application. The same packages making up a single release candidate should be used for deployment to every environment.

Defining the Bounds of a Package

Most applications have more than one runtime component. Therefore, there should be more than one NuGet package in the set of packages that make up a release candidate. Each part of your application that is deployed a specific way should be packaged separately, as shown in Figure 8-2. Let's dig into how to determine the bounds of each package.

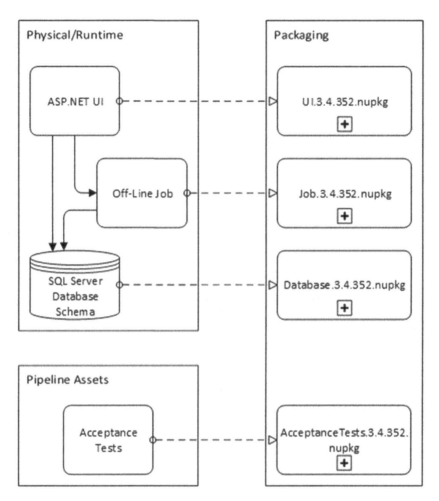

Figure 8-2. *Each runtime component of the application should have its own package*

Let's consider an application with three deployable components. The first part is a web application using ASP.NET. It is deployed to a web server or to Azure AppService. The second part is an off-line job. Perhaps a batch job or a handler service listening to a queue. These are very common, and they are deployed as Windows services or Azure Functions or WebJobs. The third is a SQL Server database. Whether on-premise or in Azure SQL, we must deploy schema and global data changes.

Each of these three components of the application run in their own memory space, in their own process, so they have differing deployment characteristics. The deployment destination is different. Because of these, each should be packaged in its own NuGet package. This allows each to be deployed to the appropriate destination while preserving flexibility. While you potentially could deploy all three components to a single server, you could also deploy each to completely different servers. In fact, you could deploy the web application ASP.NET UI to many servers in a web farm or to multiple Azure regions. The structure of your release candidate packages should map to the physical architecture of the running components of the application with a disregard to the topology of the server environment.

In addition to each application component, you will always have some additional assets that go along with the release candidate. These assets are not production code and only exist for validate of the release candidate. In Figure 8-2, you will see "Acceptance Tests." In Visual Studio, this is manifested as a project, probably NUnit or another testing framework. If the application is a web application, the tests contained in the Visual Studio project likely use Selenium in order to test the fully deployed application. Because of the need for a fully deployed application, these tests are tied to the version of the application; therefore, they belong to a certain release candidate and need to be packaged and deployed along with the other components. In our process diagram earlier in the chapter, you saw that the TDD environment is the first environment for deployments. After the application is fully deployed, the acceptance test package will be retrieved and installed on a deployment server. Then, the tests are run against the deployed release candidate running from the TDD environment. In this way, we can package additional assets for the purpose of making our DevOps pipeline more robust so that it can detect a higher percentage of defects before promoting the release candidate to the next downstream environment.

Azure Artifacts Workflow for Release Candidates

Now that you have seen how to determine the architecture for your release candidate packaging, let's see it in action. We will use this configuration for our sample application in Azure DevOps Service. In your project configuration, you will want to make sure you have Azure Artifacts as an enabled service for your pipeline.[v] Azure Artifacts is an independent product, but it's used in conjunction with Azure Pipelines. It's the storage service for the release candidate components produced by the continuous integration build.

The application we will be packaging has three deployable components that are built and versioned together:

- Web site user interface (UI)

---

[v]Dixon, n.d.

- Off-line job

- Database

In addition to these application components, this application also has acceptance tests that will be packaged and deployed. Refer back to Chapter 7 to see how a full-system acceptance test can be structured when validating a web application. In order to run these acceptance tests against our application in the TDD environment, we must package and store the version of the acceptance tests that belong to this version of the application. The version numbers must match.

Earlier, I stressed how important versioning is in a DevOps pipeline. In Figure 8-3, inspect the release candidate packages in Azure Artifacts.

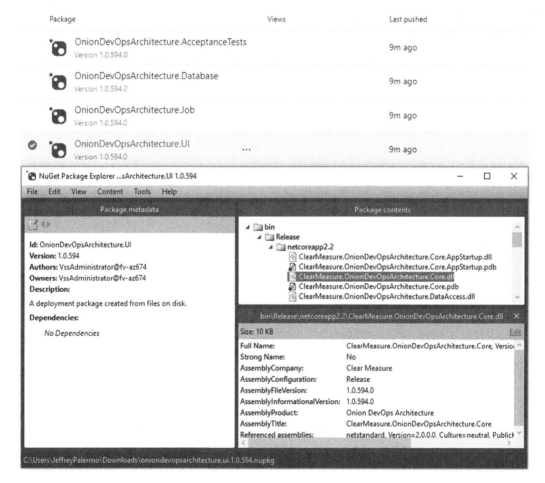

Figure 8-3. *The version of the release candidate is stamped on the NuGet packages as well as every assembly inside.*

Because the proper version number is now embedded into every assembly, your code has access to it. Whether you display it at the bottom of the screen or include it with diagnostics telemetry or logs, you'll use the version number to know whether a problem or bug was on an old version or the current one. Without the version number, you fly blind. Do not try to use date and time stamps to decipher what build you're working with. Explicitly push the version number into every asset.

Don't try to use date and time stamps to decipher what build you're working with. Explicitly push the version number into every assembly in every release candidate NuGet package.

Specifying How Packages are Created

To close the loop on how packages are made, refer back to our build script, which you will want to keep at the top level of your Git repository. Refer to Figure 8-4.

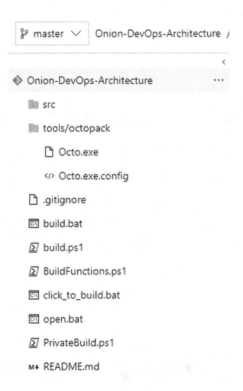

Figure 8-4. *Our PowerShell build script is stored at the top of the Git repository and is named build.ps1*

When running our private build on the local workstation, packaging is not necessary, but when this script runs as part of the CI build, packaging is the last step before the build should return success. This PowerShell function is responsible for packaging the projects as NuGet packages.

```
Function Pack{
    Write-Output "Packaging nuget packages"
  exec{
    & dotnet publish $uiProjectPath -nologo --no-restore --no-build
    -v $verbosity --configuration $projectConfig
  }

  exec{
        & .\tools\octopack\Octo.exe pack --id "$projectName.UI"
        --version $version
        --basePath $uiProjectPath\bin\$projectConfig\$framework\publish
        --outFolder $build_dir --overwrite
    }

  exec{
        & .\tools\octopack\Octo.exe pack --id "$projectName.Database"
        --version $version --basePath $databaseProjectPath
        --outFolder $build_dir --overwrite
    }

  exec{
    & dotnet publish $jobProjectPath -nologo --no-restore --no-build
        -v $verbosity --configuration $projectConfig
  }
    exec{
        & .\tools\octopack\Octo.exe pack --id "$projectName.Job"
        --version $version
        --basePath $jobProjectPath\bin\$projectConfig\$framework\publish
        --outFolder $build_dir --overwrite
    }
```

```
exec{
    & dotnet publish $acceptanceTestProjectPath -nologo --no-restore
        --no-build
        -v $verbosity --configuration $projectConfig
}

exec{
        & .\tools\octopack\Octo.exe pack --id "$projectName.AcceptanceTests"
        --version $version --basePath
        $acceptanceTestProjectPath\bin\$projectConfig\$framework\publish
        --outFolder $build_dir --overwrite
    }
}
```

Since we have four components that must be deployed, we have four NuGet packages. Notice that I am using the Octo.exe tool.[VI] OctoPack is the full name and is an open source wrapper for NuGet, and you can find the source on GitHub. NuGet was originally designed as a package format for library dependencies before it was adapted for application packaging. You can certainly use NuPack directly, but OctoPack wraps NuPack and overcomes some of the default conventions and assumptions that don't quite fit naturally when packaging an application component for deployment.

With the preceding PowerShell in our build script, we can configure Azure Pipelines as shown in Figure 8-5.

[VI]OctoPack GitHub Project, n.d.

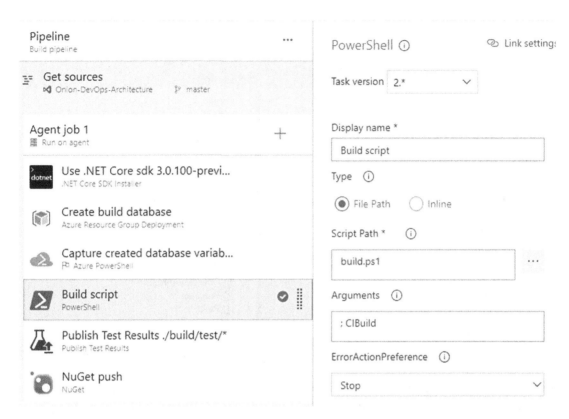

Figure 8-5. *Azure Pipelines calls the build script stored in Git in order to minimize the global step configuration*

Notice that the "CIBuild" function is being called in the build.ps1 file. This function is as follows:

```
Function CIBuild{
        Init
        MigrateDatabaseRemote
        Compile
        UnitTests
        IntegrationTest
        Pack
}
```

The Pack function is the last to be called. Then, with the NuGet packages properly created, our "NuGet push" build step places them in the Azure Artifacts services, which makes them available to any other process that accesses the NuGet feed. Refer to Figure 8-6.

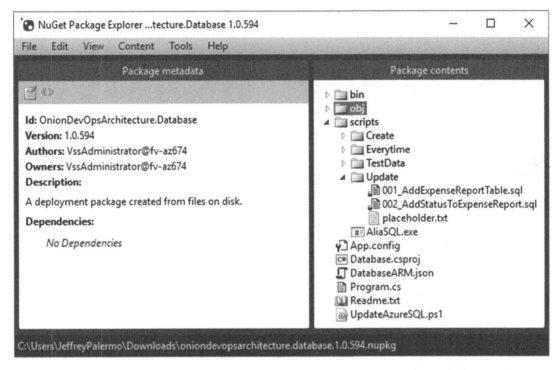

Figure 8-6. *Our database component for release candidate 1.0.594 contains the database migration scripts necessary to upgrade the schema*

Because we have the database migration tool and the full body of scripts, we are able to run the database migration process from any server we choose. And including helper ∗.ps1 files in our packages will limit the steps that must be explicitly configured in Azure Pipelines.

While YAML will become the format for all builds and releases, the tooling for that capability is not ready yet. Expect to move to YAML-based configurations at the right time. YAML will enable you to store your entire pipeline configuration in your Git repository.

Use Release Candidate Packages in Deployment Configurations

While we will go in depth on deploying in the next chapter, it is useful to know how a build or release configuration can retrieve a NuGet package from Azure Artifacts on demand, as shown in Figure 8-7.

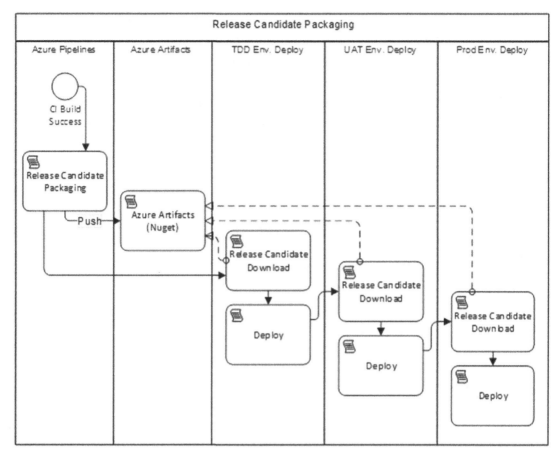

Figure 8-7. *Review of how environment deployments call out to Azure Artifacts to obtain packages*

Remember the order of our environments. In the case of the TDD environment, you will need to deploy the full application and then pull and install the AcceptanceTests package so that those tests can be run. The AcceptanceTests package lives no further than the TDD environment. If you create other types of test suites that must be run on a fully deployed environment, you would use the same pattern of packaging them as a package, storing them in Azure Artifacts, and retrieving them during deploy.

The "Download Package" step allows for easy retrieval of our set of NuGet packages for any release candidate, as shown in Figure 8-8. Because a NuGet package is essentially a *.zip file with a manifest, this step retrieves and extracts the NuGet package on the destination directory of the server that is used as the agent, whether it is a hosted agent or your own private agent. You can see how important the build number is to the pipeline. Everything ties back to the build number.

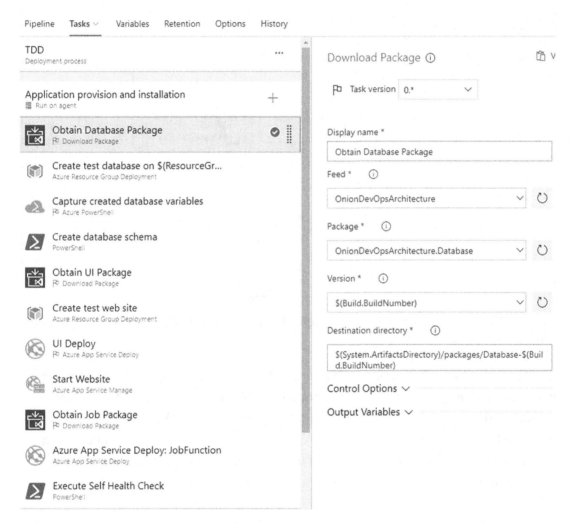

Figure 8-8. *A portion of the TDD environment release/deploy configuration*

WHAT ABOUT SHARING LIBRARIES?

If your Visual Studio solution contains a class library that you'd like to share with other teams or other applications, treat it the same as an application component. Package it as part of the CI build. Push it up to Azure Artifacts. Other developers with access of that NuGet feed will be able to pull the library in just like they do with public NuGet packages. And when you have a new build of the library, the feed will automatically receive the library as a result of the new build.

Wrap Up

In this chapter you learned how to package your application as a release candidate, consisting of a set of NuGet packages. Our rules of thumb are

- Build once, deploy many.

- Flow the build number through everything as the official version number.

- Use NuGet for your package format.

- Archive your release candidates in Azure Artifacts.

- Package test suites that must execute in a deployed environment.

- Package and publish shared libraries through Azure Artifacts.

Bibliography

(n.d.). Retrieved from OctoPack GitHub Project: `https://github.com/OctopusDeploy/OctoPack`

(n.d.). Retrieved from Microsoft Docs: Testing with Selenium: `https://docs.microsoft.com/en-us/azure/devops/pipelines/test/continuous-test-selenium?view=azure-devops`

Dixon, H. (n.d.). *Deep dive into Azure Artifacts*. Retrieved from `https://azure.microsoft.com/en-us/blog/deep-dive-into-azure-artifacts/`

Duvall, P. M. (2007). *Continuous Integration: Improving Software Quality and Reducing Risk.* Addison Wesley.

Kruchten, P. (n.d.). Retrieved from Architectural Blueprints—The "4+1" View Model of Software Architecture: `www.cs.ubc.ca/~gregor/teaching/papers/4+1view-architecture.pdf`

Wells, D. (n.d.). *Acceptance Tests.* Retrieved April 3, 2019, from Extremeprogramming. org: `www.extremeprogramming.org/rules/functionaltests.html`

CHAPTER 9

Deploying the Release

Perhaps you have skipped ahead to this chapter rather than reading all previous chapters. That's ok, but the other topics were intentionally placed ahead of this one. It is true that until we actually deploy bits to an environment, no one can use them. However, the deployment pipeline is where all prior techniques provide their value of squeezing out defects, so they are not promoted to our users. In this chapter, you will learn the model for designing your deployment pipeline, the types of environment to configure therein, and the types of activities necessary during deployment.

Designing Your Deployment Pipeline

In order to determine the proper structure of your deployment pipeline, you will have to decide how many environments to configure and the differences between them. Before we dive in to that topic, let's consider some principles that will guide those decisions:

- **Build one, deploy many**

  Regardless how many environments you have, you will deploy the same release candidate, produced from a single continuous integration build many times, once (at least) per environment type. Do not do anything that rebuilds or recompiles from source once a version enters deployment activities. If there is a problem anywhere, consider the release candidate dead, correct the problem, and proceed with a different versioned release candidate.

- **Do nothing on production for the first time**

  Design the deployment pipeline so that every unique activity necessary in your deployment be performed in at least one pre-production environment before that activity is executed on

© Jeffrey Palermo 2019
J. Palermo, *.NET DevOps for Azure*, https://doi.org/10.1007/978-1-4842-5343-4_9

production. For example, if your production environment runs on a web farm with several batch job servers and a large SQL Server cluster, it would not be prudent to have single-server configurations in all pre-production environments. Additionally, no files destined for production should be created or changed after the continuous integration build has packaged the release candidate. Everything necessary for the production deployment should be put into the release candidate packages at the end of the CI build. If you find something is missing, stop the line, add the missing piece to the code base, and let the CI build package up another release candidate that includes all that is necessary.

- **Shift left on pipeline capabilities**

  In deployment of application components as well as configuration of settings and data, push logic into script files that are stored in the application's Git repository. While the CI build configuration and the deployment steps will allow for running scripts that are stored in arbitrary locations, you create global and temporal dependencies through this tactic. Make sure that as many commands, scripts, and logic as possible are sources from the Git repository and the packages that make up the release candidate that is being deployed.

Determining Environments

Our industry has many terms for server environments. Everyone has production. Also uses are the following:

- Local

- Sandbox

- Dev

- Integration

- Test

- User

- UAT

- QA

- QC

- Acceptance

- Staging

While there is no standard, the pre-cloud set that seems to be commonly known are development, testing, staging, and production. With the advent of easily creatable and modifiable environments, any notion of standardized environment names and stages has weakened. We will attempt to sidestep this confusion and talk about the purposes of various environments.

In a DevOps environment, you will never have fewer than three (3) deployed environments for the team. Consider the table in Figure 9-1.

Distinct Environment Types			
Environment Attribute	TDD	UAT	PROD
Purpose	Automated Verification	Manual Verification	Ongoing Operations
Audience	Engineering Team	Internal Customers	External Customers
Quality Control	Acceptance Testing	UX Testing	Automated Alarms
	Env. Recreation	Exploratory Testing	Health Checks
	Health Checks	Database Migration	Tracer Bullets
	Database Recreation	Health Checks	
	Security Testing	Observability Validation	
	Scale/Perf Testing	Other Manual Testing	
	Reliability Testing		
	Other Test Suites		

Figure 9-1. *The three distinct types of environments in a DevOps pipeline*

This table shows the three types of environments you will need when designing your deployment pipeline. You are free to have as many of each type as you like, but you will never have fewer than one of each of these three types. Everyone understands production. It exists for the people who derive value from using your software. The next environment before production is for any type of manual testing. We will call that UAT because it is focused more on the users than the engineering team. Finally, we have an environment that is only for automated verification of all kinds. To remove ambiguity from other environment names that have been used in the past, we call it the TDD environment, short for test-driven development. In the TDD environment, no humans are allowed. If a human were to attempt to use this environment, they would find it being created and destroyed at a rate that precluded any valuable usage.

Let's see some examples one could use when determining how many of each type to select.

Production

In the case of production, you could choose to provision a dedicated production environment for each customer or have all of your customers use a single production environment. You

UAT

You can have a single manual verification environment if your organization is small. Or, you might have several different user or stakeholder groups that might benefit from having a dedicated environment of this type so that they can choose the cadence by which to accept the next release candidate that is ready. You might also decide to provision another environment of this type for exploratory testing of a particularly large data set – looking to verify if the system provides a snappy user experience even with a very large database.

TDD

This type of environment is suitable for complete automated construction and destruction. Every successful build should case a new deployment to this environment type. Because you may have many feature branches in play at a time, your CI build should be configured to be parallelizable – that is, multiple builds happening, one per active branch. And because each build causes a deployment to this environment type, you can have multiple instances of this environment being created at one time. For example, if you and a colleague each commit changes to your feature branch at the same time, you want the build, packaging, and deployment to your TDD environment to happen quickly without waiting on your colleague. You accomplish this by having the naming of the environment parameterized by your build or branch and creating an instance of the TDD environment dedicated to your build. Then, your acceptance tests execute (pass or fail), and the environment is destroyed.

Assigning Validation Steps to Environments

You are in control of how many actual environments to have in your DevOps pipeline. You will never have fewer than three, but depending on how many of each type you choose, you may have more. It's also your choice which environments to place in series and which to place in parallel. For example, if two stakeholder groups each need a dedicated UAT (manual verification) environment, you may decide that each can receive the new release candidate at the same time and work on validating it in parallel. In this example, you would provision two environments (or keep the environment around permanently) and deploy to each environment at the same time. From a process perspective, you would wait until each group had validated the release candidate before deploying to production. Here is a way to think about what types of activities might be appropriate for performing in each environment type.

Environment Deploy Steps			
	TDD	UAT	PROD
Migrate Database	✓	✓	✓
Deploy Application	✓	✓	✓
Run Health Check	✓	✓	✓
Load Static Data	✓	✓	✓
Load Test Data	✓	On-Demand	X
Recreate Environment	✓	On-Demand	X
Recreate Database	✓	X	X
Run Acceptance Tests	✓	X	X
Deploy Unattended	✓	X	X
Destroys Environment	✓	X	X

Figure 9-2. *Each environment type is built for different deploy and validation steps*

The table in Figure 9-2 illustrates the deployment and validation steps that are appropriate for each environment type. As we move from automated validation (TDD) to manual validation (UAT) to production, we perform fewer steps. The design of the progression through environments is intended to front-load as many validation checks as possible in order to find problems. "Shift left"[1] is a statement of value that has grown in popularity within the DevOps community. The purpose of the Shift Left type of thinking is to design a process that finds as many defects as early in the process as possible. Both preventative and removal methods are used to cause the software product to be more defect-free the further down the process it progresses. In the previous table, the TDD environment includes a full spectrum of activities, from creating the environment from scratch to building the database from nothing to running the full acceptance test suite. The UAT environment has some on-demand options for when you need to either

---

[1]Shift Left to Make Testing Fast and Reliable, n.d.

recreate the environment or reload test data, but we will always need to deploy the new version of the application and migrate the database. This last point cannot be stressed enough. Manual validation environments should always be deployed completely automatically. This includes the database and data stores along with all the application components. This is practice for an unattended production deployment. We do not want to do anything in production for the first time. And we do not want any manual steps in the production deployment process.

Deploying Data Changes Across Environments

Let's face it. The database has some unique challenges in DevOps. Application components do not have any state. They can be destroyed and put back easily. Storage components must preserve data for years. When we discuss "the database," the same thinking and principles will apply to any data store, whether it be a relational database engine, blobs, tables, json collections, or merely a directory of files on a network share. This data must be guarded and preserved through many, many deployments of application components. The schema, or the structure within which the data is organized, must be continually upgraded and modified while preserving the integrity of the database. Early in this book, we covered in detail the process of database migration tools. During deployment, you must think about the data needs of the different environment types. To move through this topic, let's review the different types of data to be managed in our DevOps environment, as shown in Figure 9-3.

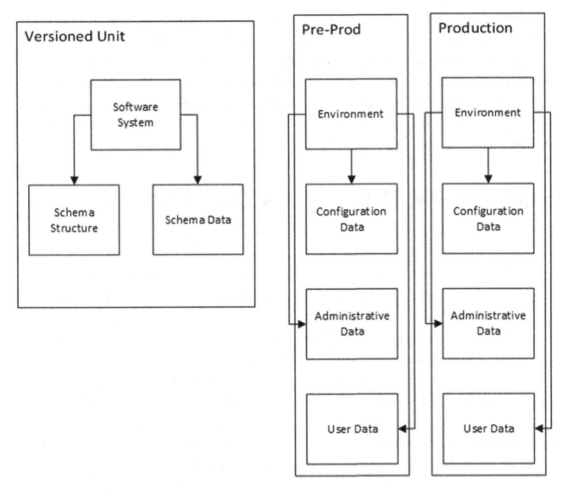

Figure 9-3. *Each of the four unique types of data is managed in different ways*

In a software system, we can subdivide all data and data concerns into four distinct types. These types are managed differently in our DevOps pipeline. Let's review them:

- **Schema**

  The schema, or the structure of the data, is owned by the software system and should be exactly the same in every environment. This includes SQL Server stored procedures, views, indexes, functions, and the like. The schema should be versioned and stored with the application code.

- **Schema data**

  This data is architecturally part of your schema and should be the same across environments. For example, standard lists are in this category. These lists can populate drop-down boxes in your application. Common name prefixes (Mr., Mrs., etc.) are a good example. These are defined during development. This schema data should be created and deployed with schema changes while being stored in the version control system along with the application code.

- **Configuration data**

  Configuration data belongs to the environment itself. It should not be stored with the application code because it is potentially different from environment to environment. Some of it may be sensitive in nature, such as passwords, tokens, and credentials. Some of this configuration data might be in an XML or JSON configuration file. Other configuration data might be stored in a database table. The storage location does not change the nature of the data or that it changes environment to environment. Because of this, it should be deployed to the environment when the application and database are deployed. The automated deployment process should handle the process of retrieving the configuration data meant for the environment and deploying it properly, whether it be poking a string into an XML file or inserting a record into a SQL Server database table.

- **Administrative data**

  Administrative data is owned by the organization supporting the environment. A common example of this is top-level user accounts or customer header records. In many applications, if not a single user account record exists, the software cannot do anything. At a minimum, a global administrator record might need to exist to enable functions to light up. Administrative data can differ by environment, but it doesn't have to. Because it is determined by the organization supporting the environment, it could be the same across two environments and then differ on another. This data should be deployed to the environment automatically and should not be stored with the application code because it likely contains credentials.

- **User data**

    User data belongs to the users who create the data. It is different from environment to environment. This is the type of data you are most familiar with. It is constantly growing, constantly changing as people use the system. It should be preserved across deployments. All automated database migration processes and tools are designed to preserve the integrity of user data.

In the previous figure, separate the ways to handle data into production and pre-production. The user data in our two pre-production environments (TDD, UAT) are not end user or customer data sets. In UAT, the set of user data has been built up or curated by a stakeholder group (or perhaps transformed from a production backup with sensitive information expunged). This set of data can be reloaded on demand from its source. In our TDD environment, the user data might be nothing. Because each automated acceptance test will be responsible for setting up the records needed to run the test, there might be absolutely no user data to deploy. And that would be just find. After the acceptance tests run, the database would contain quite a bit of user data because each test scenario and application transaction that executes will create user data.

Choosing Your Runtime Architecture

For any given application with many logical components, you will have several viable runtime architectures. In the 4+1 architecture,[II] the physical layer is meant to depict the structure of how the application is running in hardware. Therefore, if we have decided that we are using Microsoft's hardware, in Azure, in a particular region, we still must decide and specify which Azure services to use to run each component of our application. Consider our logical architecture in Figure 9-4.

[II]Kruchten

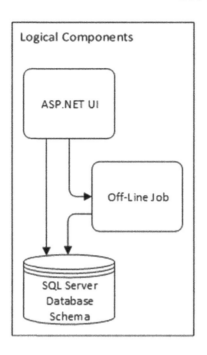

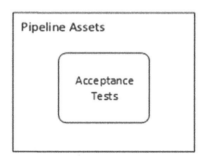

Figure 9-4. *The logical architecture of our application*

Our application has three logical components, at its highest level along with an acceptance test suite that must be deployed somehow in order to execute against the application in the TDD environment. With this application, we have a great number of options when choosing how to design a suitable environment, as shown in Figure 9-5.

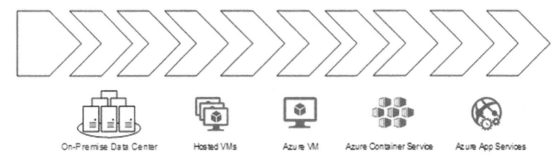

On-Premise Data Center   Hosted VMs   Azure VM   Azure Container Service   Azure App Services

Figure 9-5. *Each application can be deployed on a spectrum of environment types*

Consider the spectrum of options here. We could choose any number of options for deploying our application. The options on the left give us more control but also more responsibility and maintenance. The options toward the right constrain the scope of the computing resources that we can control but also relieve us from more responsibility and maintenance. Because we control less of the computing environment, we are responsible for less maintenance. As the options move to the right, you have fewer APIs and resources available to your application. As an example, if your web application uses a custom font for rendering a screen, it will be incompatible with Azure App Services, which do not provide the ability for installing fonts on the underlying servers. But if your application only makes use of APIs available in that environment, it's the most maintenance-free way to run your web application and off-line job.

We have already established that we will not be mounting physical servers into a cabinet in our own data center – but that option would run our application just fine. We could contract with a regional hosting company and ask them to provision some virtual servers for us. We would also provision some VMs in Azure. We would likely configure a few web servers, one or more servers to run the off-line job, and then we would need a SQL Server cluster for our database. We can likely use any server as a host for our acceptance test suite while it executes.

If we do not want to manage a server operating system, we can reach for containers or PaaS (Platform as a Service) in Azure. Windows containers are growing in maturity but retain some challenges. Linux containers are more mature and are an option if you are targeting Linux for your .NET Core applications. Progressing further than containers are the PaaS services such as Azure App Services. These can host web applications, off-line jobs, as well as a container image. If the Azure cloud had a personality, Azure App Services might say, "Don't ask too many questions. Just give me your code. I'll run it for you." The industry is certainly moving from the left side of the spectrum to the right side.

How far and how fast you and your team move are completely up to you and the software you are currently operating. For this book, we will be deploying to the runtime architecture shown in Figure 9-6.

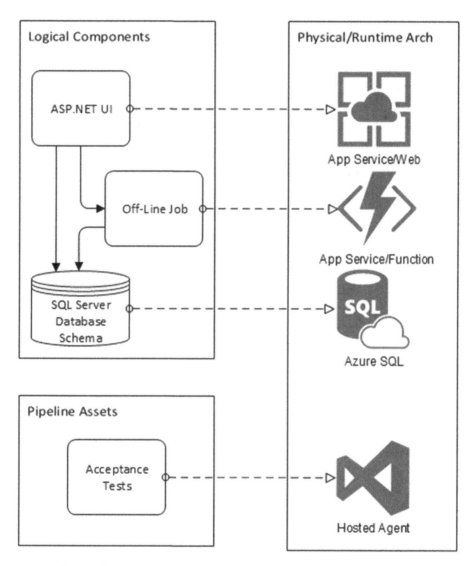

Figure 9-6. *Physical architecture has been specified for our application*

For this book's example application, we are choosing Azure App Services for the ASP.NET UI, which is a web application. The off-line job will be deployed as an Azure Function and hosted in App Services. The SQL Server database will be run in Azure's SQL database service. The acceptance tests will be deployed to the hosted agent provided by Azure Pipelines. The tests can execute from there.

Implementing the Deployment in Azure Pipelines

Now that we have decided our environments and the physical (or runtime) architecture for our application, the next step is to extend our pipeline from our continuous integration build and configure deployments across our three environments. Once it is configured properly, the overview will look like the following in Figure 9-7.

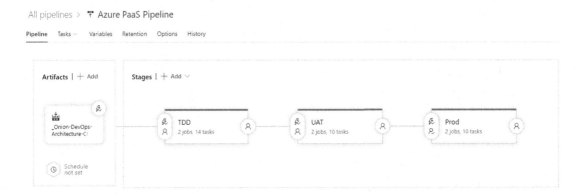

Figure 9-7. *Our release configuration contains three environments and is triggered from the CI build*

We see that there are four key parts to our pipeline's release configuration. Let's take them one at a time:

- **Artifacts**

  The release needs to know what artifacts are available to it. There are several options in the tool, but this is where you will specify the build configuration that represents the CI build for your application. You will configure the release to automatically begin upon success of that build.

- **TDD stage**

  The release can have multiple stages in series, in parallel, or both. This is the smallest, shortest pipeline you will have for any of your applications. The TDD stage corresponds with the TDD environment that is completely automated and where your automated full-system acceptance tests run.

- **UAT stage**

  The UAT stage represents the deployment of the application to the UAT environment.

- **Prod stage**

  The Prod stage represents the deployment of the application to the Production environment.

Next, we will move through each of the screens that need to have some configuration set for them.

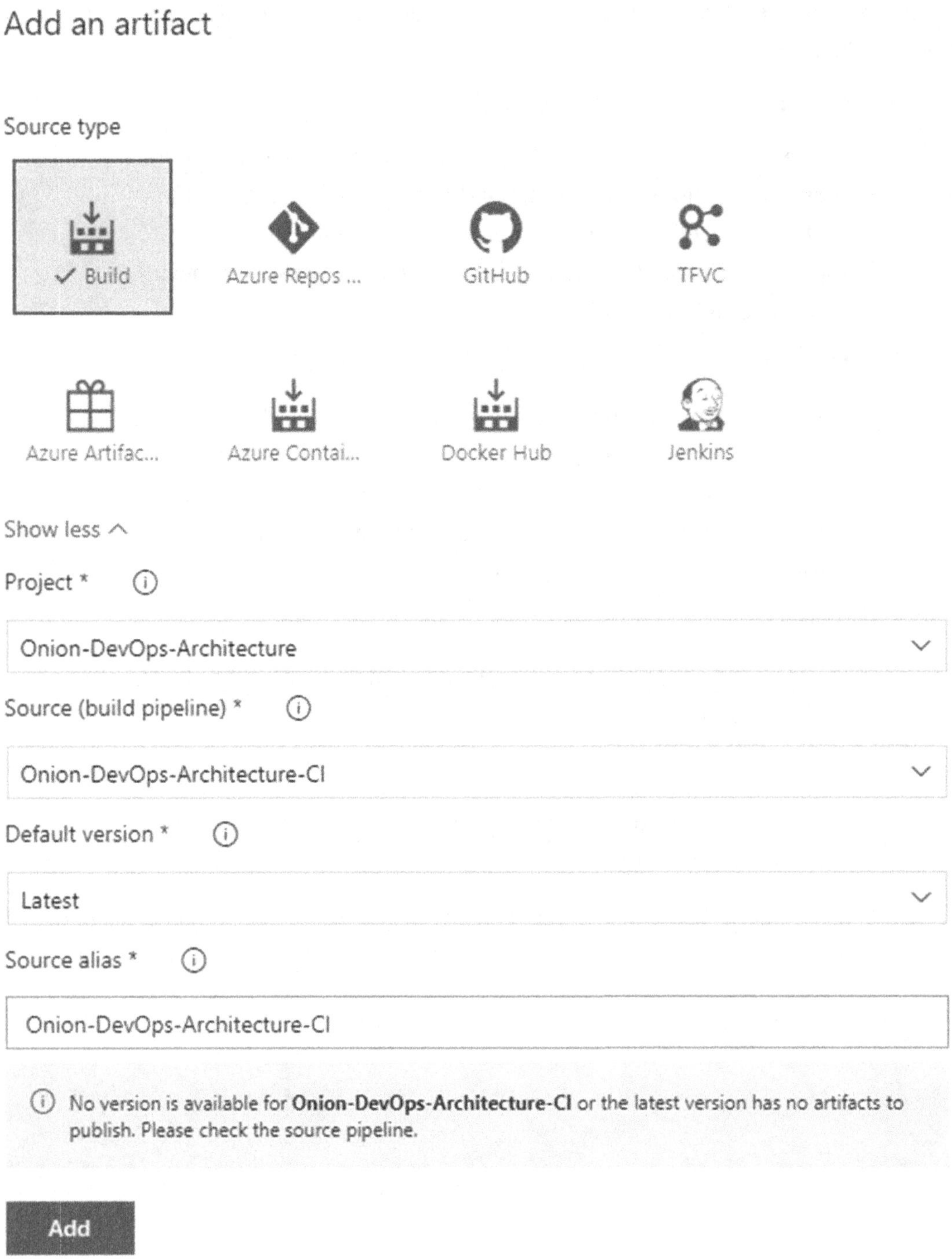

Add an artifact

Source type

Show less ∧

Project *   ⓘ

Onion-DevOps-Architecture   ⌄

Source (build pipeline) *   ⓘ

Onion-DevOps-Architecture-CI   ⌄

Default version *   ⓘ

Latest   ⌄

Source alias *   ⓘ

Onion-DevOps-Architecture-CI

> ⓘ No version is available for **Onion-DevOps-Architecture-CI** or the latest version has no artifacts to
> publish. Please check the source pipeline.

Add

Figure 9-8. *Specify the CI build that will be triggering the release*

Figure 9-8 contains the settings needed to wire up a CI build with an auto-triggered release. Use the "Latest" default version so that your release configuration works with any build from any branch that might be active. In this way, you can maintain a single CI build configuration and a single release configuration.

The property page of the build artifact contains two important settings. The first is to enable creating a release every time a new build is available. The second important setting is the Build branch filters. **While this might appear as a drop-down, put the mouse cursor in it and type an asterisk (∗).** This will ensure that builds that come from every branch will cause the release to trigger. You need this in order to deploy the pipeline to the TDD environment and run acceptance tests. Each stage/environment also includes branch filters so that you can exclude branch-based release candidates from progressing any further down the pipeline, as shown in Figure 9-9.

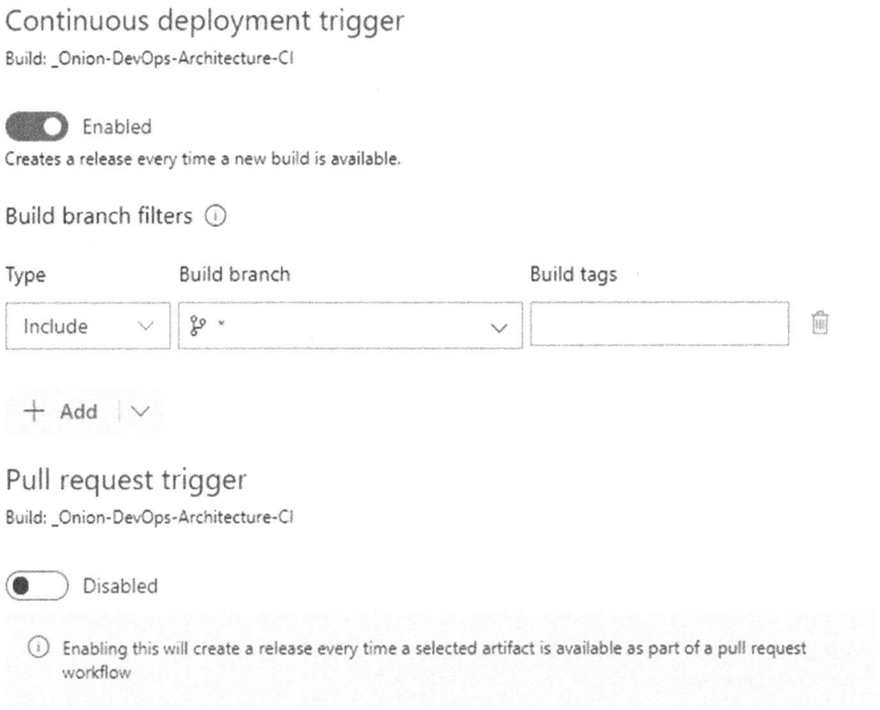

Continuous deployment trigger
Build: _Onion-DevOps-Architecture-CI

Enabled
Creates a release every time a new build is available.

Build branch filters ⓘ

Type	Build branch		Build tags	
Include ∨	⅋ ∗	∨		🗑

\+ Add ∨

Pull request trigger
Build: _Onion-DevOps-Architecture-CI

Disabled

ⓘ Enabling this will create a release every time a selected artifact is available as part of a pull request workflow

Figure 9-9. *Enable continuous deployment to automatically trigger the release*

For the TDD environment, leave all the settings at their defaults and make sure that this environment automatically triggers after release, as shown in Figure 9-10. This is the only setting you need. Azure Pipelines has filters and different logic points in several places, so unless you are changing it for a reason, leave the defaults as they are.

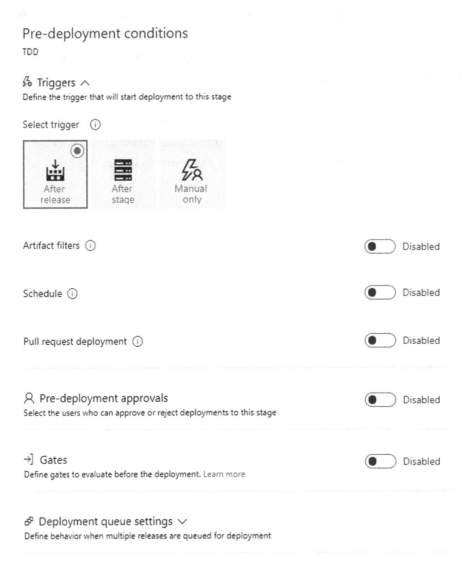

Figure 9-10.   *The pre-deployment conditions for the TDD environment*

When you configure the TDD environment, as shown in Figure 9-11, you'll have three sections because our application has three components that are packaged. We have the web site, the off-line job, and the SQL database. This portion retrieves the

NuGet package for the application component being installed. It extracts and installs that component properly and moves on to the next component. At the end, you execute the health check that calls the appropriate URL or API so that the application can run the built-in routine that checks to see if everything has started and is online.

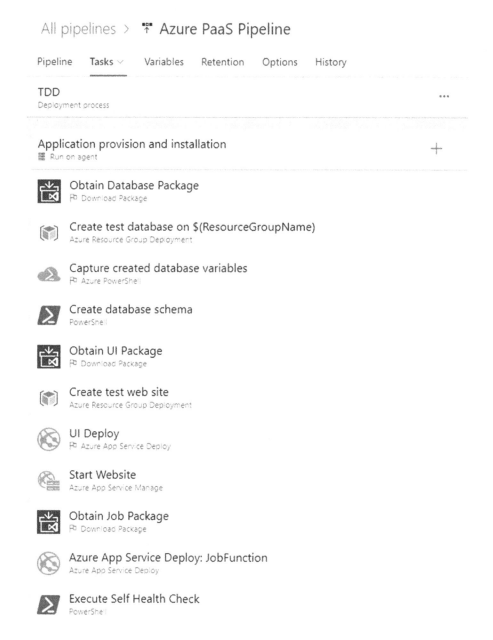

Figure 9-11. *The TDD environment deployment process*

Each stage (think environment) can have multiple "jobs" configured. The second configured job is all about running some type of automated validated. Our application has a full-system acceptance test suite that uses Selenium to drive a web browser, as shown in Figure 9-12. The tests operate within the NUnit runtime and are executed through the VsTest adapter. Since our tests are packaged in a NuGet package and stamped with the same version number as the rest of the application, we use the same method to retrieve the right test suite for execution. After the tests run, pass or fail, we run an Azure Resource Manager deployment and destroy the resource group with the TDD environment that was created at this stage in our DevOps pipeline. That last step is important because you will be executing multiple build and release cycles per day per developer. If you don't remove the resources in Azure that are created, you will run up an Azure bill; however, you are likely to hit Azure subscription limits, which will cause your deployment to fail with an error that will take time to debug.

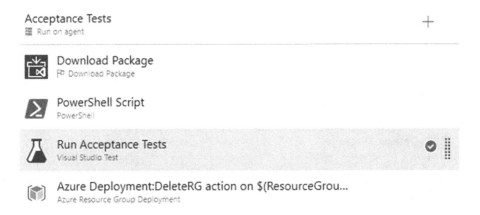

Figure 9-12. *The second major task for the TDD environment is to run the acceptance tests*

CREATING THE TDD ENVIRONMENT WITH ARM

The example application that comes with this book contains ARM (Azure Resource Manager) templates that will create the environments that are suitable for deployment. The TDD environment does not need environments that are scaled to the level that production needs. Because of this, it can often work just fine to provision a scaled down environment by parameterizing the tier of resources to choose. For example, in our TDD environment, we create an App Service resource using the Free tier. We can do this over and over, run our acceptance tests, and validate that the new release candidate continues to function well. But we need to take care that we destroy the environment when we are finished with it. If we fail to do this, we won't run up our bill because we are using the Free tier. But Azure has a limit of how many Free tier resources can be active at any one time. These limits are not guaranteed and can be changed at any time. Needless to say, if you are perpetually creating new environments without destroying them, you will encounter the limit regardless of what level it happens to be. Then your pipeline will begin to fail, and the error message may or may not lead you to the root cause quickly. The best rule of thumb is to clean up after yourself. For the TDD environment, this means destroying the environment and the end of the deployment process, after you have run the appropriate test suites.

While this chapter cannot highlight every setting in the release configuration's steps, this book's digital resources include full exports of the builds and release configurations. In addition, you can refer to the Azure DevOps Services public project at `https://dev.azure.com/clearmeasurelabs/Onion-DevOps-Architecture`.

Deploying an Application Component

Before we move on, let's look in detail at the process of retrieving an application component from Azure Artifacts and deploying it. For this section, we are going to select the most complicated component of most applications. This is the SQL database. In order to deploy the database, we will need to have all required assets available to us, and we will need to create the database itself in the TDD environment.

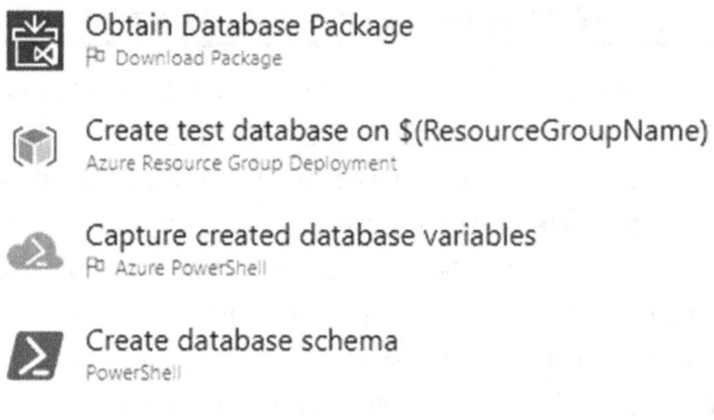

 Obtain Database Package
Download Package

 Create test database on $(ResourceGroupName)
Azure Resource Group Deployment

Capture created database variables
Azure PowerShell

Create database schema
PowerShell

Figure 9-13. *The four steps that make up a provisioning and deployment of the SQL database*

The four steps in Figure 9-13 are responsible for on-demand provisioning of a SQL database and the creation of the schema. The following is the full YAML listing.

At the time of writing, YAML configuration is available for builds but not for release configurations.

```
steps:
- task: DownloadPackage@0
  displayName: 'Obtain Database Package'
  inputs:
    feed: '<some guid>'
    definition: '<some guid>'
    version: '$(Build.BuildNumber)'
    downloadPath: '$(System.ArtifactsDirectory)/packages
                /Database-$(Build.BuildNumber)'
variables:
  ResourceGroupName:
'$(System.TeamProject)-$(Release.EnvironmentName)-$(Release.ReleaseId)'
  DatabaseUser: 'dbuser'
  DatabaseName:
```

```
'db-$(Release.EnvironmentName)-$(Build.BuildNumber)-$(Release.ReleaseId)'
  DatabaseEdition: 'Basic'
  DatabasePerformanceLevel: 'Basic'
- task: AzureResourceGroupDeployment@2
  displayName: 'Create test database on $(ResourceGroupName)'
  inputs:
    azureSubscription: '<redacted>'
    resourceGroupName: '$(ResourceGroupName)'
    location: 'South Central US'
    csmFile: '$(System.ArtifactsDirectory)/packages
    /Database-$(Build.BuildNumber)/DatabaseARM.json'
    overrideParameters: '-databaseLogin $(DatabaseUser)
-databaseLoginPassword $(DatabasePassword) -skuCapacity 1
-databaseName $(DatabaseName) -collation SQL_Latin1_General_CP1_CI_AS
-edition $(DatabaseEdition) -maxSizeBytes 1073741824
-requestedServiceObjectiveName $(DatabasePerformanceLevel)'
variables:
  ResourceGroupName:
'$(System.TeamProject)-$(Release.EnvironmentName)-$(Release.ReleaseId)'
- task: AzurePowerShell@3
  displayName: 'Capture created database variables'
  inputs:
    azureSubscription: '<redacted>'
    ScriptType: InlineScript
    Inline: |
     $azureRmResourceGroupDeployment = Get-AzureRmResourceGroupDeployment
         -ResourceGroupName "$(ResourceGroupName)" | Sort-Object Timestamp
         -Descending | Select-Object -First 1

     $azureRmResourceGroupDeployment.Outputs.GetEnumerator() | ForEach-
     Object {
         $variableName = $_.key
         $variableValue = $_.value.Value
         Write-Host
```

```
            "##vso[task.setvariable variable=$variableName;]$variableValue"
        Write-Host "$variableName $variableValue"
    }
  azurePowerShellVersion: LatestVersion
        - powershell: |
$env:DatabasePassword="$(DatabasePassword)"
& $(System.ArtifactsDirectory)\packages
        \Database-$(Build.BuildNumber)\UpdateAzureSQL.ps1
        workingDirectory: '$(System.ArtifactsDirectory)\packages
        \Database-$(Build.BuildNumber)'
        displayName: 'Create database schema'
```

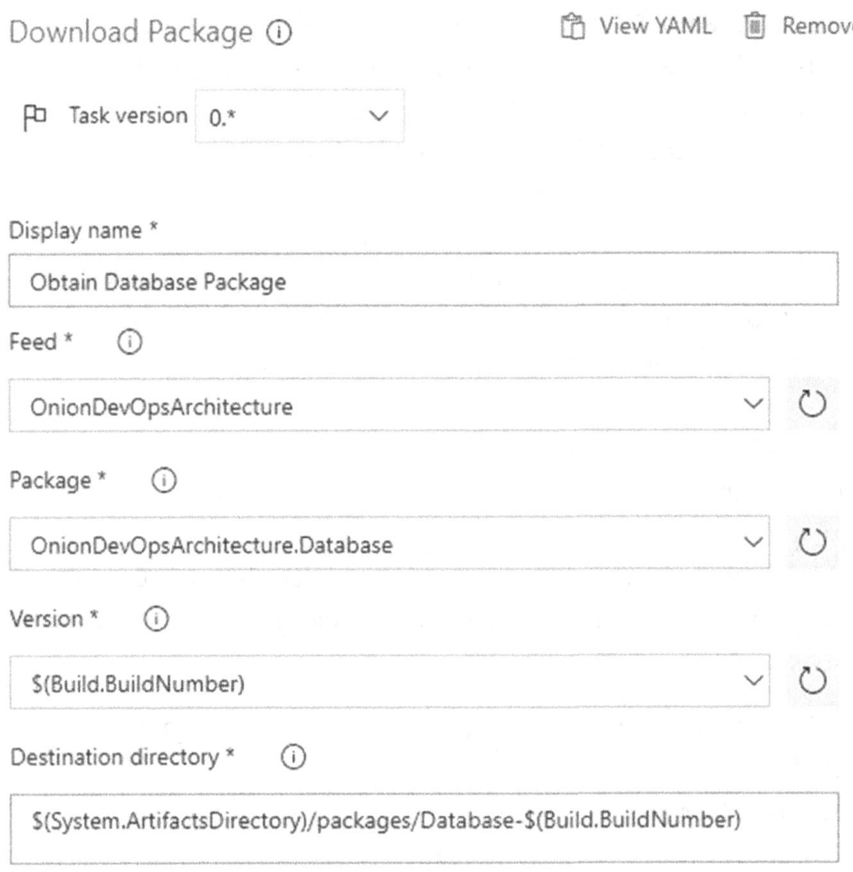

Download Package ⓘ   📋 View YAML   🗑 Remove

🏳 Task version 0.*   ⌄

Display name *

Obtain Database Package

Feed *   ⓘ

OnionDevOpsArchitecture   ⌄   ↻

Package *   ⓘ

OnionDevOpsArchitecture.Database   ⌄   ↻

Version *   ⓘ

$(Build.BuildNumber)   ⌄   ↻

Destination directory *   ⓘ

$(System.ArtifactsDirectory)/packages/Database-$(Build.BuildNumber)

Figure 9-14. *Download Package step configuration*

The preceding YAML configuration can be quite cryptic if you haven't worked with it much. Figure 9-14 represents the customized properties of the Download Package task. This task downloads the specified NuGet package from Azure Artifacts and expands the contents into the destination directory specified. Keep in mind that we will have multiple releases happening at once on multiple branches, so we want to parameterize anything that creates environments so that we don't accidentally create any global dependencies. In order to obtain the NuGet package for the release candidate we want, we specify the full name of the package: OnionDevOpsArchitecture.Database. Then, we must specify the version that we would like to retrieve. In this context, we have the current $(Build. BuildNumber) available to us, so we specify that.

Because we configured our CI build as an artifact dependency, we have the variables of that build available to us in the release configuration. The variable we will use throughout the pipeline is $(Build.BuildNumber). Everything hinges on the build number.

If you are someone who likes to know exactly what is happening at all times under the covers, you may want to install the Azure Pipelines agent to your own workstation so you can closely observe the directories used and where files are placed. For historical reasons, the agent for most people will be downloaded in a file name "vsts-agent-win-- x64-#-#.#.zip" where # is the latest version number. If you are experimenting, you are free to install as many instances of the running agent as you like. Make sure you extract and run the zip file to separate locations in order to do that.

The next step for our database deployment is to create the Azure SQL database in our TDD environment, as shown in Figure 9-15. At the top, you will notice $(ResourceGroupName). We haven't covered variables yet, but this variable is set to the value of

`$(System.TeamProject)-$(Release.EnvironmentName)-$(Release.ReleaseId)`

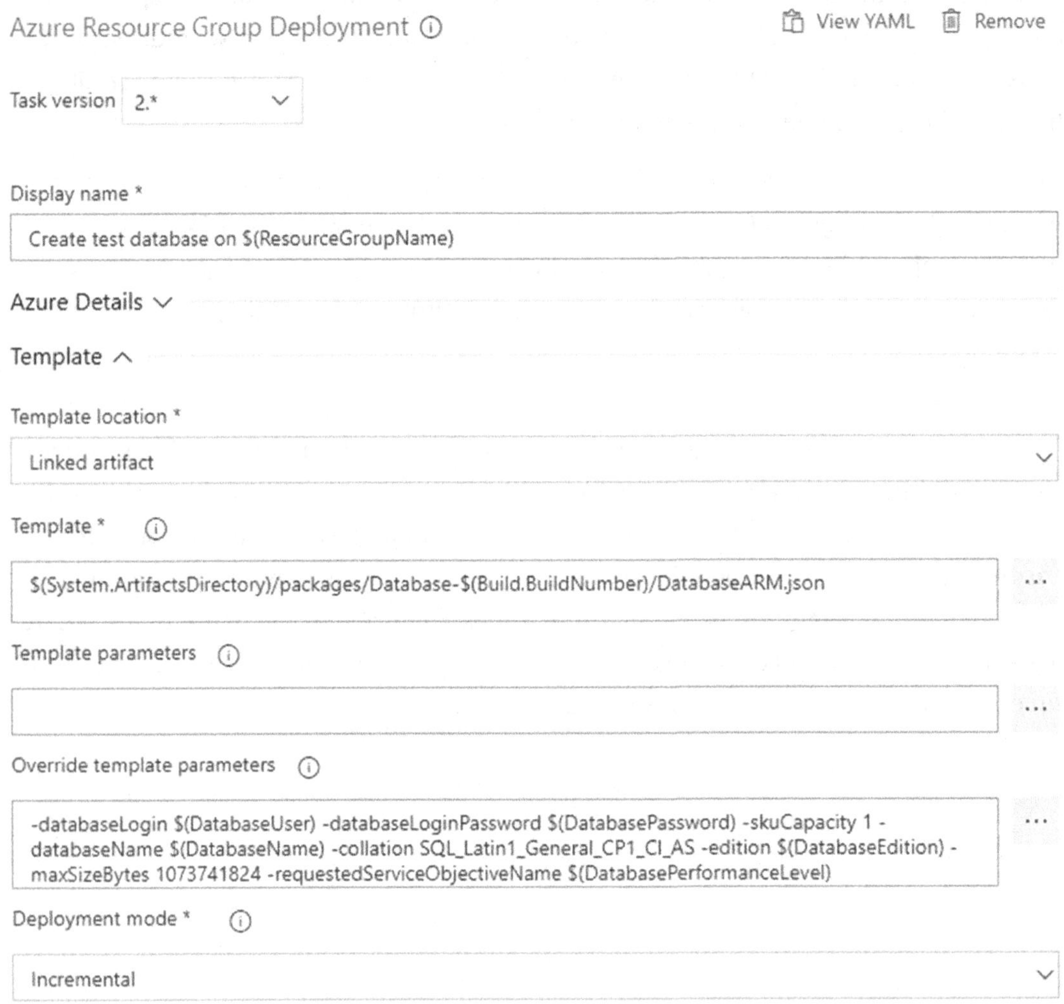

Figure 9-15. *Creating the SQL database in Azure uses an ARM template*

We do not want to hard-code these things. Many TDD environments may be provisioned simultaneously since feature branches make use of environment creation and acceptance test execution. We take enough other variables and construct a resource group name that is guaranteed to be unique. Every Azure resource we create for this versioned deployment in the TDD environment will go in this resource group. When we are finished, we destroy the resource group, and we can be confident that we have cleaned up appropriately. Notes that we embed three pieces of information in this variable:

- Team project name (by convention, we never put spaces in a team project name)

- Environment name

- Release ID (we don't use BuildNumber since resource group names can't contain dots)

As we specify the other properties, we didn't have enough space to show the basic Azure settings, but you'll specify your authenticated Azure subscription and the region you are targeting. Then you will specify the path to the ARM template file. This file was extracted by the OnionDevOpsArchitecture.Database NuGet package, so you have it available to you. This ARM template is stored in the Git repository and is owned by the "Database" Visual Studio project. You can reference the full file details by downloading the code that accompanies the book. This ARM template has some variables that have been externalized as parameters so that the deployment process can control the settings. You can see the "Override template parameters" text area. We are specifying several of these settings in order to make the ARM template generic and reusable across other applications that need an Azure SQL database. Through these variables, we can control the database edition, size, and so on.

The next step is to capture the variables that we need in order to create our database schema, as shown in Figure 9-16. We have just created a new Azure SQL database, but we don't know how to access it. A new SQL Server database must be created to house any databases, and those always have a unique hostname. From the execution of our ARM deployment, we loop through the outputs of the resource group deployment and capture them as variables that can be used in subsequent steps of our deployment.

In this case, we will capture an output named "resourceGroupUniqueString". Because of this, we now have the server name that can be used to execution our schema migration tool. We construct a variable $(DatabaseServer) by using the following value:

```
databaseserver$(resourceGroupUniqueString).database.windows.net
```

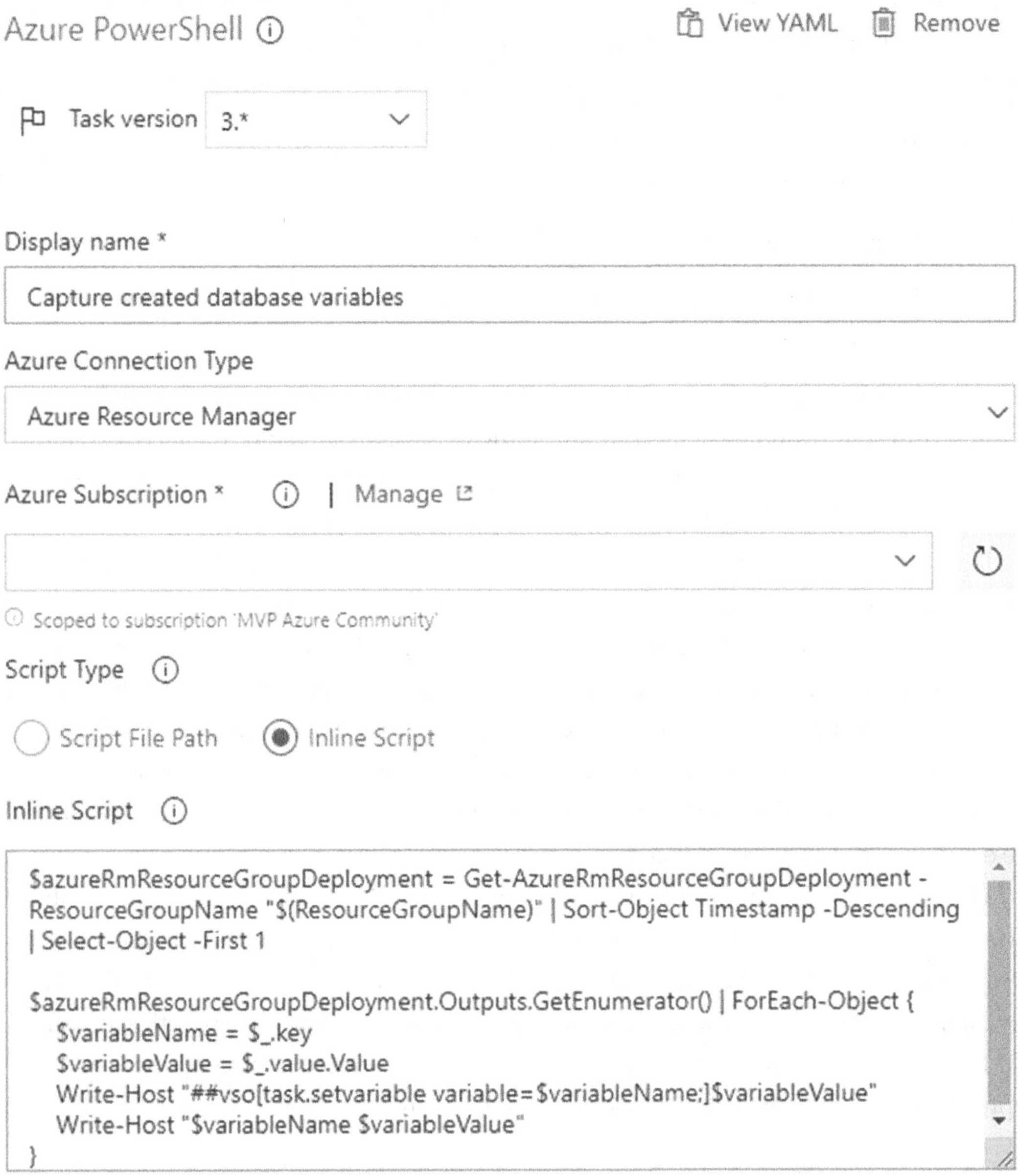

Azure PowerShell ⓘ   📋 View YAML   🗑 Remove

🏳 Task version 3.*   ⌄

Display name *

Capture created database variables

Azure Connection Type

Azure Resource Manager   ⌄

Azure Subscription *   ⓘ | Manage ↗

                                                            ⌄   ↻

ⓘ Scoped to subscription 'MVP Azure Community'

Script Type   ⓘ

◯ Script File Path   ⦿ Inline Script

Inline Script   ⓘ

```
$azureRmResourceGroupDeployment = Get-AzureRmResourceGroupDeployment -
ResourceGroupName "$(ResourceGroupName)" | Sort-Object Timestamp -Descending
| Select-Object -First 1

$azureRmResourceGroupDeployment.Outputs.GetEnumerator() | ForEach-Object {
    $variableName = $_.key
    $variableValue = $_.value.Value
    Write-Host "##vso[task.setvariable variable=$variableName;]$variableValue"
    Write-Host "$variableName $variableValue"
}
```

Figure 9-16. *We capture output variables after our SQL database is created*

Azure SQL uses this pattern for hostnames to the database server. With this variable captured, we can proceed to access our newly created database server.

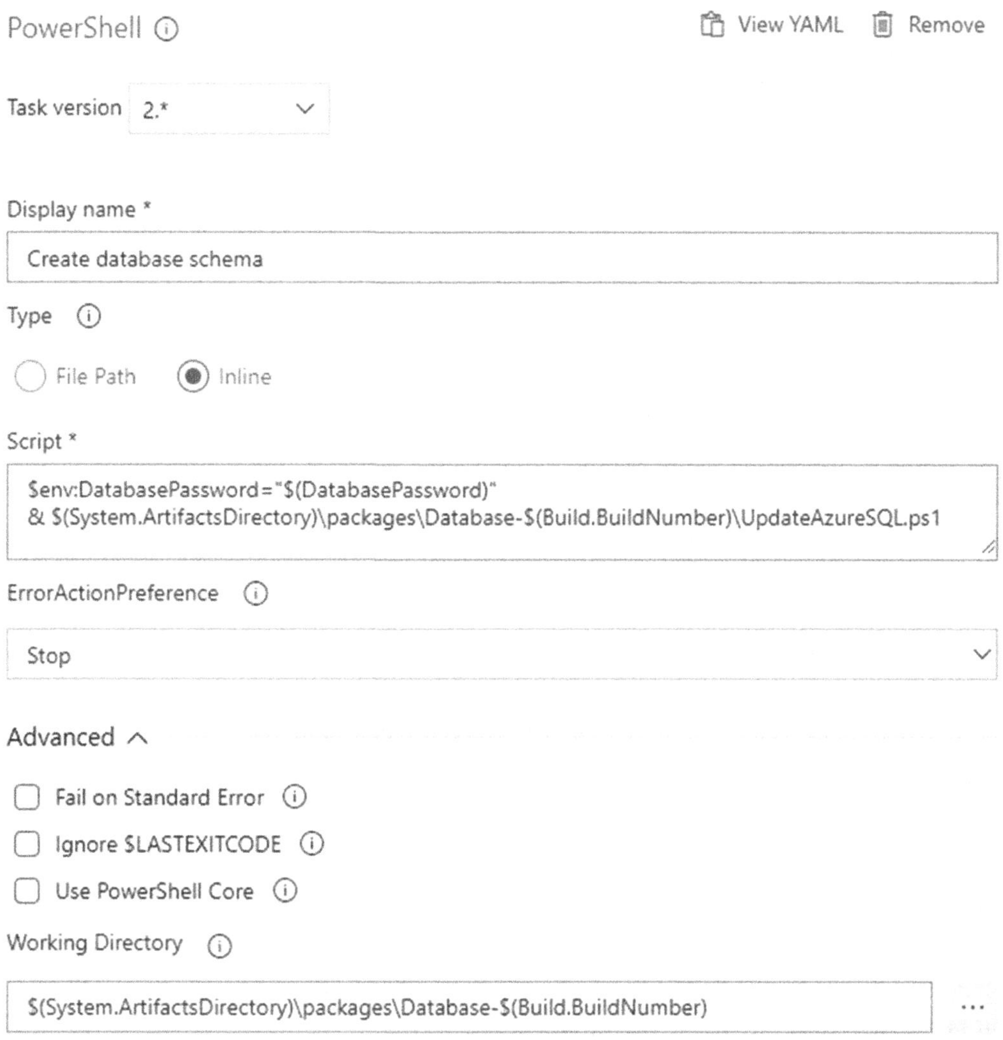

PowerShell ⓘ   📋 View YAML   🗑 Remove

Task version   2.*   ⌄

Display name *

Create database schema

Type   ⓘ

○ File Path   ● Inline

Script *

$env:DatabasePassword="$(DatabasePassword)"
& $(System.ArtifactsDirectory)\packages\Database-$(Build.BuildNumber)\UpdateAzureSQL.ps1

ErrorActionPreference   ⓘ

Stop   ⌄

Advanced ∧

☐ Fail on Standard Error   ⓘ
☐ Ignore $LASTEXITCODE   ⓘ
☐ Use PowerShell Core   ⓘ

Working Directory   ⓘ

$(System.ArtifactsDirectory)\packages\Database-$(Build.BuildNumber)   ⋯

Figure 9-17. *The step of our database deployment that creates the full database schema in the TDD environment*

This PowerShell task is another example of "shift left" as we take the logic that needs to execute and push it into our Visual Studio solution. In order to run it, we need to make available the sensitive credential stored in the $(DatabasePassword) variable. Variables marked "secret" do not automatically become environment variables. Our PowerShell snippet explicitly makes it available as an environment variable to the current process. Other variables in plain text are automatically available as environment variables. The UpdateAzureSQL.ps1 file is part of the code and comes from the database NuGet package that was stored in Azure Artifacts with our release candidate. The contents of this *.ps1 is as follows:

```
#
# UpdateAzureSQL.ps1
#
$DatabaseServer = $env:DatabaseServer
$DatabaseName = $env:DatabaseName
$DatabaseAction = $env:DatabaseAction
$DatabaseUser = $env:DatabaseUser
$DatabasePassword = $env:DatabasePassword

Write-Host "Executing & .\scripts\AliaSQL.exe $DatabaseAction
$databaseServer
$databaseName .\scripts $databaseUser $databasePassword"

& .\scripts\AliaSQL.exe $DatabaseAction $DatabaseServer $DatabaseName
.\scripts $DatabaseUser $DatabasePassword
```

The PowerShell scripts is very straightforward. We pass in location and credentials in order to access the SQL Server and create or update a particular database name. Our database migration tool, AliaSQL,[III] accesses the script stored in the .\scripts\ folder and executes them in order to build the database schema.

Several automated database migration tools exist at the time of writing. The best commercial tool is Redgate's SQL Change Automation (SCA). Other free OSS options are DbUp and Roundhouse.

[III]JeffreyPalermo.com, n.d.

One more setting that is important to running PowerShell scripts that are bundled in your release candidate's NuGet package is the working directory. As you can see in Figure 9-17, we set the working directory to be the directory where our NuGet package has been extracted. By doing this, the authoring and maintenance of the PowerShell script are simplified. It's a normal assumption that the script would use relative paths to the path where it exists. By doing this, our script can work well in all of the places and environments where it may be executed. With the execution of this command, our TDD environment now has a complete SQL Server database with the full schema and schema data loaded. We have the full connection string, and it's ready for use. The other application components follow the same pattern:

- Retrieve NuGet package

- Extract NuGet package in a working directory

- Poke any configuration variables

- Provision server/cloud environment

- Install application component

- Start application component

Now that you know the pattern to install your application, let's turn to automatic validation in the TDD environment.

Running Test Suites Using a Release Configuration

Now that our application is deployed, the value of the TDD environment is the automatic execution of our acceptance tests. Our example application that comes with this book contains a number of simple acceptance tests, validating that we can add new expense reports and list them out on the screen. We use the NUnit test framework with Selenium's web driver through the Chrome browser. Here is a listing of our test code:

```
using System;
using System.IO;
using System.Reflection;
using ClearMeasure.OnionDevOpsArchitecture.Core.Model;
using ClearMeasure.OnionDevOpsArchitecture.IntegrationTests;
using NUnit.Framework;
```

```
using OpenQA.Selenium;
using OpenQA.Selenium.Chrome;
using Shouldly;

namespace ClearMeasure.OnionDevOpsArchitecture.AcceptanceTests
{
    public class GetAllExpenseReportsTester
    {
        private string _appUrl;
        private IWebDriver _driver;

        [OneTimeSetUp]
        public void Setup()
        {
            _appUrl = new DataConfigurationStub().GetValue("AppUrl",
                Assembly.GetExecutingAssembly());
            _driver = new ChromeDriver(".");
            new ZDataLoader().LoadLocalData();
        }

        [OneTimeTearDown]
        public void Teardown()
        {
            _driver.Close();
            _driver.Quit();
            _driver.Dispose();
        }

        [TestCase("000001",
            TestName = "Should add new expense report numbered '000001'")]
        [TestCase("000010",
            TestName = "Should add new expense report numbered '000010'")]
        [TestCase("000100",
            TestName = "Should add new expense report numbered '000100'")]
        [TestCase("001000",
            TestName = "Should add new expense report numbered '001000'")]
        [TestCase("010000",
            TestName = "Should add new expense report numbered '010000'")]
```

```
[TestCase("100000",
    TestName = "Should add new expense report numbered '100000'")]
public void ShouldBeAbleToAddNewExpenseReport(string
expenseReportNumber)
{
    void ClickLink(string linkText)
    {
        _driver.FindElement(By.LinkText(linkText)).Click();
    }

    void TypeText(string elementName, string text)
    {
        var numberTextBox = _driver.FindElement(By.
        Name(elementName));
        numberTextBox.SendKeys(text);
    }

    Console.WriteLine($"Navigating to {_appUrl}");
    _driver.Navigate().GoToUrl(_appUrl + "/");
    _driver.Manage().Window.Maximize();
    TakeScreenshot($"{expenseReportNumber}-Step1Arrange");

    ClickLink("Add New");

    TypeText(nameof(ExpenseReport.Number), expenseReportNumber);
    TypeText(nameof(ExpenseReport.Title), "some title");
    TypeText(nameof(ExpenseReport.Description), "some desc");

    TakeScreenshot($"{expenseReportNumber}-Step2Act");

    _driver.FindElement(By.TagName("form")).Submit();

    TakeScreenshot($"{expenseReportNumber}-Step3Assert");

    var numberCells = _driver.FindElements(
        By.CssSelector(
        $"td[data-expensereport-property=\"{nameof(ExpenseReport.
        Number)}\"]
        [data-value=\"{expenseReportNumber}\"]"));
```

```
        numberCells.Count.ShouldBeGreaterThan(0);
        numberCells[0].Text.ShouldBe(expenseReportNumber);

    }

    private void TakeScreenshot(string fileName)
    {
        var chromeDriver = ((ChromeDriver) _driver);
        chromeDriver.GetScreenshot().SaveAsFile($"{fileName}.png");
        TestContext.AddTestAttachment($"{fileName}.png");
    }
  }
}
```

We use a DataConfigurationStub() in order to clear out the database in the TDD environment and preload it with a few records. We use the same NUnit test to run six test cases. The steps his test progresses through are

1. Navigate to the home page.

2. Find and click the "Add New" link.

3. Find the Number text box and type in a value.

4. Find the Title text box and type in a value.

5. Find the Description text box and type in a value.

6. Submit the form.

7. Find the row of the table and the Number column.

8. Make sure the value of the Number is the expected value.

This test follows the Arrange, Act, Assert[IV] convention that is a bedrock principle of test-driven development. As this test executes, it will open the local Chrome browser on the server and execute these steps. Let's take a look at how this is configured in Azure Pipelines.

[IV]Beck, 2002

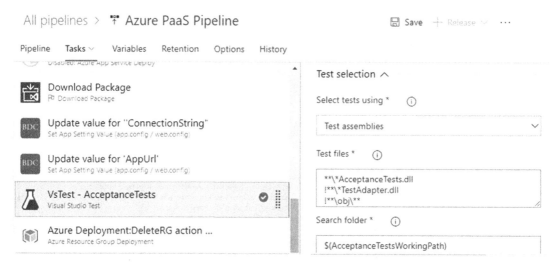

Figure 9-18. *Full-system acceptance tests are run just like any other NUnit/XUnit test suite*

Once we download the NuGet package, which contains our acceptance test suite, perform a few key steps:

1. We extract the package onto a working path on our Azure DevOps agent server.

2. ConnectionString and AppUrl config settings are poked into the test suite's configuration file.[v]

3. VSTest task is run against our *AcceptanceTests.dll assembly, which contains our tests.

4. No fourth step – because we use VSTest, the test output is automatically captured by Azure DevOps as a test run.

Before we proceed further, let's examine the NuGet package for our acceptance tests, as shown in Figure 9-19.

---

[v]Build & Release Tools from Benjamin Day, n.d.

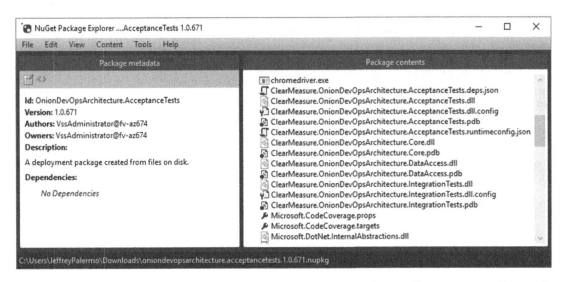

Figure 9-19. *The acceptance test package contains the Selenium driver as well as the test assemblies*

Notice that chromedriver.exe is contained in the package as well as the test assemblies and the config files that go with them. There are more dependent assemblies that don't fit in the screenshot, but everything necessary for the tests to run is here. Besides the NUnit test code and the VSTest Azure Pipelines task, we are also integrating some of the built-in features of Azure Test Plans. Notice in the previous code the line:

```
TestContext.AddTestAttachment($"{fileName}.png");
```

Azure Test Plans keep track of all test runs, the tests, and the results of each. And each test that is run can archive any arbitrary file attachment. In the case of full-system acceptance tests that run through a browser UI, one of the most useful attachments is a screenshot of every screen the test sees as it runs. Our test scenario in C# is instrumented with calls to the ChromeDriver to take a screenshot, and then we save the file and attach it to the TestContext. When VSTest runs these tests, it collects all the information and archives it in Azure Test Plans. Let's take a look at this one step at a time. First, we can see the results of our CI build.

On this build summary page shown in Figure 9-20, we can see the successful build and that the deployments to TDD and UAT are successful. We can also see that the deployment to Prod is ready and waiting (but will not proceed without a manual approval).

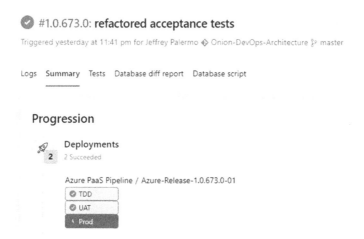

Figure 9-20. *The build summary page shows that this build has been deployed across environments*

When we click over to our TDD deployment from the build page, as shown in Figure 9-21, we can see information about the release and drill into each environment to see details about what has happened.

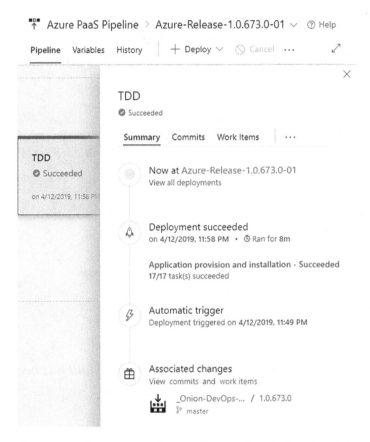

Figure 9-21. *The TDD release view shows the top-level details of the TDD deployment*

Beyond looking at the Logs of your deployment, which is critical in debugging it until it works properly, the Tests tab is your access to the world of the acceptance tests, as shown in Figure 9-22. In our example, we have six tests. In business-critical applications, you will have over a hundred. A good rule of thumb is to ask yourself if every text box and every button on every screen are being interacted with by your acceptance tests. You don't want basic functionality gaps. You don't have to look for every edge case, but you do want basic coverage. Next, let's select and click the last test in the list, "Should add new expense report numbered '100000'".

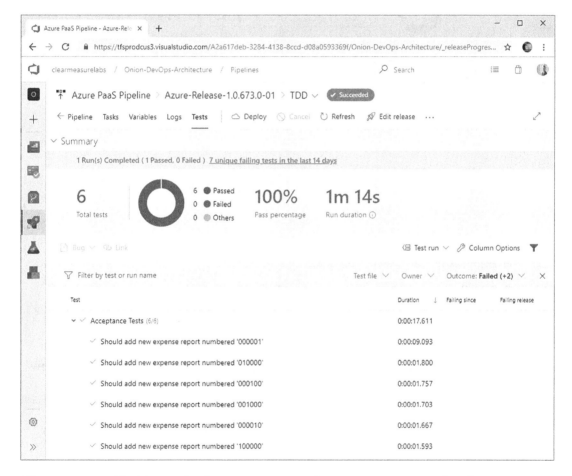

Figure 9-22. *The Tests tab gives us access to the acceptance tests that have run*

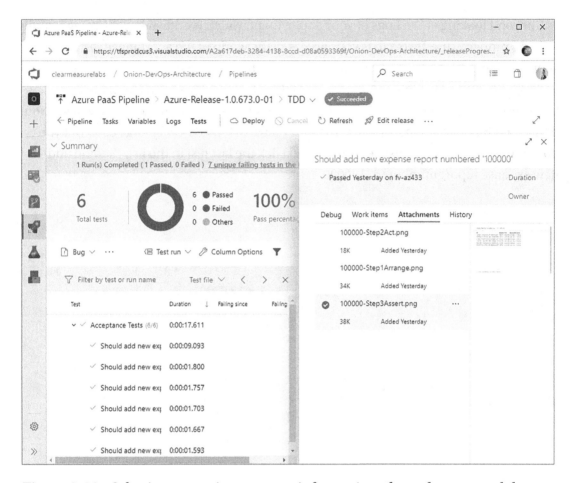

Figure 9-23. *Selecting a test gives us more information about that test and the run of it*

While you can associate work items with tests and see the history of it, most of the time you want to run tests and just know that they passed. The value comes when a new commit breaks a test, and now you have to figure out why. This is where attachments come in. Because we took screenshots while the Selenium tests were running, we can refer back to them if something goes awry. You can see here in Figure 9-23 that we can see a preview of what the screen looks like when we are running the asserts of the test. Let's look at that screenshot more closely.

With this capability, if the test fails, we can see what has changed on the screen, as shown in Figure 9-24. Because you are finding elements with CSS selectors or names, you may choose to store the full HTML page source as an attachment. It is completely up to you.

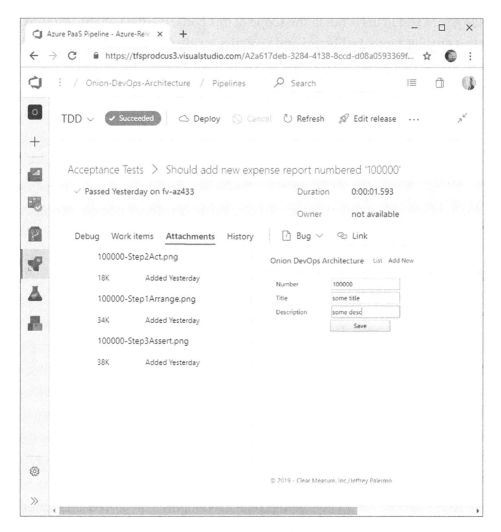

Figure 9-24. *Expanding the attachment view shows a full preview with the ability to link a work item to log a bug*

With Selenium and ChromeDriver, you can capture a screenshot of the page as your acceptance tests are running. Everything inside the window will be captured and stored as an attachment to the test run.

While Azure Test Plans is not in the scope of this book, the data on the test runs themselves enables more dashboard and analytics inside the Azure Test Plans product. As you accumulate more tests, you will likely start asking questions such as

- Why do some types of tests seem more brittle than others?

- Why are some tests slower than others?

- Why did some tests get removed?

- Why is our ratio of tests to code changing over time?

Without these metrics, you don't have the ability to consider these questions.

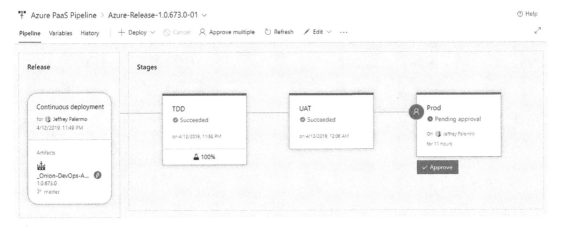

Figure 9-25. *The complete pipeline looks like this when it is functioning properly*

Once your TDD environment is being created, configured, deployed, and tested, the other deployments in your pipeline follow suite. You can create and deploy as many environments as you like depending on the audience of people who need to participate in software validation and testing. You will see a 100% next to the beaker icon on the TDD environment. This signifies that a test suite ran and that all tests passed. It would show less than 100% if any tests were ignored.

Differences in the UAT and Production Environments

While the deployment process for the TDD environment should be the same as UAT and Prod, you will have some key differences in order to maintain all the branching capabilities for trunk-based development. First, the UAT state deployment needs to be configured to ignore release candidates generated by feature branches, as shown in Figure 9-26.

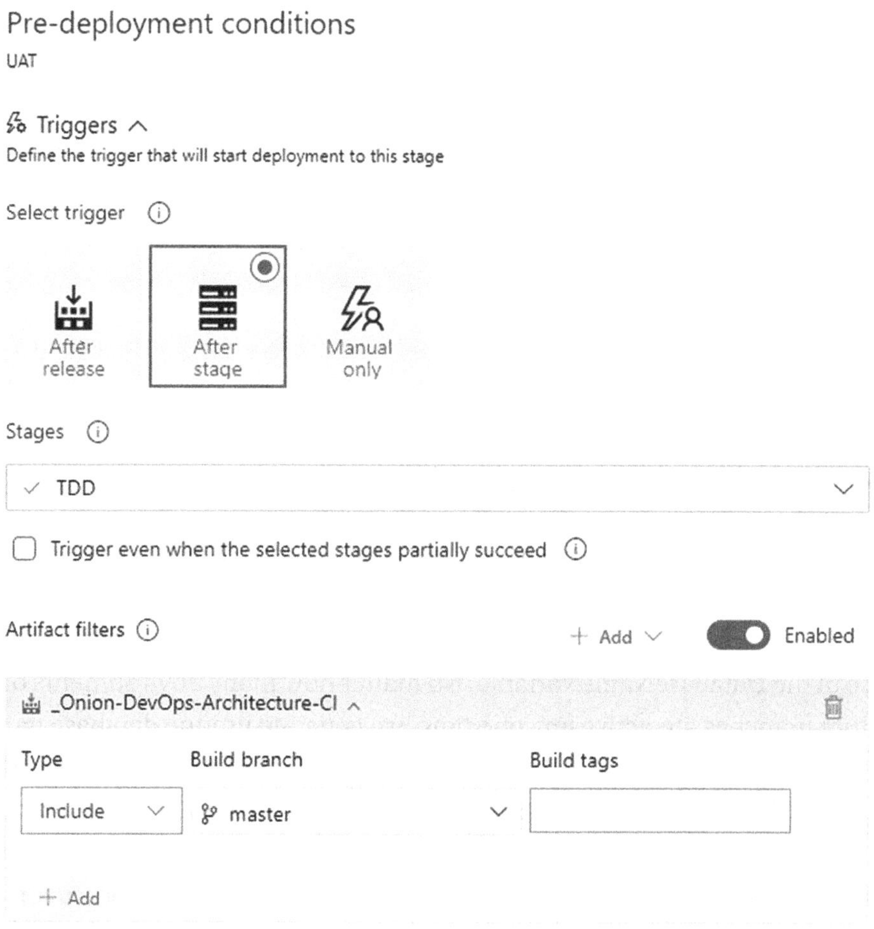

Pre-deployment conditions
UAT

⚡ Triggers ∧
Define the trigger that will start deployment to this stage

Select trigger ⓘ

After release	After stage ⦿	Manual only

Stages ⓘ

✓ TDD	⌄

☐ Trigger even when the selected stages partially succeed ⓘ

Artifact filters ⓘ   + Add ⌄   ⬤ Enabled

🏗 _Onion-DevOps-Architecture-CI ∧   🗑

Type	Build branch	Build tags
Include ⌄	⿻ master ⌄	

+ Add

Figure 9-26. *The UAT environment should only deploy release candidates generated by the master branch*

Every environment depends on the release candidates generated by a particular build. You can filter how a deployment is triggered by adding filters. In this case, we want the UAT environment to be automatically deployed when the TDD stage succeeds but only if the release candidate came from the master branch. Most of the time, stakeholders outside the development team want very stable release candidates that are fully integrated. It is your choice to modify this if it is appropriate for deploying some of these feature branch release candidates. Other differences in the UAT stage are not process differences but variable differences.

Name	Release	TDD	UAT	Prod
AcceptanceTestsProjectName	AcceptanceTests			
AcceptanceTestsWorkingPath	$(System.ArtifactsDirectory)/packages/$(AcceptanceTestsProjectName)-$(Build.BuildNumber)			
AppInsightsName	$(System.TeamProject)-ai-$(Release.EnvironmentName)			
AppUrl	https://$(UrlName).azurewebsites.net			
ConnectionString	Server=$(DatabaseServer):Database=$(DatabaseName):Persist Security Info=False:User ID=$(Datab...			
DatabaseAction		Rebuild	Update	Update
DatabaseEdition	Basic			
DatabaseName	db-$(Release.EnvironmentName)-$(SourceBranchName)-$(Build.BuildNumber)-$(Release.ReleaseId)			
DatabasePassword	********			
DatabasePerformanceLevel	Basic			
DatabaseServer	databaseserver$(resourceGroupUniqueString).database.windows.net			
DatabaseUser	dbuser			

Figure 9-27. *Variables can be different per stage or the same throughout the release*

Figure 9-27 is a subset of the variables used to deploy and test the application along our DevOps pipeline. Most of the variables tend to be the same in every stage because the environment name is able to be used to construct variable values. For example, take notice of the DatabaseName variable. No matter how many environments or how many feature branches are active any one time, we generate unique database names to prevent collisions. The environment name and even the branch name are embedded in the DatabaseName so that we can provision as many environments as needed. The DatabaseAction is different. The DatabaseAction variable has no default value for the whole release. Instead, we specify different values so that our process runs our database schema migration tool with the right command-line arguments. In the TDD environment, we want a completely new database built from scratch. This proves that we aren't relying on anything in the environment in order to have a database that can pass our acceptance tests. In the UAT environment, we do not rebuild the database. Rather, we preserve the database and data and update it by running only the *.sql files that have not yet been run on that environment. This is signified by the "Update" value. When this completely successfully, we have a high degree of confidence that when we run the same routine on production, the data will be preserved, and the schema will be updated properly. Next, examine the different configuration for the Production deployment stage.

Because you're going to be creating many releases, you need variable values that are going to be resilient to the repetitive nature of DevOps.

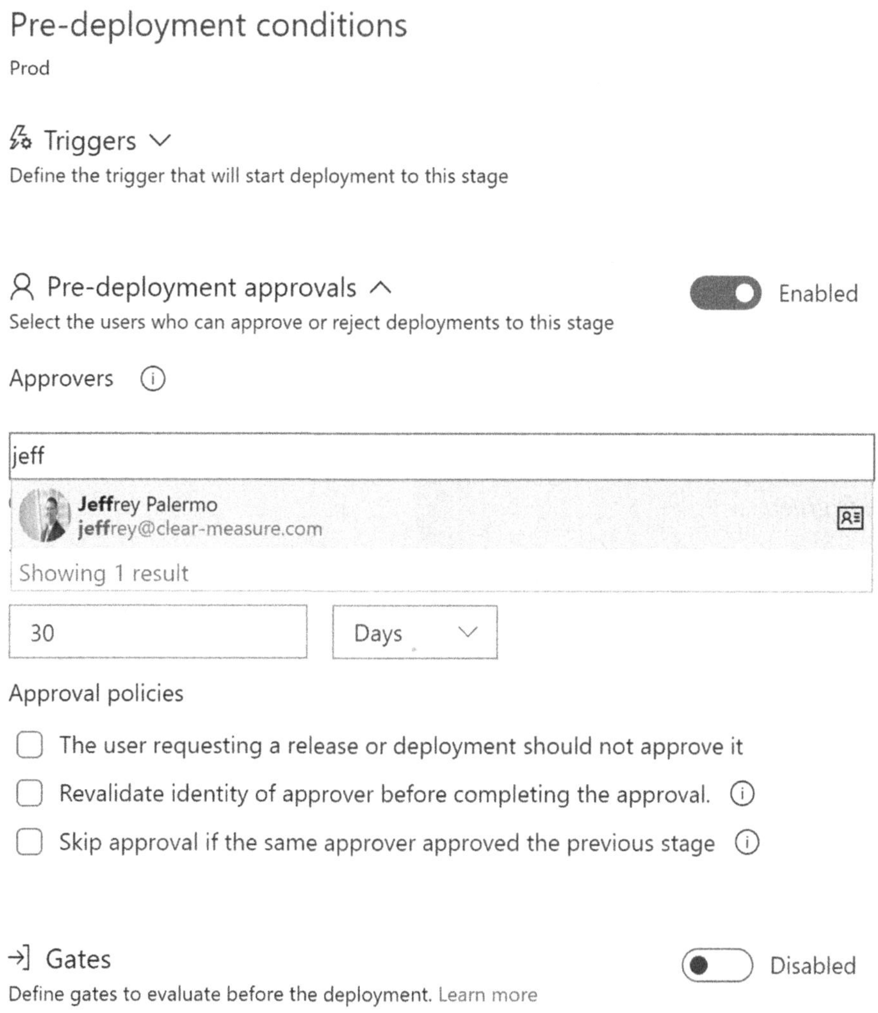

Pre-deployment conditions
Prod

⚡ Triggers ⌄
Define the trigger that will start deployment to this stage

👤 Pre-deployment approvals ⌃   ⬤━ Enabled
Select the users who can approve or reject deployments to this stage

Approvers ⓘ

jeff

Jeffrey Palermo **jeff**rey@clear-measure.com	🔳
Showing 1 result	

30		Days ⌄

Approval policies

☐ The user requesting a release or deployment should not approve it

☐ Revalidate identity of approver before completing the approval. ⓘ

☐ Skip approval if the same approver approved the previous stage ⓘ

→] Gates   ⬤━ Disabled
Define gates to evaluate before the deployment. Learn more

Figure 9-28. *The production configuration specifies an approver*

The approver for a release stage can be an individual, multiple individuals, or a group. You have several options. In addition, you can enable the Gates feature which provides the ability to build in some business logic to determine if the deployment should be allowed to proceed. The combination of configuration options provides a robust method by which to restrict the ability to automatically or manually, with approval, deploy to the production environment. Upon approval and the satisfaction of any gates or filters, the deployment stage is queued. Refer to Figure 9-29.

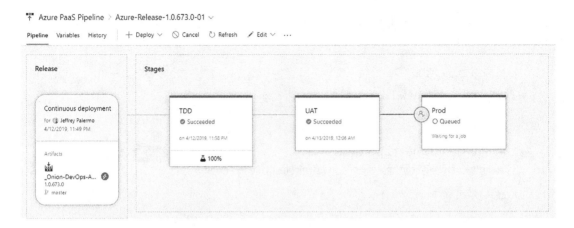

Figure 9-29. *The production stage will queue the deployment as soon as manual approval is given*

If a previous release has been placed in the approval queue, the new release will wait for it. If you see the preceding screen unexpectedly, look for a previous release that has not been approved. Chances are that some other releases are in the queue for this release stage.

Upon approval of the production deployment, you will see the progress auto-updating on the screen, as shown in Figure 9-30. You can watch it as it executes or close the window and come back later. Because you have placed a call to the built-in application health check, you will know, if the deployment reports success, that all parts of the application along with their dependencies have been deployed and that everything is online and functioning properly.

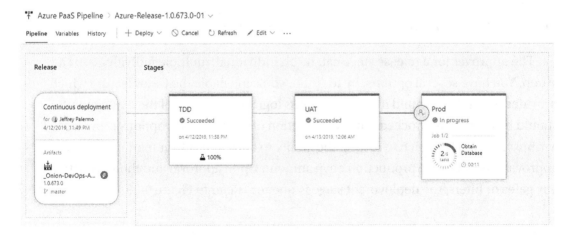

Figure 9-30. *You can see the progress of the deployment when it is executing*

Wrap Up

In this chapter, you learned how to design your deployment pipeline, and you saw the experience of executing a properly configured release configuration. It's important to determine the correct number and type of environments. You also assigned validation steps to each environment including a built-in application health check. You learned about the different types of data that is deployed or provisioned with a deployment, and you reviewed the different options you have within Azure for running code in Azure PaaS services or others. Finally, you saw the various touch points in the release configuration, including the impact of variables on the execution of the deployment steps. And you learned how to integrate a full-system acceptance test suite into your TDD environment, both for releases from feature branches as well as from master. Next, we'll take a look at how to properly operate, monitor, and support our applications as they run in production and are used by our customers.

Bibliography

Beck, K. (2002). *Test Driven Development: By Example.* Addison-Wesley Professional.

Build & Release Tools from Benjamin Day. (n.d.). Retrieved from `https://marketplace.visualstudio.com/items?itemName=bendayconsulting.build-task`

JeffreyPalermo.com. (n.d.). Retrieved from AliaSQL – the new name in automated database change management: `https://jeffreypalermo.com/2014/01/aliasql-the-new-name-in-automated-database-change-management/`

Kruchten, P. (n.d.). Retrieved from Architectural Blueprints—The "4+1" View Model of Software Architecture: `www.cs.ubc.ca/~gregor/teaching/papers/4+1view-architecture.pdf`

Shift Left to Make Testing Fast and Reliable. (n.d.). Retrieved from Microsoft Docs: `https://docs.microsoft.com/en-us/azure/devops/learn/devops-at-microsoft/shift-left-make-testing-fast-reliable`

CHAPTER 10

Operating and Monitoring the Release

Once our software changes are deployed and running in production, we have just begun. Consider our model for DevOps that was introduced at the beginning of this book in Figure 10-1. We must have a strategy for operations. Then we must execute that strategy consistently and measure to ensure what we expect is happening. Our DevOps cycle around the outside calls out learning as a feedback into planning for future changes. Through operating the software with real customers using it, we can

1. Verify that our customers can accomplish their goals

2. Learn what is the best change to make next

© Jeffrey Palermo 2019
J. Palermo, *.NET DevOps for Azure*, https://doi.org/10.1007/978-1-4842-5343-4_10

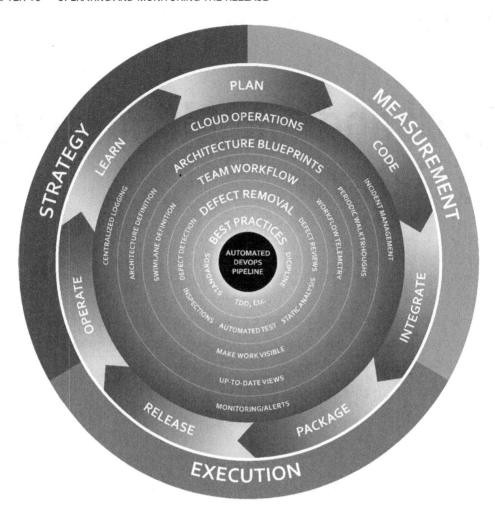

Figure 10-1. *Onion DevOps Architecture provides a model for a complete DevOps environment*

In the cycle around the outside of the onion, the release stage is just past the halfway point of the cycle. After releasing software to our customers, we must operate it well, learn how it's performing, and then funnel that learning back into future plans. This chapter will cover the fundamentals for operating our .NET software in Azure.

Principles

In discussions around quality and testing, a desirable trait of a software system has become known as **testability.** Software architects and engineers can have discussions about the design of a system and the components therein and evaluate the testability of the design. When operating a software system in Azure, or any environment for that matter, a desirable trait for the system is **observability**. Here are the principles:

- **Know what your software is doing at all times**

  It is not enough to know that a server is up, or that a web site is online. If any function of the system no longer functions as needed, then a customer is down. We should think in terms of our customers and their goals. If customers cannot do work, then the customer is down, even if the technical parts of our system are up. With that lens, we can ask ourselves "what do we need to know so that we are confident that our customers are up?"

- **Listen to what your system is saying**

  Through the various types of telemetry, you can have your software system emit, it speaks. Listen for what the system is asking for. Eric Hexter, a visionary in DevOps Diagnostics, related, when he presented to the Azure DevOps User Group,[1] that through telemetry, the system can ask for nonfunctional features or for maintenance. Through examining the logs and metrics, we can discover work that needs to be done on the system. This work might not show up in regular product backlogs.

Many teams discuss the level of logging that should be a part of the software. In addition, many already have some type of alerting in place. If trouble tickets or problem reports come in from customers, that is one sign that the **observability** sophistication of the system is lacking. Consider the work in this area an insurance policy. It does take investment of effort, time, and some money on products in order to achieve success in this area. This insurance policy has a premium that must be paid for the return on risk avoidance. If this is neglected and the insurance premium not paid, your organization will pay the full losses of a business disruption. This is another instance of the "Shift Left" way of thinking where we can design observability into the system that will yield better service to our customers.

---

[1]Hexter

Sam Guckenheimer has discussed observability and the importance of it on an Azure DevOps Podcast interview.[II]

Architecture for Observability

While this chapter cannot cover all techniques or forms that observability can take, we will focus on the basics that are universally application to what this author believes if >80% of .NET applications in the business world. Let's start with the types of telemetry that should be emitted from your software:

- **Metrics/performance counters**

  Many of these are built into the Azure platform, but if you are using queues, you will want to capture queue length, for example. Another useful metric is number of users by type currently using your system in the past hour/ day. These types of trends can be used to trigger alarms. For example, if your normal usage drops off unexpectedly, you might be having a technical issue that needs to be investigated.

- **Log messages/log files**

  While the most common type of telemetry, this is not consistently done. Every operation or transaction a system executes should be logged. Further, log files and log messages from various components should be aggregated and centralized into a repository that can be queried as a whole in order to provide a complete picture of what the system is doing.

- **Heartbeats**

  Is it alive? Heartbeats can come from the outside or be built directly into application components themselves. These are signals and synthetic transactions that are built-in health checks. For example, if a critical integration is between the application and a payment processor, it is useful to know that the connection with the payment processor is functional. Integrations are notorious for breaking, and heartbeats that test these on a constant basis can alert us before a customer, frustrated, notifies us that a software feature is not working.

[II]Guckenheimer, 2018

Figure 10-2 illustrates the architectural model for observability in Azure. While many products exist in the marketplace that can collect, aggregate, and search telemetry, we will focus on the capabilities built into Azure.

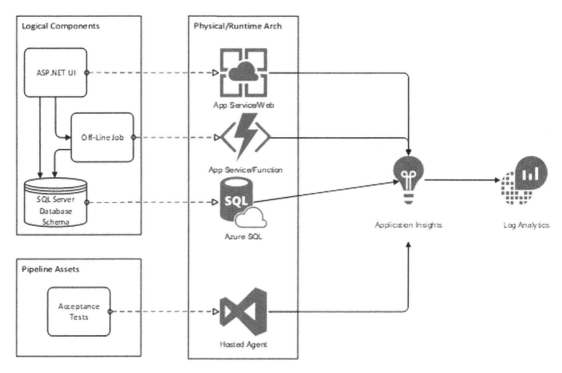

Figure 10-2. *Each application should send telemetry and diagnostics information to a single Application Insights service*

Application Insights has the capability to gather a wealth of information from every running component of your application, including the DevOps pipeline itself, which is part of your system. One of the ways we improve the observability of our software is to collect all available information in the same place. Application Insights provides that. If you have never used Application Insights before, referred to also as AppInsights, Microsoft has a great overview in its documentation.[III]

[III]Microsoft, n.d.

As you have seen in our DevOps pipeline, we have a stable production environment, one or more UAT environments, and a whole host of TDD environments that are constantly being created and destroyed. You will want the data in AppInsights to be durable across changes to environments. Consider the following environment architecture.

By providing each environment type with an AppInsights instance, we can tune queries for each environment type to the audience. For example, our TDD environment will have environments come and go as new builds are produced. By capturing performance metrics while full-system acceptance tests execute, we might be able to detect when runtimes of transactions change by more than a certain percent. This could be indicative of a performance slowdown from version to version. In addition, our production AppInsights repository should have alerts configured on it. Refer to Figure 10-3.

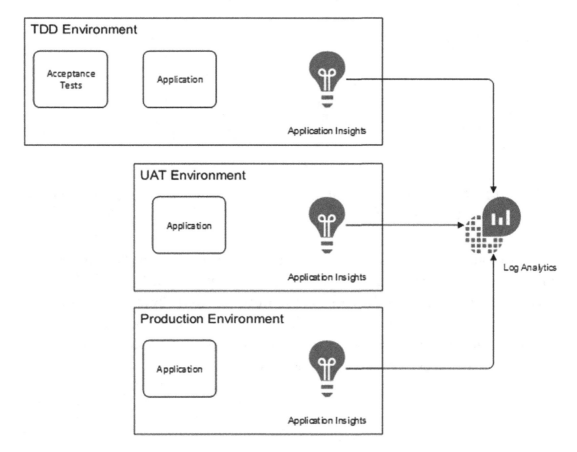

Figure 10-3. *Each environment benefits from an AppInsights instance, which can then be aggregated to Log Analytics or other analytics sink*

The intent of AppInsights is for there to be one AppInsights service per application. While you can add custom tags to telemetry to facilitate filtering out environments in a single AppInsights instance, the service was not designed with that in mind. The service was designed to collect telemetry from a single application. That is, one versioned, complete unit of software. If you have broken your software into multiple Git repositories with multiple DevOps pipelines, you can still use a single AppInsights service for the software system running in production. To make this decision, you must ask yourself what kind of queries you will want to execute against the data and how you'd like the data to be segments. For our example application, we have multiple components that will send telemetry to a single AppInsights instance for each environment. In total, we have three AppInsights services, one for each environment. Now that you can see the relationship between application components and AppInsights, let's begin enabling observability in our software.

Jumpstarting Observability

While we are destroying and recreating TDD environments – and UAT environments from time to time – we want AppInsights to be durable. Because of this, we place the AppInsights services in a separate resource group from the environments that might be destroyed.

Figure 10-4. *Resource Group*

These services live in their own resource group "Onion-DevOps-Architecture-diagnostic". You can name this resource group whatever you like. This resource group will live a long time, in contrast to your pre-production environments, as shown in Figure 10-5. Once we have our AppInsights in place, it is time to prepare the application for the sending of telemetry. First, you will add the AppInsights NuGet packages to your projects in Visual Studio. ASP.NET projects have some quick start tooling to help with this, but you can add these packages to any projects you like. In our Visual Studio solution, we have kept the dependencies of the Core project very minimal – essentially this library contains plain old C# objects (POCOs). Because of these, we will choose the UI and Core.AppStartup projects to receive the AppInsights dependency, as shown in Figure 10-6.

☐ 💡	Onion-DevOps-Architecture-Prod-AppInsights	Application Insights	South Central US
☐ 💡	Onion-DevOps-Architecture-TDD-AppInsights	Application Insights	South Central US
☐ 💡	Onion-DevOps-Architecture-UAT-AppInsights	Application Insights	South Central US

Figure 10-5. *Each environment type has a dedicated AppInsights instance in the same region as the environment*

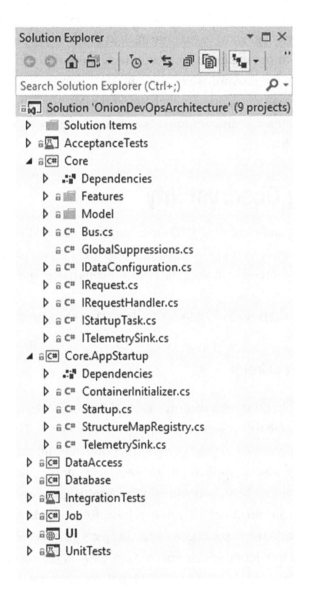

Figure 10-6. *The Core project is just POCOs without dependencies, so AppInsights will be added to Core.AppStartup and UI*

The NuGet package to select is Microsoft.ApplicationInsights.AspNetCore. This package is appropriate for code running in Azure AppServices, including WebJobs and Azure Functions. There are other packages for software running on Windows VMs, but if your application is .NET Core, you just need this one.

Once you have the AppInsights NuGet package available to you, you will want to find an architecturally suitable place in your application to observe the transactions happening so that the information can be emitted to AppInsights. In this application, we already have an implementation of a bus patter whereby user intent is packaged as a C# message (object). Command and query objects are sent "down" the bus for execution. We can add some interception code in our TelemetrySink class here:

```
using Microsoft.ApplicationInsights;
using Microsoft.ApplicationInsights.DataContracts;

namespace ClearMeasure.OnionDevOpsArchitecture.Core.AppStartup
{
    public class TelemetrySink : ITelemetrySink
    {
        public void RecordCall<TResponse>(IRequest<TResponse> request,
            TResponse response)
        {
            var telemetryClient = new TelemetryClient();
            EventTelemetry telemetry = new EventTelemetry();
            telemetry.Name = request.GetType().Name;
            telemetryClient.TrackEvent(telemetry);
            telemetryClient.TrackTrace(request.GetType().Name +
                ":- " + request.ToString(), SeverityLevel.Information);
        }
    }
}
```

If you have not yet explored the source code of this book's example application, the following code is from the ExpenseReportController ASP.NET MVC controller action:

```
public IActionResult Index()
{
    var command = new ListExpenseReportsCommand();
    ExpenseReport[] reports = _bus.Send(command);
```

```
    var orderedReports = reports.OrderBy(report => report.Number);
    return View(orderedReports.ToArray());
}
//..//
public class ListExpenseReportsCommand : IRequest<ExpenseReport[]>
{

}
```

The code in the user interface takes the request from the user and sends that down the bus. The request is to list the expense reports. This class implements the IRequest<T> interface. Our TelemetrySink has access to every request that flows through the application, and in a few lines of code, and records a trace for that request and a custom event. In your application, you might extract even more information about what the application is doing, the users performing the action, and other pertinent elements for querying later. In addition to this code, take care to ensure that the appsettings.json file does not send telemetry from a workstation to an environment's AppInsight's instance. In fact, take care not to accidentally commit to Git any Instrumentation Key from the AppInsights resource. The appsettings.json file might look like the following:

```
{
  "Logging": {
    "LogLevel": {
      "Default": "Debug"
    }
  },
  "AllowedHosts": "*",
  "ApplicationInsights": {
    "InstrumentationKey": "bogus value"
  }
}
```

By putting a fake value in ApplicationInsights.InstrumentationKey, you will ensure that no telemetry can be sent from local developer workstations. Instead, you can try out and validate your telemetry by running the application in Debug (F5) mode.

The Application Insights Search window can be a bit hard to find, but it allows you to develop your diagnostics capability locally without having to connect to Azure. You'll want to make sure you are exporting the telemetry that you think you are. When you run the application in debug mode, you can examine not only the telemetry that you add but also the phenomenal amount of data that is automatically captured for you. Refer to Figure 10-7.

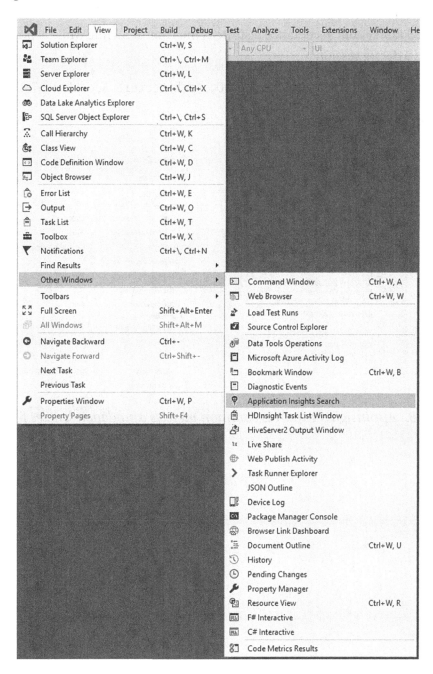

Figure 10-7. *The AppInsights window can be used to see telemetry on a local workstation without connecting to Azure*

257

You added the Custom Event at the top of Figure 10-8, but you did not add anything in order to have the SQL statement that was run from the application to the SQL Server database captured. This view allows you to search across any number of attributes to learn more about your application. To dig into more data, you can run your full suite of automated full-system acceptance tests from the command line while capturing the telemetry in a debug session:

```
dotnet vstest .\ClearMeasure.OnionDevOpsArchitecture.AcceptanceTests.dll
```

(Refer to Figure 10-9).

Figure 10-8. *AppInsights captures common metrics and dependencies for you*

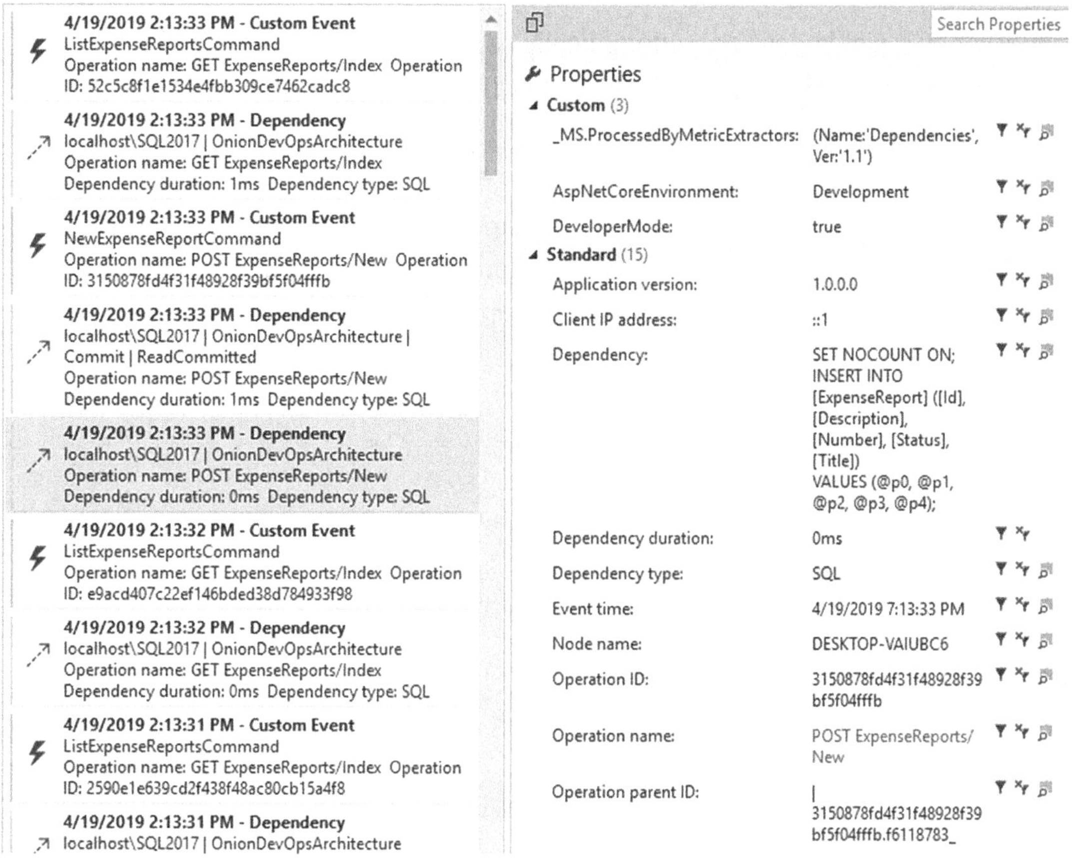

Figure 10-9. After running the acceptance tests, you can see all the telemetry captured in Application Insights

If you run the preceding command from the folder of the acceptance tests assemblies, you can amass quite a bit of telemetry to search. You will want to take a break for a cup of tea or coffee as you wait for your browser window to stop flashing across your screen as all the Selenium tests exercise your application as fast as it will go.

It's interesting to note that Application Insights does not automatically capture any data, parameters, or arguments. Therefore, you will have to add code to explicitly do that. When you do, take care that you are exporting any sensitive data field to a monitoring system that might have different data security controls that the production database. Then, once you are satisfied that you have a useful iteration of telemetry for your application, it's time to link the application with the various environment specific AppInsights services in your Azure subscription.

Application Insights does not automatically capture any user data or SQL parameters. If you need parameters captured, you will add that directly, taking care of sensitive data fields.

For the execution of our deployment, it's important to know when new release candidates were promoted from one environment to another. For this, you will add a Release Annotation task to your deployment steps.

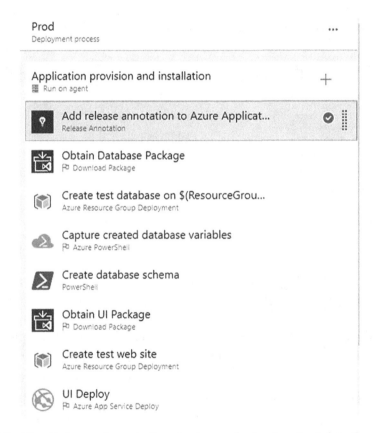

Figure 10-10. *The Release Annotation task marks in AppInsights the deployment*

You will want to place this as the first task so that even if the deployment fails, Application Insights receives a marker that a deployment was started. In this way, AppInsights records that a version started deploying even if the deployment fails in the middle. At some later date when reviewing a period of exceptions and bad failures, you won't have to strain your memory to remember that a bad deployment was associated with a period of elevated exceptions. Within the "UI Deploy" step, you will also add the appsettings.json file to the JSON variable substitution text area so that your variables will be evaluated for JSON substitution.

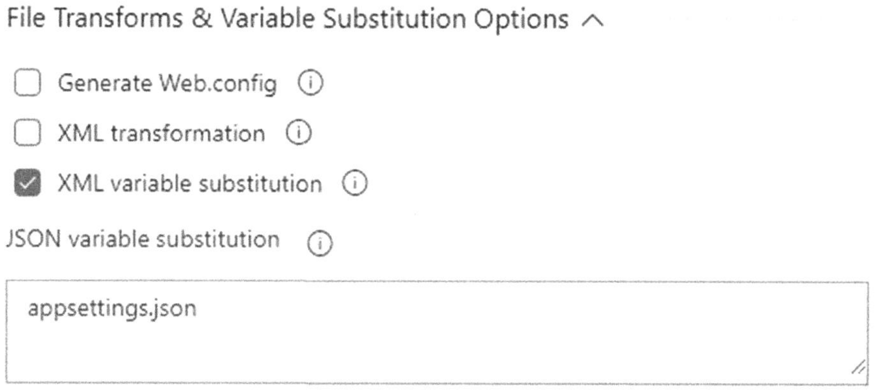

File Transforms & Variable Substitution Options ∧

☐ Generate Web.config ⓘ

☐ XML transformation ⓘ

☑ XML variable substitution ⓘ

JSON variable substitution ⓘ

```
appsettings.json
```

Figure 10-11. *The AppInsights Instrumentation Key resides in the appsettings.json file*

Once this is configured, and after adding a properly named variable with the InstrumentationKey per environment, your release configuration is ready to deploy. Refer to Figure 10-12.

ApplicationInsights.InstrumentationKey	********	TDD
ApplicationInsights.InstrumentationKey	********	UAT
ApplicationInsights.InstrumentationKey	********	Prod

Figure 10-12. *Each of the environments needs its own InstrumentationKey*

When your next release runs, you'll be able to see release markers and telemetry from each of the environments. Beyond the production observability you gain, it can also be useful to find nonfunctional defects like scalability issues. As your acceptance tests run, your release candidate receives its first full-system exercise.

Our example application has only a handful of acceptance tests, so the data captured is only from those; however, when you have multiple feature branches executing releases in parallel, and you have multiple TDD environments created an operating at once, you'll see all that in Figure 10-13. The searches will be able to correlate versions.

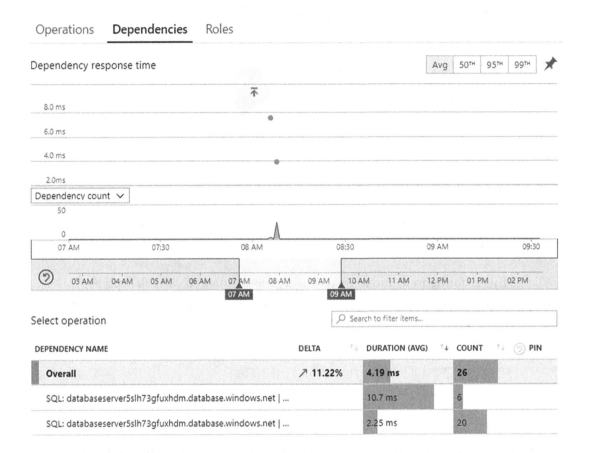

Figure 10-13. *Our TDD environment's AppInsights performance view now shows our release marker that is correlated with the run of the acceptance tests*

Stamping and embedding version numbers in every .NET assembly in your application have downstream benefits and consequences. The telemetry in Application Insights records version numbers. Make sure the version number is available.

If you click the release marker within the Azure portal, you can see detailed information about the release that deployed the application that is responsible for the recorded telemetry.

The release marker includes hyperlinks back to the release and the Azure DevOps project for the application that is emitting the telemetry, as shown in Figure 10-14. The BuildNumber, which originated in the continuous integration build, is here with every bit of telemetry recorded in Application Insights. You have now connected code in Visual Studio, stored in Git with live captured usage data in Azure environments.

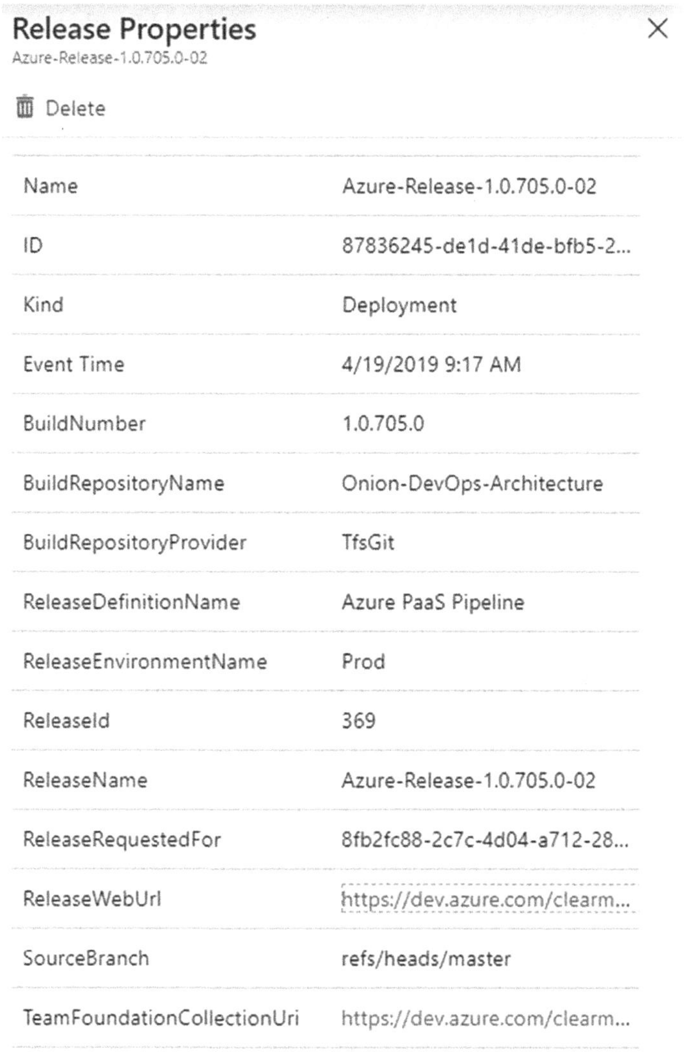

Release Properties

Azure-Release-1.0.705.0-02

🗑 Delete

Name	Azure-Release-1.0.705.0-02
ID	87836245-de1d-41de-bfb5-2...
Kind	Deployment
Event Time	4/19/2019 9:17 AM
BuildNumber	1.0.705.0
BuildRepositoryName	Onion-DevOps-Architecture
BuildRepositoryProvider	TfsGit
ReleaseDefinitionName	Azure PaaS Pipeline
ReleaseEnvironmentName	Prod
ReleaseId	369
ReleaseName	Azure-Release-1.0.705.0-02
ReleaseRequestedFor	8fb2fc88-2c7c-4d04-a712-28...
ReleaseWebUrl	https://dev.azure.com/clearm...
SourceBranch	refs/heads/master
TeamFoundationCollectionUri	https://dev.azure.com/clearm...

Figure 10-14. *The release marker in AppInsights is recorded with a wealth of information about the release that deployed the application*

Wrap Up

You did it! You've been through the entire DevOps process on .NET for Azure. The term "DevOps Process" is discussed in some circles as if it is a simple thing. You can see from this text that there are numerous concepts, decisions, and steps that all go together in order to make the "DevOps Process" function. When put together properly, the team moves fast, can make changes when needed, and is able to operate the software well. You may wish to do some of the steps differently than the guidance in this book. If you already have a fully operational DevOps environment with at least all the capabilities illustrated in this book, then you are on your way to mastery. Implement your ideas. If you do not yet have a fully functioning DevOps environment with at least these capabilities, this author's recommendation is to implement DevOps "by the book." Then, once you can operate in very short cycles of code changes to stable deployments in a production environment, make your changes. Use the concept of ShuHaRi[IV] as you progress down your DevOps journey. Refer back frequently to the online public project that accompanies this book at `https://dev.azure.com/clearmeasurelabs/Onion-DevOps-Architecture`.

Bibliography

Fowler, M. (n.d.). *ShuHaRi.* Retrieved from MartinFowler.com: `www.martinfowler.com/bliki/ShuHaRi.html`

Guckenheimer, S. (2018, 9 24). Sam Guckenheimer on Testing, Data Collection, and the State of DevOps Report. (J. Palermo, Interviewer) Retrieved from `http://azuredevopspodcast.clear-measure.com/sam-guckenheimer-on-testing-data-collection-and-the-state-of-devops-report-episode-003`

Hexter, E. (n.d.). *DevOps Diagnostics w/ Eric Hexter (Azure DevOps User Group).* Retrieved from `www.youtube.com/watch?v=60-17phQMJo`

Microsoft. (n.d.). *What is Application Insights?* Retrieved from Microsoft Docs: `https://docs.microsoft.com/en-us/azure/azure-monitor/app/app-insights-overview`

[IV]Fowler, n.d.

Afterword

This text builds on a host of prior industry work. None of the ideas in this book are inventions or completely original. This book represents a synthesis of ideas from all corners of the software industry across multiple platforms. Coupled with experience, success, and failure, this book provides the best rules of thumb that can be mustered at this time.

The following is a short summary of the prior works and events that were highly influential in the experience that led to this book.

In 2001, a group of software industry leaders met at a ski resort to mull over the problems in their field that had been building throughout the 1990s and the infamous dot-com bubble of the late 1990s. This group produced the *Manifesto for Agile Software Development* (`www.agilemanifesto.org`). These principles have redefined the way the industry organizes and executes software development work. A fundamental premise of agile development is to organize and perform work in much smaller batches than had previously been used in the late 1990s. Now, units of software delivery called "sprints" or "iterations" are commonly discussed. Many organizations run in cadences of iterations that are 1–3 weeks in length. The unit of software changes has likewise shrunk. Now developers target changes that can be accomplished in the current iteration, and many teams experiment with just how small software changes can be while keeping the software stable and releasable at all times.

In 2004, Michael Feathers wrote *Working Effectively with Legacy Code*. The book was released in the years following the *Manifesto for Agile Software Development*, and it addressed a common situation that many organizations were faced with: How can I change my software when every change generates at least two new defects? As teams were attempting to make changes and restabilize their software, they realized that previous engineering methods were insufficient when attempting to drive cycle times down to less than a month. Feathers describes methods for breaking apart code bases that were never intended to execute outside of a completely integrated production environment. The author summarizes that without running the software within automated test harnesses, any piece of software, however new, is destined to become

© Jeffrey Palermo 2019
J. Palermo, *.NET DevOps for Azure*, https://doi.org/10.1007/978-1-4842-5343-4

labeled as "legacy code;" unchangeable, brittle, and expensive to maintain. He described techniques illustrating how to insert seams into existing code in order to retrofit tests. Then, armed with tests that protected the functionality, the software could be changed with less fear. Michael Feathers was also the author of some early unit testing framework for C++, namely, CppUnit.

In 2006, Paul M. Duvall, Steve Matyas, and Andrew Glover wrote *Continuous Integration: Improving Software Quality and Reducing Risk*. This influential work illustrated a method that some in the industry had been perfecting called *continuous integration* (CI). This method sought to run an automated build of the software application every time any change was committed to the version control system. The book illustrates some specific engineering methods that have to be adopted. A ground-shaking inclusion was the premise that the continuous integration build must include building and testing dependencies that an application owns, including relational databases and other storage mechanisms. The authors dedicated an entire chapter (Chapter 5) to *continuous database integration*.

Additionally, in 2006 Martin Fowler penned an article titled *Continuous Integration* (www.martinfowler.com/articles/continuousIntegration.html). In this article, he proposes some standards for a continuous integration build:

- Maintain a single source repository

- Automate the build

- Make your build self-testing

- Everyone commits to the mainline every day

- Every commit should build the mainline on an integration machine

- Fix broken builds immediately

- Keep the build fast

- Test in a clone of the production environment

- Make it easy for anyone to get the latest executable

- Everyone can see what's happening

- Automate deployment

While many in the industry were innovating new and better methods for shortening cycle time, 2006 was the year when successful and proven methods were being shared openly and published widely. Continuous integration included the automated deployment of software releases. In the years that followed, continuous *integration* became known as continuous *delivery*, expressly implying the inclusion of software deployments all the way to end users in production environments. Some refer to the method as *CI/CD*, illustrating the confusion that exists to this day about where CI stopped and CD started. Both refer to the full process of integrating source code from multiple developers and providing new working software to end users. However, in the common lexicon, most refer to the "CI build" and then refer to a CD *pipeline* that deploys across successive environments. Historically, however, continuous integration, as a method, in 2006 included automated deployments to production.

The year 2009 saw another seminal work published. Jez Humble and David Farley authored *Continuous Delivery: Reliable Software Releases through Build, Test, and Deployment Automation*. This book cited the 2006 book on continuous integration and pulled the story forward by proposing methods by which to not only build continuously but also to continuously deploy to downstream environments. More proven methods for handling deployment scenarios were included. The stages proposed in this book are

- Version control

- Commit stage

- Automated acceptance tests

- Manual validations

- Release (production)

This process is much more high level, but the commit stage includes the private build and the integration build, and the automated acceptance tests are prescribed to be run against a fully deployed pre-production environment.

In 2009, the term *DevOps* was coined by Patrick Debois when he organized the first DevOpsDays conference in Ghent, Belgium. The current body of DevOps-focused works and events has grown substantially over the last 10 years.

Index

© Jeffrey Palermo 2019
J. Palermo, *.NET DevOps for Azure*, https://doi.org/10.1007/978-1-4842-5343-4

Printed in the United States
By Bookmasters